Grounded

How to Solve the Aviation Crisis

Captain Shem Malmquist
& Roger Rapoport

Grounded
How to solve the aviation crisis

Captain Shem Malmquist & Roger Rapoport

ISBN: 978-1-7345042-3-1
ISBN: 978-1-7345042-4-8 (ebook)
ISBN: 978-1-7345042-5-5 (audiobook)

Library of Congress Control Number: 2020940136

Cover design: James Sparling, Lexographic
Typeset in Masqualero, 10pt on 13pt by Lexographic, Chicago

Printed in the United States of America

First print edition: January 2021.

Published by
Lexographic Press
500 S Cornell Ave, Unit 6a
Chicago IL 60615

A Curt Lewis Aviation Book

lexographicpress.com

For our children.

We are so proud of you.

Gweneth, Travis, Sara, Ethan, Avin, Preston, Jonathan, Elizabeth and William

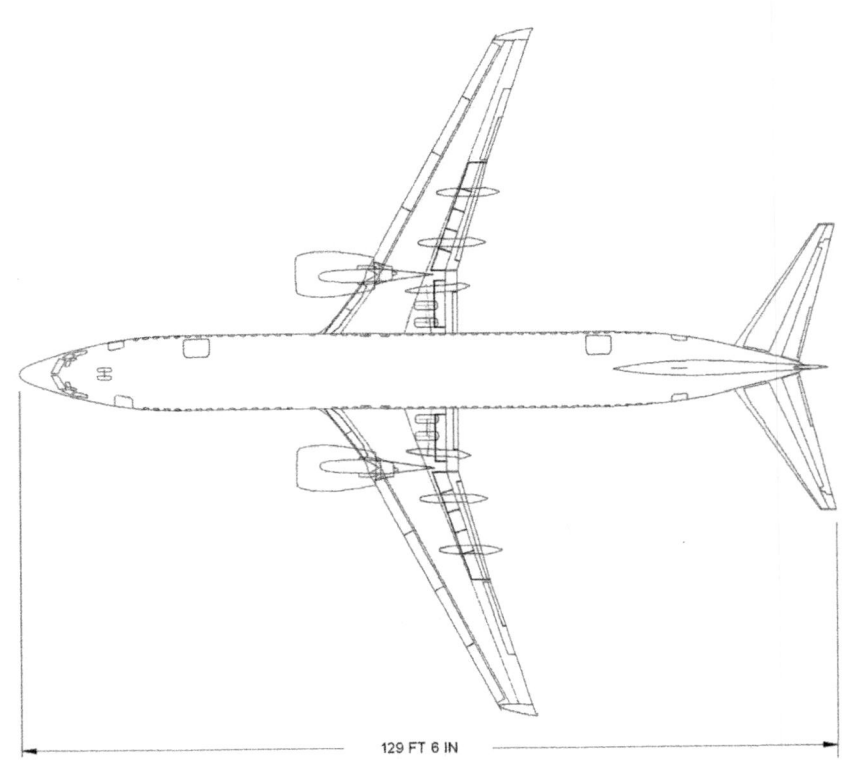

129 FT 6 IN

Contents

"I don't think we're ever going to lose money again. We have an industry that's going to be profitable in good and bad times."

Doug Parker
American Airlines CEO
September 28, 2017

"If a farsighted capitalist had been present at Kitty Hawk, he would have done his successors a huge favor by shooting Orville down."

Warren Buffet
Letter to investors May 2, 2020

FOREWORD
Curt Lewis

n their 2017 book on Air France 447, Angle of Attack, Captain Shem Malmquist and investigative reporter Roger Rapoport posed a question everyone who flies or thinks about flying is asking: What will it take to make sure that getting on a plane is as safe as it can be?

Their diligent analysis of that event, based on years of research and interviews with top aviation officials and scientists worldwide made it clear that automation will never rule out risk. Well-trained flight crews are essential to making sure that unexpected challenges can be correctly handled in real time. Sadly that message did not get through to the Boeing team writing and designing the requirements for the 737 MAX or the regulators at the FAA overseeing the airplane's certification. The result, once again, were accidents that could have been prevented.

Now in the midst of a Covid-19 pandemic, the industry faces a new crisis in confidence, even among seasoned flyers who depend on reliable air travel. Until there is a safe and effective vaccine, air carriers around the world will be struggling. Finding a way to eliminate the risk of viral infection in the air transportation system will require a new industry paradigm created in partnership with governments around the world.

For Malmquist and Rapoport these challenges also create an opportunity. As you'll see in these pages, badly overdue reforms could help make the airlines a model for other industries heavily dependent on effective automation. What works for the airlines could also be successful in the energy and transportation industries, as well as health care, construction and manufacturing.

Step-by-step this book lays out promising ideas on software and system safety that will bring an end to decades of unfortunate automation surprises. An optimistic look at achievable solutions, this book is also a great read on one of the central concerns of our time. Science is a continuous learning process. Solutions lead to new ideas and inevitably lead to greater creativity. That dialog, so important to all of us who fly or want to fly, begins right here.

Curt Lewis, PhD

Editor, Flight Safety Information, October 2020

CHAPTER 1

The Golden Age of Aviation

A s they like to say in the airline business, it's never too early to break out the champagne. From the *bon voyage* party thrown by friends to the pre-board flute handed you in the VIP lounge, a premium vintage is a perfect way to get you off the ground.

In the fall of 2018, the hard working women and men of the airline industry had good reason to break out the bubbly. With passengers worldwide boarding at a record pace, it was celebration time for the airlines, manufacturers, regulatory agencies, shareholders, banks and the industry's infallible lobbyists.

Thanks, in part, to the emerging middle class in countries like China, Indonesia and India, as well as promising markets such as Africa, the world's airline industry was outpacing world economic growth. After netting a record $37.6 billion in profits during fiscal 2017, the carriers had rebounded dramatically from the tragic events of 9/11 and the recession of 2008-2009. Out in France's *foie gras* country, Airbus was booming. Across the pond, competitor Boeing's 737 MAX was selling like hotcakes, breaking industry records. With MAX orders pushing toward an astonishing 5,000 planes, the American manufacturer was spending billions buying back its own shares soaring toward an all time high.

The same was true for American carriers conservatively projected to net an unprecedented $116 billion in profits for the second decade of the 21st century. Not a bad return on investment for an imaginative industry that netted an average profit of less than $6 per ticket sold. Ancillary items such as baggage and cancellation fees, as well as cobranded credit cards, early boarding VIP lounges, tour packages, duty free items, food and, of course, champagne, were pure gold. Like slaughterhouses who sold everything but the squeal, many airlines even charged passengers for the privilege of booking a middle seat in coach.

With armies around the world still battling on multiple fronts and tens of millions of refugees struggling to escape from poverty and terrorism, the airlines remained uniquely positioned to thrive in a divided world. Except for rogue nations like as North Korea, the carriers' balance sheets appeared immunized from the vicissitudes of dictators, international tariff wars, Brexit, Russia's encroachment on the Ukraine and Syrian genocide. When warfare erupted airlines easily diverted around the trouble spots. Anomalies such as the 2014 disappearance of a Malaysia Air 777 or the apparent Russian missile attack on another jet flown by the same carrier soon fell to the back pages. Even global warming wasn't an economic threat as airlines moved toward more fuel efficient aircraft and encouraged passengers to make voluntary contributions toward carbon offsets.

Although a mere two percent of the world's population traveled regularly by air, carriers were the beneficiary of generous government economic support such as a wide ban on government fuel taxes. World leader Boeing paid a modest eight percent tax on income and Airbus enjoyed broad financial support from European nations. State subsidies provided billions for international airlines based in the Middle East, China, Russia and India. The resilience of the airlines over the past century transformed our world. Quick and affordable transport made it possible for superpowers like China to become central to the pharmaceutical, auto and computer industries. Haute couture sewn in Guangzhou on Friday could be showcased the following night on a Milan Fashion Week runway. By air it was possible to go virtually anywhere in the world within a day or two. College kids on spring break could easily lounge on exotic Bora Bora beaches while their parents explored the Himalayas. The $100 billion cruise industry made it easy to see the Northern Lights or the penguins on the coast of Antarctica.

The road to automation.

Humankind's evolution from the world of crude hand tools to automation is a credit to scientific geniuses like Leonardo da Vinci and the Wright Brothers. From Thomas Savery, the inventor of the steam engine, to August Pitot who created the eponymous pitot tube (a device that measures the velocity of air via impact pressure) we all owe a debt to the brilliant scientists, engineers, mathematicians, and physicists who opened the door to the marvelous machines and discoveries which transform our world. Their brilliant thinking and ground breaking scientific work has improved the quality of life around the world.

When corporate board members at companies like Boeing earn $355,000 a year they can thank their lucky stars for these creators who paved the way for technology that appears to work seamlessly. Billionaire investors who have made it possible for Silicon Valley to rival Wall Street are similarly indebted to the innovative scientists and engineers who helped create these transformative companies. Today the Boeing/Airbus aviation manufacturing duopoly can endlessly tout the achievements of an industry that believes safety is always job number one.

Some of what the self-congratulatory aviation industry is saying rings true, despite the fact that thousands of people have died in more than 60 commercial airplane accidents during the past decade. All kinds of airlines, including some of the very best, have coped with tragic crashes we believe could have been prevented. This book is dedicated to those who lost their lives and to bringing an end to these aviation disasters with a promising new approach to aviation safety management. It is also dedicated to the millions of people working in commercial aviation who share that goal.

Every time technology fails and lives are lost there is a rush to pin the tail on someone. Or as University of California sociologist Fred Block, deftly explains:

"One of the ways that people have coped with the anxieties of living in such a dangerous world is to imagine that the sources of chaos and disorder are ancient and archaic, and that they are gradually being displaced by a new and rational social order that can stabilize the planet."

A key part of this process is finding someone to blame for what went wrong. We have spent a long time thinking about this. No matter which side of the political fence you are on, or where you sit on an airplane, blame is always a waste of time. Simply dismissing an accident as someone's fault does not prevent the next accident. It makes more sense to focus on understanding why controls in place at the time of these accidents failed and how to make these controls work better.

No one, with the possible exception of a sociopath, wants to see people get sick or die on an airplane. Everyone we know in aviation is dedicated, 100 percent, to protecting the lives of the traveling public. Reducing the carbon footprint of global aviation with readily available technology is yet another shared goal. Even people we disagree with deserve to be treated with respect. Our differences focus on the conflicting assumptions that contribute to a meaningful conversation about the future of aviation.

In most cases the power to make decisions comes from the consent of the governed. Democracies such as the United States, France, England and Germany shape the international aviation industry. There is a reason why Democrats and Republicans, libertarians, capitalists, communists, CEOs and union leaders all fly on the same planes made by Boeing and Airbus. We believe, as Fred Block explains, that when it comes to boarding a plane, most passengers feel a sense of invulnerability. If we saw aviation otherwise many of us would not go to the airport.

Ask the scientists

We know that in science, ignorance is never bliss. People managing safety systems must always be technical experts. The problem at the heart of this book is essentially a control issue or, to put it another way, a lack of control. All too often regulatory agencies are reactive, rather than proactive, because the people in charge lack relevant training and experience in aviation. Managers who come from the accounting world or the financial services industry, as well as agency leaders who have never flown a plane, can be victims of their own inexperience. Leaders who aren't current on the latest technology may be unable to objectively evaluate important changes.

All too often experts, especially type-rated pilots, who know what they are talking about, don't always get the respect or attention they deserve. Unlike the dawn of the "space race" in the 1950s, when America rushed to put a man on the moon, respected scientists are being challenged by non-scientist influencers. Indifferent to badly-needed STEM education, political leaders who don't know what they are talking about try to get reelected on an anti-science platform. Government experts and well-informed whistleblower pilots are grounded for spurious psychiatric exams aimed at undermining their laudable safety initiatives. Lobbyists, special interests, campaign contributors, spouses, former business associates, even well-meaning friends of elected officials, can undermine scientific objectivity. Every step of the way this trend threatens to undermine independence in aviation.

Fred Block's troubling "new and rational social order" promises that past disasters won't be repeated. When a new, state-of -the-art, plane crashes in the South Atlantic or Indonesia, we are reassured that this will never happen again. When we watch a documentary about the Spanish Flu of 1918-1919, we don't expect this kind of pandemic to reoccur in our lifetime. Guardians at the gates, campaigning for the reduction of CO_2 emissions from aircraft, struggle to gain a following. For better or worse governments and industry tend to be reactive, not proactive.

The great irony is that even when all parties are doing their job correctly accidents can happen. And the reverse is also true—when some things are going wrong, accidents may not happen. This paradox explains why it's so important that all voters and political leaders question the most commonly held assumptions about the future of safe air travel.

We believe an effective solution begins with a science-based approach in the offices of our elected leaders as well as the nation's transportation agencies. Great leadership means this: The people managing the air transportation system must fully understand the industry and make critical decisions based on a broad scientific foundation. Anything that interferes with this process directly contributes to dangerous control problems.

Principal issues at the heart of our book, the grounding of the worldwide Boeing 737 MAX fleet, and the sharp decline of air travel due to the Covid-19 virus, took place in less than two years. Rather than seeing these events as anomalies, we believe they are the culmination of a dangerously misleading business strategy based on outdated government requirements and regulations. Critics at agencies such as the National Transportation Safety Board and public health agencies have been waving red flags for years. The lack of an effective contact tracing system in aviation was a direct result of a well-financed industry lobbying campaign. Along with accident investigators at the French BEA, we have been arguing for over a decade that failing to address the automation problems pinpointed by the loss of Air France 447 would lead to a similar computer crash. Does it seem a little weird that the same government that is happy to spend $82 million on a manual for the President's Air Force One is not able to catch an obvious software system error that led to two devastating crashes and the worldwide grounding of more than 350 American made jets? Who could have imagined that asymptomatic people traveling unrestricted by air and other modes of transportation would transmit Covid-19 to the far corners of the earth?

All too often problems in aviation begin with erroneous assumptions made in good faith. By extension, any technology-dependent industry ignoring new risks introduced by the latest avionics is vulnerable. It takes a very special kind of expert to make sure these "upgrades" are safely introduced. The painful irony is that the hubris of the technology evangelists frequently handicaps the industries they are trying disrupt or improve, making it harder for those on the ground, and in the air, to do their job.

Instead of trying to blame governments, politicians, regulatory agencies or world health organizations for these problems, we need to see this crisis as a valuable teaching tool for future generations. The safety challenges playing out in aviation are the canary in the coal mine, a useful warning for high tech industries and governments everywhere. In a short time we can empower leadership able to make aviation safer. Finding an effective way to restore confidence in air travel is the goal of this book.

CHAPTER 2
Selling The Airplane

"Humans are confused when something that has always been reliable and trustworthy fails."

Gary Helmer,
Chief, Safety Division,
National Transportation Safety Board

From the Wright Brothers bicycle shop in Dayton, Ohio, to the Boeing factory floor in Everett, Washington, aviation has made our imaginations soar. Around the world, children are lulled to sleep by classic books written by legendary pilot Antoine de Saint-Exupéry. The beautiful people flying first class, tucked in to their lie-flat seats, arrive on the Riviera in the early morning light, raring to go. Those who plan their trip from China right, can arrive home in Los Angeles before they took off.

With the airlines moving the equivalent of the world's population every ten years, it's hard to think of an industry that better defines the delicate balance between human performance and automation. Brilliant people build these elegant machines that do precisely what they are programmed to do. They don't fall asleep on the job or stage walkouts and never second-guess the boss.

All who fly benefit from the spirit of cooperation and trust defining this industry. Unlike the cruise lines, the railroads or car manufacturers, the airlines have consistently positioned themselves as the safest way to travel. For an airline passenger en route to a honeymoon in Bali or a cruise on the Yangtze river, there is little reason to be afraid.

Now, it is true that since 1918 there have been 27,011 aviation commercial, general aviation and non-combat military accidents taking over 156,000 lives. Since 1958 more than 29,000 people have died in over 1,525 commercial airline accidents. More than 1,000 passengers have died on five airlines. Since its founding Aeroflot has lost 11,299 passengers followed by Air France at 1,756 and Pan Am with 1,655. American Airlines accidents have taken the lives of 1,450 while United's count stands at 1,217.

While the learning curve has been steep, the International Air Transportation Association's CEO Alexandre de Juniac is reassuring:

"Flying remains one of the safest ways to travel and is getting safer. Based on the 2019 fatality risk, on average, a passenger could take a flight every day for 535 years before experiencing an accident with one fatality on board."

This view sidestepped the FAA's own analysis of the Boeing 737 MAX two months after the October 2018 Lion Air crash. Making it clear that no manufacturer is perfect, the agency forecast up to 15 fatal crashes of this aircraft, one every two to three years, if Boeing failed to improve the aircraft's flight control software. With a century of experience building airplanes, it was clear that even the world's most successful manufacturer remained vulnerable. We will explore the control problems that grounded the MAX in detail later in this book.

Even though aviation accidents have been declining, building and retaining consumer confidence in air travel today is hard work. Certainly this is nothing new for the industry that has relied on visionaries who know how to get the job done.

One of them was Boeing's Tex Johnson who some believe may have been the inspiration for Major T.J. "King" Kong in Stanley Kubrick's *Dr. Strangelove*. This intrepid test pilot is best known for a flyover at Seattle's Lake Washington on August 7, 1955. Skeptics, disillusioned by the recent collapse of the British Comet program, watched in disbelief as the 707 prototype, went in to a perfect barrel roll at 490 miles an hour.

This stunning unscripted stunt—Johnson was supposed to have merely done a pass for the crowd of 250,000—was duly noted worldwide thanks to the assembled press corps. Watching from a boat full of business executives, Boeing CEO William Allen barely caught his breath before the $16 million plane circled back for a second barrel roll.

"What did you think you were doing up there yesterday," Allen demanded of Johnson the following day at Boeing headquarters. Johnson, sensing his job might be on the line, knew the answer. "Selling the airplane."

By 1958, thanks in part to a big defense department purchase for a military version of the 707, Boeing had the backing and orders needed to launch the aircraft that put the commercial jet age on a firm footing. Faster flights meant the planes could do more turns per day, sharply boosting revenue for the airlines. Within a decade, US passenger rail services had been abandoned and even the vaunted Eisenhower interstate highway system was meeting its match with new budget airlines focusing on short hops. For many passengers one day round trips were the new norm. Commuter marriages were easier than ever.

Airlines around the world confidently ordered planes from these American manufacturers who enjoyed an enviable reputation for quality and safety. When the commercial plane business sank, military orders backstopped Boeing, McDonnell Douglas and Lockheed.

As the industry grew, a series of unfortunate accidents, especially the crash of a TWA Super Constellation and a United DC-7 over the Grand Canyon on June 30, 1956 led to the launch of the Federal Aviation Agency two years later. The FAA took over many of the functions of the Civil Aviation Agency, while accident investigation remained the job of the Civil Aviation Board.

In 1965 the FAA's administrator, Najeeb Halaby, wrote President Lyndon Johnson recommending that the nation's transportation agencies be shifted from the Commerce Department to a new cabinet level department. He believed the nation needed, "a point of responsibility below the President capable of taking an evenhanded, comprehensive, authoritative approach to the development of transportation policies... to assure reasonable coordination and balance among the various transportation programs of the government."

The following year Congress created the new Department of

Transportation. The nation's fourth largest federal agency, it took over the FAA, the Roads Agency, mass transit, the Coast Guard, the Highway Administration, the Federal Railroad Administration, and the St. Lawrence Seaway Development Corporation. At the same time aviation accident investigation was moved from the Civil Aeronautics Board, to the new National Transportation Safety Board, tangentially under the DOT.

Johnson's pick for America's first Secretary of Transportation was a good friend, Alan Boyd. The former Florida Railroad and Public Utilities Commissioner had also led a winning campaign for Senator George Smathers. In 1959 Boyd joined the Civil Aeronautics Board and two years later he was assigned to handle the investigation of a Convair 380 crash in Texas.

The plane, en route from Austin to the LBJ Ranch late on the evening of February 20, 1961, hit a hill in a rainstorm seven miles short of its destination. Vice-President Johnson had been scheduled to return to Washington on this aircraft the following morning with the two pilots who died in the crash.

Boyd was impressed by Johnson's persistence: "God, he was on the telephone at 8 every morning, 'What the hell do you know, what are you finding?' It ultimately came down to one thing, nothing happens to jeopardize the insurance for their families."

Boyd, who had piloted a C-47 that dropped American paratroopers in France on D-Day, was a tireless advocate for the airlines at the Civil Aeronautics Board.

"The U.S. flag carriers (American, Pan Am, Northwest) all had antitrust immunity," he said years later. "Jets had come out. The

13

International Air Transport Association was meeting." Boyd encouraged the airlines to "support this new proposal, because you're going to save a hell of a lot of money (with jets) and you should pass along some of it (to passengers in the form of lower fares)."

Under the aegis of the Department of Transportation, the FAA was tasked with promoting commercial aviation while also making sure flying was safe. Trying to oversee the booming airlines, the manufacturers and companies building components was an overwhelming job. Instead of hiring an army of government safety regulators to march into factories and hangers across the land, the FAA created a new class of Designated Aviation Representatives. While the manufacturers paid the DARs, they actually represented the FAA. Their job was to work with the airlines and companies like Boeing and Lockheed to ensure compliance with government standards. FAA managers were always available to resolve disputes between the DARS and these companies.

Managed largely by leaders like Boyd who had direct experience in the aviation world, the DOT and the FAA did an impressive job overseeing a world where engineers committed to safety enjoyed the respect of their employers. At the same time the FAA staff worked closely with production teams available any time to discuss unexpected challenges.

As sociologist Fred Block explains, teamwork is essential to building machines that consist of more than a million parts.

"With technologically complex products, ramping up to mass production is the last and often most critical step of research and development. The firm needs some of its best engineers working on the shop floor with production workers. Moreover, this is not just a one-time

challenge; such products are likely to be repeatedly upgraded and modified, so there will be continuous changes to the techniques of mass production."

As the FAA's job expanded exponentially there was also an important corollary to Block's thesis. Success depended on an engineering perspective that gave the end user the ability to effectively evaluate new systems in real time. Controls ruling out error needed to be built in to these machines. Unlike workers in other industries, flight crews did not have the luxury to troubleshoot system critical challenges when they were in the air. With extensive hands-on military training, experienced aviators were able to use their thorough understanding of aerodynamics to fly out of emergency situations.

Out of an abundance of caution the industry worked hard to develop new systems that would protect aircraft carrying large passenger loads. The catch was that any change, no matter how minor, had the potential to trigger unexpected consequences beyond the scope of emergency checklists. As a result the FAA's designated aviation representatives worked closely with the manufacturers on the review process, a process that included many test flights.

As systems grew more and more sophisticated, with flight automation replacing traditional analog controls such as conventional (steam) gauges and hydraulic systems, it became harder and harder to evaluate the avionics.

The challenge, says Dr. Gary Helmer, chief of the safety division at the National Transportation Board, is that, "Technology can extend way beyond the capacity of humans to verify potential problems."

This could be difficult, as one senior Boeing designated aviation representative told us:

> *"As society progressed there was more need to modify airplanes. Since the life of a modern airplane is virtually unlimited, the FAA's job was to make sure that these new systems worked. Unfortunately some of them backfired and contributed to accidents."*

Overwhelmed by manufacturers eager to certify new planes, systems and upgrades, the ranks of the DARs soared into the thousands. This was the only way the FAA could keep up with an explosion of avionics pouring into the agency for fast approval. This public/private partnership system was built on mutual trust with manufacturers long dominated by an engineering culture.

In the mid-1980s Boeing bought out competitor McDonnell-Douglas. The technical experts who created groundbreaking designs were suddenly under the thumb of managers eager to cut costs and boost return on investment. At the same time the Department of Transportation and the FAA began hiring more and more outsiders who lacked the kind of industry expertise that people like Alan Boyd brought to the new agency.

Eager to build a team spirit that would attract the best and brightest, and ward off labor strife, the FAA hired psychologists to run retreats. Among the experts brought in to enhance the agency's corporate culture was psychologist Gregory May, hired in 1984 to conduct training sessions programs. He received $1.4 million for training FAA employees over the next eight years through no-bid contracts and private sessions for agency officials.

An investigation by the DOT's inspector general found that May, who claimed to have trained up to 4,000 employees, had an imaginative approach to stress management. One of his favorite techniques was tying up employees for 24 hours at a time with bed sheets, forcing them to go to eat, sleep and even go to the toilet together. One instructor was required to share a bed with her boss. The instructor verbally abused others.

May's DOT training program triggered a lawsuit filed by controller Douglas Hartman who sued, claiming he was required to sprint through a group of women who "groped him" while verbally demeaning his sexuality. Another controller received $75,000 from the FAA after suffering "extreme trauma" during a diversity session. A federal investigation, which led to the firing of the agency's personnel chief, proved to be a major distraction for agency officials committed to protecting the traveling public.

Congressman Robert Dornan (R-CA) who investigated the scandal told *Newsweek*: "It makes me want to ride the train."

With the introduction of more automated cockpits, new fly-by-wire planes introduced by Airbus, and the cutting of flight crews on short and medium length flights from three to two, the FAA worked closely with the industry to make flying safer. No longer subject to Dr. May's verbal abuse, the Department of Transportation worked hard toward its ultimate goal, the elimination of plane crashes from sea to shining sea.

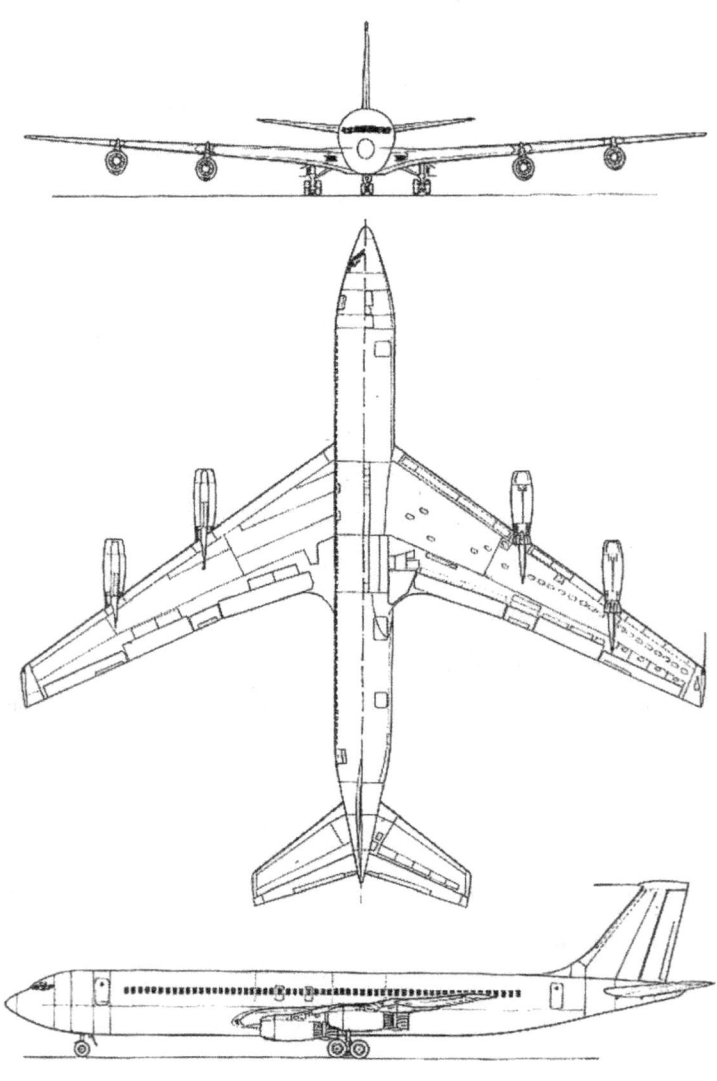

CHAPTER 3

When Automation Rules: Losing Our Sense of What is Happening

ngineering practices have not changed significantly since the time of the steam locomotive. This profession was brought to life by engeniators—a Latin word describing people who created devices. They were practical craftsmen and artisans dating back to the ancient Greeks. In Italy Leonardo Da Vinci bore the title of Ingegnere Generale. These innovators investigated why methods and designs worked. Their skills were applied for the public good, from aqueducts to waterways to bridges. They were the original civil engineers. The millions who earn their living from flying, maintaining and managing tens of thousands of commercial aircraft are heirs to the pioneering work of these remarkable engeniators.

With the scientific revolution, engineering adopted a new approach to solving problems. Mathematics became an integral part of design. More precise measurements and predictions became central to more reliable designs. For the first time it became possible to calculate

19

in advance the forces involved in the design. This resulted in great savings of time and expense. The earlier in the design process problems can be eliminated by engineers, the easier they are to fix.

While science can be purely theoretical, engineering is always associated with practical application. This is one of the reasons why it took so long for engineering to become a scientific profession. Theoretical scientists, who didn't really want to get their hands dirty, viewed engineering as a second-class profession.

Based on the early work of geniuses such as Descartes, science discovered that one way to approach many types of problems was to break them up into their component parts. This atomization, or analytic decomposition, of the whole resulted in many rapid advances and quickly became the accepted method for examining problems and devising solutions. It is much easier to sort out the workings of a simple system rather than that of the entire system, just as a single cell's structure is less complex than the entire body of a person. If each part of the machine is reliable, then the entire machine should be reliable.

Machines created up through the mid-1950s were fairly simple electro-mechanical devices. It was relatively straightforward to look at each component and, as long as each one was reliable, to conclude that the entire system would be reliable. This was bolstered by the creation of statistical methods where, if one had the historical data, fairly accurate predictions could be made on the reliability of simple components. By "simple" we mean they must truly be a random, or stochastic, process. Like a coin toss, the probability of the failure of a metal part can be calculated.

While all scientific progress is built on the works of others, the creation of the practical applications in modern statistics is often attributed to William Gosset, Head Brewer and later Head Experimental Brewer for Guinness. The company was, at the time, increasing production and seeking ways to ensure quality after the volumes grew too large for each batch to be sampled. The brewers were able to determine metrics such as the percentage of soft resins in a batch but couldn't confirm what those numbers meant in terms of consistency across batches. While people were already using small samples to estimate the outcomes, they didn't know how accurate those estimates were. Gosset, who had studied natural sciences and mathematics at Oxford, was asked to investigate. He first determined, based on studying the matter, that just two samples could provide a close measurement 80% of the time, with three there was an 87.5% chance, and with four that number increased to 92%. While this was useful he did not know the mathematical basis for this measurement and so he spent two years working with Karl Pearson's biometrics lab at University College, London to find the answers.

While Pearson was later credited with establishing the entire field of statistics, it was Gosset's work that led to the "law of errors" for small samples. Interestingly, due to the concerns of Guinness, he could not publish under his own name, so in the end, published under the name "Student", and his "invention" we now call "Student's t-distribution".

This work was wonderful for testing the quality of manufactured products, and with computers the work has become more accurate. Using historical data we can calculate to a fine degree the probability of failure, or success. However, this approach works only for those types of products subject to random distribution. This fact has been widely ignored, as most of the standards written required entering a statistical probability to obtain approval. In more complex systems where it is impossible to create statistical rates of failure (such as software), these numbers were estimated. Obtaining real numbers for complex systems and critical system components is impossible.

How did engineers and designers lose sight of the critical fact that statistics cannot be applied to everything, especially complex systems that are central to our lives?

Through the first part of the 20th century, science and philosophy were closely intertwined. Newton, Faraday and Einstein were considered to be "philosopher-scientists", committed to the scientific process. Einstein insisted that science without philosophy was primitive and muddled. To their credit, engineers understood the philosophy underlying the scientific method.

The intertwining of these two fields began to diminish by the second half of the 20th century. Perhaps this explains the unfortunate move towards new methods for analysis of complex systems that simply were not up to the task. First was the previously discussed desire towards atomization to the component level. To a true philosopher-scientist, the flaw in industry's march toward analyzing components and later applying statistics becomes obvious. Absent the philosophical aspect, we are left with people applying methods by rote without questioning the methodology chosen to solve the problem. In so doing they created a problem that has led directly to the never-ending story at the heart of our book. Again and again, basic assumptions have been made, based entirely on a failed theory of probability. The result is automated system failures that happen too quickly for humans to intervene and prevent tragic accidents.

A few keen observers saw and understood this problem by the late 1950s when more complex systems were being created. They knew statistics that work well when applied to mechanical components were not yielding the same reliable results for entire systems. They also saw that components acting together or reacting to other components could result in completely different system behavior.

These people were still thinking as philosopher-scientists, looking more deeply into the problems instead of just applying already learned methods. A new field, system theory, was created to help understand these interactions.

As these experts began studying this problem, the computer revolution was getting underway. Universities never caught on to teaching system theory and over time the system engineers reverted back to what they were comfortable with—analytic reductionism. The designers believed that even if a machine had thousands or millions of parts it was still possible to analyze each part separately and then combine them to get a statistical value of system reliability. It was comfortable; it was what they had learned in school.

The airline industry expected there should not be an accident more than once every ten million hours. The reasoning was that if the most critical parts were reliable to one failure every 1,000,000,000 hours the entire system would hit the ten million hour target. The system also relied on pilots to manage those aspects which the engineers could not address, as well as those scenarios engineers did not envision during the design process.

Despite the earlier work in cybernetics, there was an increasing reliance on statistics by the late 1960s. Computers supported enhanced statistical analysis and a reversion to analytic reductionism. That method could work for those systems relying on mechanical components, in part because numbers are very convincing.

Decision makers failed to understand the limitations of statistics. They insisted on having a numerical probability, and engineers dutifully complied (a problem that continues to this day). This was perfect for boards of directors who lacked a scientific background and are chosen for their celebrity status, government, or political connections— Caroline Kennedy on the board of Boeing.

This error would compound itself and ultimately open the door to junk science. People became so enamored with numbers that they began applying them to probability situations which were clearly outside the ability of statistics to capture. As the philosopher/scientist era ebbed, the application of statistics to non-stochastic processes was coupled with a strong desire to have a numerical value for success. To this day statistics are required to be used on many applications where they simply will not work.

The naïve unquestioned application of these methods has led to many self-defeating assumptions. One of the best examples and a key focus of our work is the application of statistical analysis to computerized systems. A complex computer is analyzed like any other hardware component, but it has little in common with those simple parts.

The popular belief is that computers never make errors, which is generally true, but not in the way most people believe. Computers will reliably do what they are designed to do which unfortunately is the problem system designers all too often don't understand. The designer may not have considered the actual scenario in which the computer finds itself. When writing software code, computer programmers must rely on the requirements provided, which are based on assumptions about situations a computer will encounter while accomplishing a goal.

This is a little like writing a detailed step-by-step set of instructions and recipes for an elaborate dinner. If all happens the way you expect, the dinner will turn out perfectly. But what happens if an ingredient is missing and needs to be substituted, or the oven's temperature is a bit off? A real cook can adjust for these aspects, but a computer never does more than it was programmed to do. Software designers must take into account every variation they can think of. Problems arise when the situation varies based on the actions of other software and human reactions. Anything can happen in this unpredictable environment.

Unfortunately, computers are frequently seen as a panacea for any complicated problem. Software is cheap to add, much cheaper than making changes to the design itself, and can accomplish a great many things. But in safety-critical systems the devil lies in the assumptions. In one infamous case, a radiation medical device, the Therac-25, massively overdosed six people. Unfortunately, the designers did not consider how humans would actually use the system, or the problems that might occur when things failed to go as expected. The assumptions were wrong.

Another case involves keyless cars. The system detects the driver's "fob" and enables the start switch to work. All this is fine, but several problems have occurred. One happens when a driver finds the accelerator sticking while on the highway. In a traditional vehicle the driver would simply turn the key, but this car has no a key. It has a button. Can the driver just push the button and shut it off? It's not that simple, because the designers decided that if the car is in gear and the button were accidentally pressed the sudden shutdown of the engine could be a hazard. As the engine stops running, the car slows down. The likely loss of steering and braking were certainly not what the designers wanted.

As a safety feature, the system requires the driver to hold the button down for perhaps 3 seconds or tap the button several times (models vary). Unfortunately most people do not read the manual and as a result they push the button repeatedly in an attempt to shut the engine off, all to no avail. In another case a driver might park in their garage, place the keys on the kitchen counter and not realize that the newer quiet engine is still running. This has led to carbon monoxide poisoning.

There is another important aspect of assigning computers control. The more we automate the more we remove the human from the "loop." This is, of course, intentional. After all, what would be the point of automating a system if we still expect a human to closely monitor it? Unfortunately the unexpected consequences of this approach can make it difficult or impossible to stop the damage triggered by automation failure.

If a pilot is not monitoring an automated system then we blame the pilot. We automate cars, such as the Tesla's "automatic pilot," but then blame the driver when he become distracted or places too much trust in the system. Adding a computer to the mix leads us, as humans, to lose some of our sense of what is happening.

As an example, if a person is adjusting the flame on a gas stove they have direct control over the flame, and they can visually see the flame and know how much their input affected the size of the flame. However, if we remove our visual on the flame and now rely on a computer to tell us how big it is, we are now dependent on that computer's programming. If we have also ceded control of the flame to the computer, we have also now ceded control of the size.

At this point both our perception and control is moved back a step. Assume the computer is deciding how much flame is required to increase the rate of cooking. Now it also needs to know something about the size of the pot. It's also important to realize what is in inside the pot as well as the quantity. Things start getting complicated quickly. If the assumptions given to the computer are inaccurate the outcome is not what we want.

While a person knows how much is in the pot and what is in it, the computer is dependent on what we tell it or what it is sensing via whatever sensor scheme it might be connected to. Further, how it is cooked is now left to the whims of the person who came up with requirements for the computer. All this might be fine if one does not know how to cook, but how well does it work for a master chef who knows better than the computer what is needed for a great meal?

The size of the flame is being controlled both by the person and the computer, a problem that can lead to conflicts, as well as unexpected outcomes. The same is true for any computer-controlled system. That said, we also know that we can increase functionality with computers. A computer allows us to have a lot more features. We also can have the flame on high until the water boils and then automatically go to a low simmer. That will help us avoid burning a stew when we get distracted chopping vegetables.

Understanding how these complex systems are actually working, and figuring out what went wrong when they don't work, has become a lot more challenging. If the food burns on our automatic stove, was it the fault of the cook or the automatic system? How do you sort this out?

We have been living with false confidence that we can better understand our world through simplification. When things went wrong on the stove we thought we could dissect all the components and figure out the culprit. However, when there are multiple actors who all influence how the other parts behave, it does not work.

Encountering a complicated problem, we break each component down, solve each sub-component and put it back together. Children are taught how to apply this idea to math problems at a fairly young age. We take that logical method and extrapolate it to most complex problems we come across. The truth is this only works part of the time. Consider that math problem we can solve by breaking it down. Now imagine what would happen if every time we start solving that sub-component all the other sub-components become something else. Now add in yet another layer. Imagine that when we put all the subcomponents back together they come out to something entirely new and there is no way to accurately predict what that new evolving thing is. Each tweak of some minor aspect changed the entire outcome. It does not take too much imagination to see what our imaginary stove would do if we had multiple computers and multiple people all trying to work on the same pot of stew!

These are the types of problems impacting advanced technologies. A pilot that has no way of knowing what the flight controls are actually doing, but is still blamed for anything that goes wrong, is one consequence of this failure system. This is the situation we have seen at too many accidents. Consider the choices of what information a chemical plant operator needs to do his job. The operator is dependent on the decisions made by people who designed the system long before it became operational. If some circumstance has changed in a way that the designers did not anticipate, the operator may not be able to prevent a catastrophe. Like our stove example earlier, the assumptions of the designers might not match the real needs of the system.

A good example is the automatic brake control in a car that stops for a small object leaving us to be rear-ended by the surprised driver behind us. Did designers trying to prevent a front-end collision really not consider the possibility of being rear ended?

Absent a major breakthrough, computers remain limited to those problems that we can well define. Even with the hype of machine learning, these limitations will be with us unless we can create boundaries to the environment and eliminate surprises. Humans are still uniquely able to manage an unexpected, poorly defined problem. We are also still the best system for solving problems that are completely novel.

Next we will look at how a failure to adapt to the unique challenges of automation has adversely impacted the airline industry.

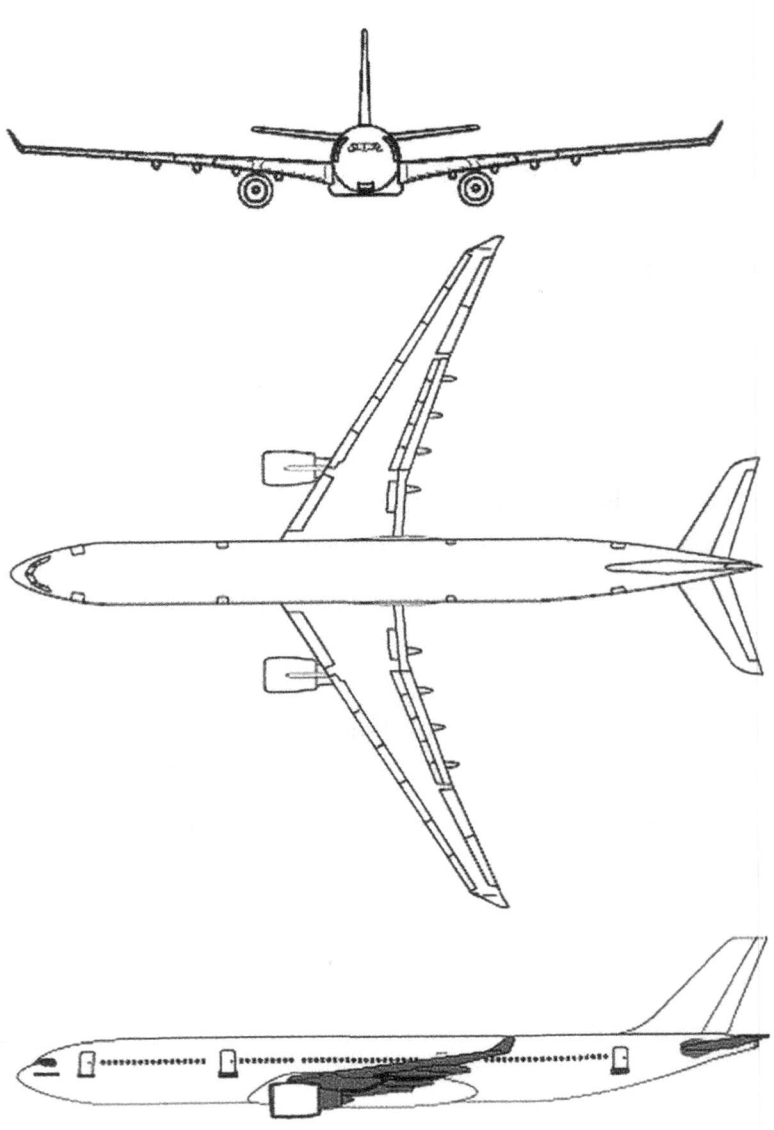

CHAPTER 4

Air France 447: The Plane That Couldn't Stall

early a decade before the first Boeing 737 MAX crash in Indonesia, another plane built by competitor Airbus was headed back to Paris from Rio in the hands of an aviation dream team, three of Air France's top pilots. They were flying an Airbus 330, an aircraft that had a perfect record over the past decade. Since it inaugural flight in 1992 over 100 million passengers, far more than the population of France, had flown about the world on nearly a million Airbus 330/340 flights.

The June 1, 2009 loss of Air France 447 was one of the most important and troubling accidents in aviation history. This event quickly called into question many of the most commonly held assumptions about the integrity of flight automation and its ability to control the aircraft with built in computer "protections." The jet was flown by a three-man crew because the eleven hour flight time required each pilot to take a required rest period. The primary focus of adding a third pilot for flights over eight hours is to ensure that the captain and the first officer are rested and alert for the approach and landing after the long flight. Because the relief pilot has more flexibility the best sleep periods are taken by the "operating" crew. Typically the captain assigns the relief first officer to take the first rest. This is a normal choice since neither operating pilot would be tired when the plane took off. The captain rarely takes the last period because that would mean he or she would still be a bit groggy during approach planning. Following industry practice on long overnight flights, Captain Marc Dubois took the second rest period after the flight departed Rio.

A little over three hours into the flight Air France 447 was in cruise at 35,000 feet approaching the equator. Nothing ominous appeared on the aircraft weather radar as the captain left the cockpit for his nap. He rang the chime in the crew rest area and the relief first officer came forward. After a brief discussion, the relief first officer took the captain's seat and the captain left the flight deck to prepare for his assigned rest. Flying at 8 miles per minute, it was not long before new convective weather activity began appearing on the radar screens. The relief first officer suggested a small turn to go around what appeared to be the heaviest storm areas. As the flight circumvented the weather, the pilots suddenly encountered what sounded like heavy rain. Shortly afterwards all three airspeed indicators went to zero and the autopilot disconnected. Over the next 40 seconds the startled pilots reacted quickly. As the first officer struggled to maintain the wings level in the storm tops, the nose of the aircraft slowly tilted up. Soon the aircraft encountered an aerodynamic stall, where the wings could not produce enough lift to sustain flight. This was triggered by the fact that the nose had been raised as the aircraft's actual speed decreased. The pilots had both lost their flight deck airspeed indications, as the twin engine jet's airspeed dropped. Why did these accomplished pilots not realize they were going too slow?

Loss of airspeed indication on their flight deck may have led them to distrust the stall warning system, perhaps assuming it was sending a false alert triggered by failure of airspeed indications. Although this is not an accurate diagnosis of the problem, it is a common misconception in today's world of automated flight. In smaller aircraft, sound can be a good indication of speed, but this is not the case with big jets. In this case, sounds such as heavy rain or hail just added to the perception of speed. In conventional aircraft the pilots can judge speed by the feel of the flight controls. Alas, this was not a conventional airplane.

Like the newer Boeing 777 or 787, the Airbus A330 is fly-by-wire. This means that pilot controls are not directly connected to the control surfaces which do not necessarily move directly with the cockpit controls as seen on older large aircraft. Although only connected via hydraulic actuators, the direct ratio of the movement of these controls to the surface position of the controls means that the aircraft will respond differently to a given control input based on airspeed.

Fly-by-wire jets do not operate like traditional planes. Aircraft pitch controls (nose up or down) work to set a desired g-rate at this altitude. This means that a neutral stick maintains the normal force of gravity. Pulling back increases the force with the wings supporting a bit more than the weight of the aircraft and pushing the acceleration upwards. Pushing the stick forward reduces the amount of lift the wings are producing and the plane accelerates downwards.

The fly-by-wire flight control computer adjusts the control surface (elevator) position to match the commanded rate. How much it needs will vary on multiple factors such as airspeed, thrust, turbulence and more. The bottom line is that there is no direct ratio between how much the pilot moves the controls and the control surface position. It is all tempered through the computers.

What does this mean for Air France 447 as it heads across the Atlantic? In this case, there is no way for the pilots to get a good sense of where they are in the "flight envelope," a term that pinpoints the parameters in which the airplane can be safely flown. There is no airspeed, no sound, no haptic feedback from the controls, really no feedback at all. Without feedback it's pretty much like walking blind through an unfamiliar house.

Of course there are other indications of an aerodynamic stall. In light airplanes the aircraft will pitch down as it stalls. Unfortunately, this is not the case for large swept wing transports where this cue is absent. Another cue is stall buffet. The air is not flowing smoothly over the wings and that turbulent flow causes the aircraft to shake. The way this happens on a large swept wing jet is much different than on a small airplane.

Because of all these problems the experienced Air France 447 flight crew never recognized that their plane had stalled. Everything that happened was beyond their training or experience. Nearly four minutes after the autopilot disconnected the airplane fell into the Atlantic ocean killing all 228 people on board.

And why?

So where did the industry go wrong? There are many layers to this.

We'll start with simulators, the ultimate high tech training tool that is so effective and efficient that many newly minted pilots outside the United States begin working on commercial jets with minimal hands on flying experience, often as little as a couple of hundred hours. Most of their actual flight training takes place on trusted simulators.

Simulators only work when manufacturers have the fundamental data required to make these machines effective for training. An inadequately trained pilot or an incorrectly programmed simulator can lead to unexpected consequences. In 2009 most of the industry didn't realize that airline simulators failed to correctly replicate an aerodynamic stall. Recognition of this problem began to revolutionize flight training. But before pilots could be correctly retrained, simulators needed to be upgraded. The challenge was making sure that ground-based simulator motion accurately replicated the sensations of flight. This upgrade would help pilots develop a much better feel for the way their big aircraft handled.

Simulator manufacturers historically concentrated on making sure the systems replicate real flight, so that any failure would reliably create the same indications for pilots that would occur in the real world. Pilots would learn how to respond to these potential failure scenarios, such as an engine fire or a hydraulic leak. If they followed the procedures, as designed by the aircraft manufacturer, the simulator would indicate the problem was under control. To do this they required the actual "boxes" from the real airplane. The instruments, flight controls and switches are all the actual components used on a real airplane. It is fed data from an artificial world, but as far as the instrument "knows" the indication is real, not simulated.

In the real world, the modeling of the actual way the airplane performs aerodynamically is entirely dependent on information provided from the aircraft manufacturer. Most of the basic flight data for normal flight or expected emergencies was provided. The simulator could accurately replicate the control forces needed for a pilot to manage an event such as an engine failure or a flight control malfunction. The problem was that modeling the dynamics of an actual stall is far more challenging. In the absence of critical airplane manufacturer data, simulator companies did not have the technical information needed to model how these modern swept-wing jets behave in a stall. Unfortunately this stall data is very difficult to obtain from an industry worried about liability. Because each stall is different, it is difficult to decide which one to use. The response from most of the aircraft manufacturers was to not provide any data. While this may sound irresponsible it's actually a classic example of everyone in a large corporation doing their job. In an industry where a single crash can have a devastating impact on a company, the legal department may understandably have the final word. Even a company that is well insured wants to minimize its liability to keep renewal rates down.

CHAPTER 5

The Simulator Challenge

To comply with new regulations put in place in the aftermath of Air France 447, the simulator companies have largely been forced to rely on data provided by third parties which never quite matches the actual data. To be sure, the data provided by third parties is better than what was previously offered but it is not quite right. The problem remains that simulators can only replicate what they are programmed to do, and many aspects of flight are still not in the "areo package." The result is that pilot training is not as good as it could be. While simulators are very valuable they do not offer a perfect a model of the real world. Models are necessarily limiting. At best they are an abstraction of the real world, and the factors a model presents are based on the designer's subjective evaluation. In the case of a flight simulator, they create a hypothetical flight. Equally important, you can't die in these forgiving machines. Simulators give pilots a second chance. Airplanes do not.

Aircraft react to all kinds of anomalies in the real world. Small variations in temperature or a few insects smashed on the wing will subtly alter the way air flows over the wings. Fortunately, the impact here is minor. By contrast a small amount of ice adhering to the wings can make a major difference. Layer on more problems like pilot fatigue or design defects and the issues become bigger challenges.

Regulars at an airport might talk about how that aircraft hangar alongside the runway can make the landing "squirrely." Winds coming from a certain direction or hot air rising from a parking lot on approach, can prompt a last-minute landing control adjustment. The aircraft reacts in ways that are not always predictable. It's impossible to anticipate these seemingly minor issues that quickly add up to major challenges. Out of necessity, the aerodynamic model for a simulator is much simpler than in the real world.

As discussed, manufacturers do a reasonably good job of mimicking real airplane behavior as long as they have reliable data. When a company is not required to provide data for their airplane in certain regimes (e.g., a full stall at high cruise altitude) that data is nonexistent. Even if they do testing, they may not have retained the data or, if they have, may not be willing to share it.

Guessing what a plane will do can be very dangerous. A classic example of this industry problem was incorrect simulator training that misled the pilots of an American Airlines Airbus 300. This flight crashed shortly after takeoff from New York's JFK in November 2001. The accident investigation revealed that a procedure created in an airline simulator recommended a new approach to handling an unexpected roll. The standard technique, using the aircraft's ailerons, was replaced with rudder deflection. Here, best intentions worked great in theory and failed dramatically in the air.

On an A300, like in other conventional airplanes, roll is normally controlled via the ailerons, which are moveable surfaces at the trailing edge of each wing. Traditionally the control wheel is turned in the direction of the desired roll. In the case of a fly-by-wire Airbus aircraft, the control stick is moved in the chosen direction.

On one wing a panel moves upwards, decreasing lift. On the opposite wing a panel moves downwards, increasing lift. In addition, on large airplanes there are spoiler panels, which deflect upwards on a wing to decrease lift. For a rapid turn, panels on the downward moving wing will be deflected upwards to further decrease lift on that side. It is also possible to roll the aircraft using just the rudder. When the rudder is deflected, the airplane initially is rotated and the oncoming air hits the aircraft at an angle. For example, if the pilot pushes the left rudder, the airplane rotates to the left. The airplane is now moving sideways in a manner called a "sideslip". When this occurs, air starts moving around the airplane in a way that increases the angle of attack of the wing—that is, in this example, on the right side. That response leads to the airplane rolling to the left. If the airplane has swept wings, as most jet airliner aircraft do, there is an additional effect. The rotation results in the wing moving forward, thus increasing the lift due to a longer effective span, as shown in the diagram below. Interestingly, there is a pervasive misconception among many pilots that the cause of the roll is not the sideslip but an increase in speed with one wing. This is yet another example of flaws in training that need to be corrected as soon as possible.

In the case of American Airlines, it looked perfect on a simulator. Unfortunately, the airline's training simulators were not programmed to replicate the excessive forces that could be encountered on a bigger plane.

EFFECT OF SWEEPBACK

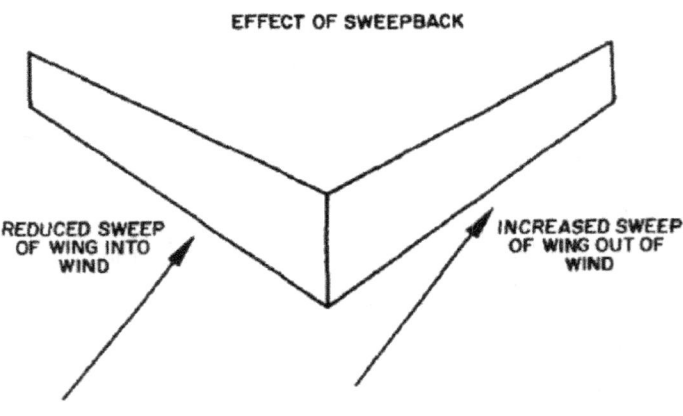

REDUCED SWEEP
OF WING INTO
WIND

INCREASED SWEEP
OF WING OUT OF
WIND

Figure 1—Aerodynamics for Naval Aviators Page 297

On departure from New York's JFK airport, the crew of American 587 ran into wake turbulence from a previous departure. Their Airbus A300 rolled to the side and the first officer, who was flying, reacted as he was trained on the simulator with a rudder input to counter the roll. The airplane rapidly rolled in the opposite direction. To stop that roll he reversed the rudder, making successive rudder inputs. Each time the nose swung, it was followed by a roll. This sideways motion put more force on the vertical stabilizer. As it swung the opposite way, the pilot made another input that backfired, doubling the force on the vertical stabilizer. Both the motion of the aircraft and large rudder input combined to drastically exceed the design limits of the vertical stabilizer. The stabilizer broke, leading to a total loss of control and crash.

Simulator concepts were modeled for training, not engineering. They created the false impression that a procedure that worked in the simulator would also succeed in the airplane. In a similar way, there were also efforts to replicate the response of large airplanes using small aircraft. While those smaller airplanes specially designed with fly-by-wire controls can mimic a large airplane response, they are still not a perfect solution to this problem in terms of replicating behavior in a stall. Similarly, some advocated using small aerobatic airplanes. While they were good fun, this approach is generally no more accurate than driving a small sports car in an attempt to replicate how a multi-trailer truck would jackknife.

Clearly improved flight simulation then is the only viable way to model a stall where the wings lose lift. Unfortunately, having the data to replicate a stall is one thing, having a simulator do it is far more difficult. As it happens, the shaking in the real airplane is so violent that for most pilots it feels like the airplane is breaking apart. It would be impossible to make this happen on a simulator without destroying it.

High altitude stall buffet feels fundamentally different than anything most pilots outside of flight testing have ever experienced. Some pilots confuse the sensation with turbulence. Unless pilots expect the possibility of buffeting, they may miss this critical stall cue. Another confusing element for pilots is the fact that buffeting encountered on small aircraft during stall recovery training is relatively mild. Many pilots expect the same for a large transport jet, not realizing that buffeting on a big jet is far stronger when stalling at higher altitudes, more analogous to the experience one might have driving at 20 miles per hour sideways across a series of railroad tracks.

The force and frequency of the vibrations is so strong that the human head wobbles uncontrollably and the flight instruments become a blur. Because this event doesn't feel like a stall, many pilots have confused this phenomenon with extreme turbulence. Perhaps some have even worried that it indicated a structural failure. Because they have never flown or trained on an approach to stall at high altitude, crews may not recognize what is going wrong. In fact, even if they have been trained there is a fair chance they will not recognize it in the real world. If you do not realize that you are in danger you won't respond correctly. It's impossible for pilots to recover from a stall if they don't realize they are already in one (absent an unintentional recovery, which has occurred on several occasions).

An unexpected stall is not entered the same way pilots experience it in training. The lead-up cues are missed in an unscripted event. Adding to the confusion is the fact that the airplane often is not actually stalling, at least at first. Instead what often occurs is that the high angle of attack creates a lot of drag. Lacking engine thrust to overcome the drag, the airplane starts to descend, often fairly rapidly. It is not quite stalling, but rather it is doing what pilots call "mushing". Failing to recognize this condition, the pilot attempts to slow the descent and then the real stall occurs.

Even if a pilot recognizes it, the fast descent rate has created a situation where a much more extreme descent is needed to recover, well beyond what the pilot was trained for. In the past this was just "powering out of the stall" as will be described below. Today it is reducing the pitch until the stall warning stops. What happens if there is no stall warning or the pilot believes it is false? In that situation the flight crew might assume, in error, that they were wrong. This would lead them to incorrectly conclude that the plane is not stalling, or guess there is another factor such as a wind shear. It's relatively easy to understand why even an experienced pilot with a perfect record might fail to recognize a stall. As humans, our brains filter out information that seems irrelevant. This protects us from becoming overwhelmed by too much information. Recognition also depends on our perception of the progress we are making toward a specific goal. If the indications that are actually occurring for a stall don't match our expectations, we may have trouble assigning them a high priority.

Another potential challenge is that modern simulators have no way to warn instructors or pilots when they have exceeded known parameters. Also, a grounded simulator's motion is necessarily limited. For example, there is no way it can replicate a prolonged "falling" sensation. Other forces are similarly compromised to varying degrees. Many people have experienced this in some of the newer amusement park rides that are really just simulators. At times the motion does not quite match the visual that is being depicted. Given this history why did it take a major Air France accident to redesign simulators in the first place? Much of the problem was due to the industry's reliance on statistical data. High altitude stalls were a rare occurrence. In addition, newer aircraft such as the A330 had automatic protection systems that when operational, made a stall virtually impossible. These protections led to overconfidence in an industry where stall training was traditionally not a priority for airlines or regulators. Before Air France 447, stall training consisted of "powering" out of the stall, adding enough thrust and allowing the airplane to accelerate. This was a nice coordination maneuver to test the skills of pilots, but of little value for the real event. The industry simply failed to recognize the need for more robust stall training. Apparently the combination of aircraft flight control protections along with better alerting systems "virtually" eliminated the possibility of getting into a stall—unless they fail. There was a certain irony here. Warning systems are built to send instant cues designed to keep humans out of harm's way. When these systems behave abnormally, we may tune these warnings out. On the other hand, crews can overreact to a nonexistent problem. A spurious warning, such as a defective nose-gear warning light, might distract a flight crew from the fact that their plane is unexpectedly descending. This actually happened to a 1972 Eastern Airlines flight that crashed in the Florida Everglades. In addition to Air France 447, there have been several other accidents which should have been an immediate wakeup call for the industry. An American Airlines crew stalled an Airbus A300 in 1997 and luckily averted a crash. In that case the pilots were not aware that the throttles had been moved below the auto throttle range and needed to be manually set as they descended to 16,000 feet. Entering a holding pattern, the power was slightly increased but not enough. The pilots were focused on avoiding the worst of several thunderstorms in the area and, as the airplane rolled into the turn, it stalled.

Fortunately, the aircraft rolled over into a steep bank and recovered from the stall naturally, with the pilots pulling out of the resulting dive. When an airplane is banked steeply the nose naturally drops. The rollover into the bank may have saved them as neither pilot recognized the plane had stalled. More recently, in the aftermath of Air France 447, an Air Asia Airbus A320, captained by a veteran pilot, crashed into the Java Sea in 2014 after stalling at high altitude.

He was busy trying to troubleshoot a faulty electrical system while flying through a convective storm. The same year, an Air Algérie MD-80 also stalled and crashed in similar weather. In this case, the engines were not putting out enough thrust due to icing over of sensors measuring pressure for the engine fuel controller. Like a carburetor, the controller uses the pressure to determine the proper amount of fuel to meter into the engine. Unfortunately, the crew did not notice the airspeed decay, probably because they were focused on convective storms ahead. These and other crashes in recent years took place on planes flown by experienced test pilots and veteran airline captains. Accident analysts were surprised that these flight crews did not quickly recognize that they were stalling. Clearly something went wrong in training.

Further complicating this situation is the fact that due to retirements, the number of airline pilots with hands-on flying experience at high altitudes is shrinking rapidly. Pilots seldom hand-fly an actual airplane at cruise altitudes. In fact, it is virtually unheard of due to the regulations enacted in recent years. When pilots actually hand flew they simply followed a flight director that kept the airplane symbol on the cross-hairs. Very often this resembled a video game with augmented controls that make the airplane easier to handle. Training regimens focused on procedures and the ability of pilots to follow them. Making sure airline pilots were versatile aviators, well-qualified to handle the unexpected with stick-and-rudder skills, was a lower priority for airlines fighting hard to attract passengers with low fares.

The rigid focus on conformity did not guarantee system safety. Airlines used the metrics from data monitoring and reporting systems to "see how well they are doing." Lower numbers were seen as a big plus. But what is this really telling us? Was the data getting better or was there just less reporting of abnormal incidents? Perhaps pilots were inadvertently being "trained" to avoid certain actions that will trigger a report, making the data look good while actual risks remain hidden. The danger was that pilots were being type rated to fly complex aircraft with a lack of knowledge or skill sets needed to fly beyond the very narrow parameters in scripted training. As a result, they finished training lacking the actual resilience and ingenuity to come up with solutions to unexpected challenges.

CHAPTER 6

The FAA: Where Perfect is Never Good Enough

"Every single member of (the) administration should be spending at least part of every day, if not thinking like a Secretary of Business, at least being mindful of their agency's impact on private sector job creation.

—Elaine Chao,
Secretary of Transportation

I n his April 2018 letter to CBS News producers, criticizing network coverage of the Federal Aviation Agency Administrator for Aviation Safety, Ali Bahrami wrote:

"We are never content with the status quo and the FAA is continually working to enhance safety for the flying public. Since 2009, there have been no fatal domestic air carrier accidents in the U.S. and commercial aviation fatalities in the U.S. have decreased by some 95 percent over the past 20 years as measured by fatalities per 100 million passengers on board."

Captain Chesley Sullenberger who brilliantly landed a crippled US Airways Airbus 320 on the Hudson River in December 2009 was thrilled by this milestone, "...something I wouldn't have thought possible 25 years ago."

Could there have been a better time to be a safety boss at the FAA? For Bahrami, who had returned to the agency the previous year after working for the Aerospace Industries Association trade group, this was certainly the best of times for his agency. With more than 50 crashes taking the lives of over 2,500 passengers in other countries during the same 2009 to 2018 timeframe, the FAA appeared to be the envy of the aviation world. An airworthiness directive from the leaders and best at the FAA had just as much credibility in Kiev or Kathmandu as it did in Seattle or Dallas. For the millions of passengers who trusted their lives to the agency's oversight every day, the FAA appeared to be government done right.

Bahrami's message resonated with the President of the United States, the first commander in chief to have actually run an airline and his Secretary of Transportation, Elaine Chao, the wife of Senate Majority Leader Mitch McConnell.

The President's empathy for the industry went all the way back to October 1988 when he bought twenty aging 727s from Eastern Air Shuttle to create the eponymous Trump Shuttle. After dolling up the carrier with faux marble sinks, chateaubriand box dinners and offering up to three drinks on the short hop from New York to Washington, he broke the cardinal rule of airline marketing: publicly trashing the competition.

As the *Daily Beast*'s Barbara Peterson wrote: "Trump decided he'd win customers away from Pan Am by scaring them. Pan Am was unsafe, he said. He had no proof of this, of course; his message was simply: 'I wouldn't fly them.'"

For Trump, who also gave passengers free chips good for his Atlantic City casinos, airline economics proved troubling. At one point he proposed breaking FAA rules by cutting flight crews from the legally required three people to two.

"I cringed every time he opened his mouth," Trump Shuttle President Bruce Nobles told Peterson.

"He really didn't understand the business and at times he said things that weren't helpful. That was his style and it really hasn't changed."

The fact that Trump Shuttle was losing money didn't stop the real estate developer from making a failed attempt to take over American Airlines. After the banks said no to his proposal he struggled to keep his tiny airline aloft. Less than three years after paying $365 million for the carrier that became his flying billboard, Trump relinquished control of the unprofitable airline to his bankers, losing his entire $20 million investment.

While Trump's ill-considered attempt to scare passengers off Pan Am didn't work, it offered a valuable life lesson: marketing is never a substitute for evidence based research. Conjecture is always a bad idea when people feel their lives might be at stake.

The American people, through their elected representatives have pushed hard to make sure that their government does its best to protect the traveling public. Public interest organizations and investigative reporters have played a key role here on everything from seatbelts to recalling Ford's fiery Pinto.

In aviation much of their focus was on the work of the Federal Aviation Agency. Founded two years after the tragic 1956 United/TWA crash over the Grand Canyon, the FAA had spent more than half a century working toward the recent record touted by Ali Bahrami in his self-congratulatory letter to CBS.

The FAA's success in the second decade of the 21st century explained why regulatory agencies around the world accepted American government certification decisions on new aircraft such as the Boeing 787. This was a bird in hand for sales teams at Boeing busy booking thousands of orders for the 737 MAX. With much fanfare this plane entered commercial service on May 22, 2017, with a flight from Kuala Lumpur to Singapore on Malindo Air, a division of Asia's largest aviation holding company, the Lion Group.

Underscoring this unprecedented success story was a shared industry commitment. From Boeing directors paid well into six figures annually for contributing their wisdom at monthly board meetings in Chicago to $9 an hour freelance software engineers telecommuting from India, everyone in the FAA supervised industry was doing their job. They all realized the industry's financial health and their livelihoods depended on the kind of safety record Ali Bahrami touted. No one wanted a crash.

Industry veterans may have felt a touch nervous about Bahrami's proud statement. It was a little like watching a perfect game in progress at Chavez Ravine or Fenway Park. Superstitious fans and broadcasters were reluctant to jinx the pitcher by breathing a word about what they were watching. This was why, for example, Southwest Airlines, did not advertise its perfect safety record.

By the time the Trump/Chao team went to work in January 2017, the FAA was the kind of agency members of congress could brag about in their constituent newsletters. While passengers complained about cramped seating, tight leg room, onerous change fees, baggage fees and seat fees, the industry touted the benefits of red tape cutting deregulation. The women and men of Congress who relied on the carriers to commute back and forth to their districts were proud of the fact that America's airlines were, year after year, among the safest in the world. Although no longer part of the Department of Commerce, federal aviation policy remained essential to the livelihoods of more than 2 million people working across the industry in every state in the land. Like the military, commercial aviation benefited every Congressional district. In return, manufacturers like Boeing paid far less taxes than the average American corporation, a mere eight percent in 2017. The astonishingly profitable airlines were so successful that carriers like Southwest were sitting on nearly $15 billion in cash.

The apparently successful collaboration between the FAA and the aviation industry buttressed the President's decision to mandate cutting two government regulations for every new one. Secretary Chao, who had arrived in America with her mother and sisters on a freighter from China, was the daughter of a shipping magnate. She and her family had been major donors to Majority Leader's Mitch McConnell's Senate campaigns in Kentucky prior to their marriage. Her lack of airline experience did not stand in the way of her becoming leader the world's most powerful transportation agency. The aviation industry and President Trump appreciated her easy access to McConnell who often held life or death power over the legislative branch. Able to stop Supreme Court appointments with a single press conference, he had singlehandedly become America's leading political roadblock, halting hundreds of House of Representatives bills from advancing to Senate debate.

The American aviation industry, under the aegis of the FAA is a lynchpin of the nation's economy including the export/import business, tourism and conventions. Air travel has helped make many smaller communities competitive with the nation's largest cities. The grand whistle-stop rail campaigns of yore have been replaced by air tours to mega rallies central to the success of politicians like Elaine Chao's boss.

Thanks to this public/private partnership American aviation has billed itself as an industrial safety role model. Boeing, like General Motors is central to our nation's military/industrial complex.

In many ways American aviation's primacy on the world market-place is a credit to the hard work of pilot and flight attendant unions, accident investigators, investigative journalists, and the Flight Safety Foundation. Tenacious lobbying of groups such as the National Air Disaster Alliance have done an extraordinary job representing the families of loved ones who perished in plane crashes.

Following the February 2009 Colgan Air/Continental Airlines turboprop crash on approach to Buffalo Airport, relatives of the victims pushed relentlessly in Congress for a series of reforms that addressed key regulatory oversights that contributed to that tragedy. Once again industry control problems had let passengers and their families down.

Pilots previously eligible to fly for a commercial airline with just 250 hours, now needed 1,500 hours of experience to qualify. New rest requirements and stall recovery training were also implemented by the FAA as part of the legislation approved by Congress in 2010. These reforms were a fitting tribute to all those lost in the Buffalo crash.

With the American industry entering the safest period in its history, manufacturers and the airlines assumed more responsibility for oversight through the FAA's Designated Aviation Representatives employed by Boeing and the airlines. The DOT and the FAA were gaining more confidence in the way these companies addressed safety challenges. Perhaps one day this concept of self-regulation under FAA guidance would extend to promising new inventions such as the driverless cars. With a "cross my heart and hope to die" commitment to their customers, entrepreneurs like Elon Musk promised they would safeguard the public as if it were their own family.

The FAA was clearly succeeding where other government agencies, such as the Drug Enforcement Agency and the Environmental Protection Agency, had let the nation down. Disasters such as the opioid crisis taking the lives of more than 45,000 Americans a year and the lead poisoning of drinking water in Flint, Michigan, documented the pressing need for more effective government regulation.

When we began writing Grounded it would have been difficult to find anyone who disagreed with Ali Bahrami's view that the FAA had clearly become the "world's preeminent air safety agency."

During research on our previous book, Angle of Attack, we interviewed Bahrami who explained the agency's response to the aerodynamic stall that led to the deaths of 228 people on Air France 447. Thanks in part to the leadership at the FAA, pilots at most airlines around the world were taking special training that taught them how to avoid the aerodynamic stall that took down the French plane en route from Rio to Paris. This course cost the airlines a pretty penny, over $100 million at last count, and it was money well spent.

The retraining process, which was completed in 2019, was well thought out. In 2016 co-author Captain Shem Malmquist was one of the first pilots to learn the new stall recovery procedure at the FAA's training headquarters in Oklahoma City. A decade after Air France 447 many pilots at major carriers now understand how to prevent the kind of aerodynamic stall that defeated that first rate French flight crew. The new approach shows pilots how to make a quick 10,000 feet dive to unstall the wings as the engines continue working perfectly.

As Bahrami and his teammates from the Department of Transportation and the White House applauded the industry, a new and completely unexpected challenge to the FAA's largely unchallenged worldwide authority was emerging. Fixing the aerodynamic stall problem that led to the Air France 447 crash was no panacea. Similar bad weather contributed to fatal 2014 Air Asia and Air Algérie crashes that killed 278 people. Clearly there was no 'one size fits all' solution to the challenges posed by high performance jets. More training was necessary to make sure pilots had the knowledge and insight to handle unexpected automation surprises.

This was all based on a kind of Hippocratic, "do no harm" oath that has long been part of the industry's moral code. A new collision avoidance system that would probably have prevented the 1956 crash above the Grand Canyon went through rigorous testing. Every step of the way evidence based analysis was reviewed by in-house FAA professionals and test pilots to insure new systems worked as designed.

Critical components typically came with multiple backup systems. Noncritical components were certified to make sure that in a worst case scenario, a failure would not limit the flight crews ability to make it to a nearby airport without incident. For example under ETOPS (extended twin operations) certification, manufacturers were required to prove that if one engine failed on a transoceanic flight, the aircraft could reliably fly to an alternate airport on the remaining engine.

The shift from the analog to the digital world began to change this trusted approach to aircraft design. The traditional control system was based on redundancy as well as the experience and ability of pilots to handle emergencies through clearly scripted checklists.

The problem is far from defeating the possibility of future accidents, automation introduced its own unique set of problems, often never seen before by the best in the business. Automation is sold on the idea that it will make our lives easier and save us money. For the end user this is certainly true. Automation also presents new and unexpected problems that make work less predictable for human operations. Instead of reducing their workload these problems can present what is called automation surprise. Because these changes typically reduce the workforce, more and more responsibility is delegated to fewer and fewer employees.

For nearly a century, movie theater projectionists essentially had two jobs. One was to make sure that the motor and the mechanical system feeding film reels into the projector worked properly: When a motor broke it was repaired. The second job required learning how to change the light bulb. With good basic training any projectionist could work at any theater because these systems were essentially universal.

In the early part of the 21st century cinemas began turning these historic film projectors into lobby museum pieces. Experienced projectionists were quickly amazed by all the new problems created by digital projectors. Computer hard drives crashed and had to be rebooted causing delays of ten minutes or more.

→ Circuit boards failed and had to be replaced.

→ Satellite delivery of films sometimes failed and there were problems with expired passwords requiring eleventh hour calls to tech support.

→ Some hard drives uploaded via a USB connection didn't ingest properly into the projector.

→ Color settings for 3D movies produced a green hue when content switched to regular films.

→ When the projectionist had a night off, assistant managers, with little or no training, had trouble solving these problems to the dismay of customers.

These technical difficulties can lead to other problems requiring a projectionist to become a jack of all technology trades. The tricky part is that even a well trained projectionist with a solid knowledge of the new system, can be undercut by a bad circuit board, a balky satellite or a hard drive that perished well ahead of its life expectancy.

When new "state of the art" systems arrive, projectionists struggle to find out what the manufacturers aren't telling them. As one veteran projectionist in Memphis told us: "Being able to handle all these new unexpected problems makes my job a lot more complicated."

In similar fashion the arrival of new computer technology and fly by wire systems suddenly eroded the primacy of the flight crew cut from three to two on short and medium distance flights. As flight engineers began disappearing in the 1980s, Airbus hard limits were set on what pilots could do. Hundreds of new checklists for emergency procedures were added to help pilots work their way out of unscripted problems.

Exciting new automation systems were sold on an argument central to the job of every executive, board member and government agency overseeing the regulatory system. Each one arrived with assurances that they could, once and for all, rule out what was believed to be the primary cause of aircraft accidents, human error. Machines, the sales force confidently told airline customers, were never distracted by a bad day on Wall Street or a child custody battle. They never hung out at bars during their off duty hours or played around with nubile interns. They were reliable and easy to upgrade via software upgrades or a quick fix at maintenance. Equally important, they saved money, making sure that the industry could win over passengers from other forms of transportation, especially on short hauls.

In some cases new systems were created that didn't require documentation in a manual or special training. Although this may have sounded a little weird to pilots who came up through the ranks, the bottom line was this: new pilots no longer had to fly fighters for a decade or longer to qualify for the right seat in the cockpit. The controls built into the plane appeared to simplify the job. Instead of demanding that pilots have many years of flying experience, the regulators could lighten up. Machine intelligence in aviation was sounding more and more like a high tech babysitter making sure newbies in the cockpit wouldn't make a mess of things.

A 23 year-old pilot could go to work for a Chinese airline with as little as a couple hundred hours of flight time. Although that was certainly not true in America, it was hard to tell a foreign customer placing a big order that they had to hire copilots with 1,500 hours of flight experience in a tight labor market. Suddenly automation, created to make

flying easier, became the rationale for cutting back hands on flight training. Effective training, the manufacturers told the airlines, could take
place on ground school and on a simulator. Experienced pilots could
master new models at home with just an hour or two on a tablet.

The FAA's primacy in aviation licensing, coupled with the European
Union Air Safety Administration (EASA), which oversaw aviation
superpower Airbus, created an uncontested duopoly. With these two
government agencies firmly setting standards worldwide in partnership
with aircraft manufacturers and airlines, governments around the globe
didn't need to perform their own due diligence. Even in countries with
strong aviation cultures like England, Germany, Canada and Australia
the FAA and EASA requirements were generally acceptable.

This vote of confidence was based in part on the assumption that
automation made new aircraft failsafe. We believe this view overlooks
the fact that humans are central to the success of all effective technology control systems. Lack of effective controls can threaten even the
most sophisticated operating system.

In most of the accidents around the world that we have studied
during the past decade it is clear that absent or insufficient controls
were always a central issue. Attempts to blame these crashes on a single
point of failure, a triggering event, a root cause or a chain of events is
dangerously misleading. Implying, for example, that most aviation accidents are the result of pilot error, diverts attention away from underlying control problems that could lead to more accidents. Blame is always
the enemy of safety.

Accepting our view at face value raises an important question.
Why did none of the dozens of accidents that took place during the

decade following Air France 447 happen on American carriers?

First, it's important to keep in mind that many other nations with outstanding airlines such as Canada, the United Kingdom, Japan and Australia also avoided commercial airline crashes during the same time frame. Second, the American experience is built on a long history of accidents that became an invaluable learning experience. It's also true that America has consistently been home to some of the best pilots in the world represented by strong unions that have done a good job promoting safety within their ranks. The National Transportation Safety Board has also been vigilantly promoting safety improvements through its "most wanted" list. The NTSB's independence and valuable criticism of the FAA on a wide range of issues ranging from MD-80 maintenance to lithium battery fires on the 787 have helped the industry succeed.

An anonymous reporting system that encourages pilots to report safety issues without fear of employer reprisal has also made a major contribution. Unlike many other countries, America encourages its pilots to speak out when they identify safety challenges. Thanks to Congressional whistle-blower protection they don't have to fear reprisal. Today's flight crews can help their own carrier and other airlines correct deficiencies that will benefits all of us.

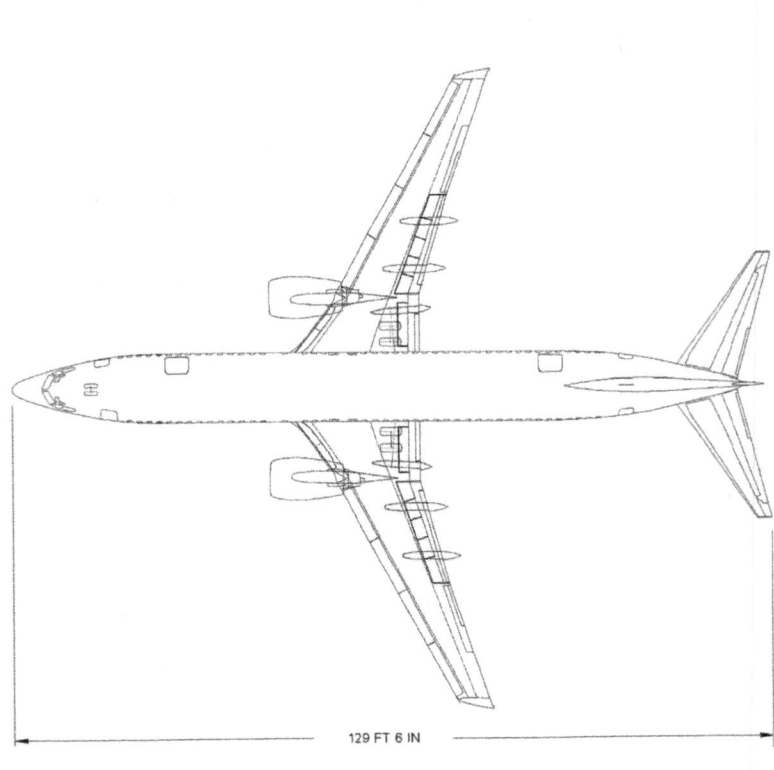

129 FT 6 IN

CHAPTER 7

Boeing's $280 Million Money Back Guarantee: The Strange Case of the 737 MAX

Thanks to remarkable aviation accident investigators, the world knows precisely why jets have hit Columbian mountaintops, plowed in to Iowa cornfields and plummeted into the South Atlantic They have worked non-stop to keep us safe and make sure past mistakes won't be repeated. Indeed, the creation of the FAA—not to mention the Transportation Security Agency—was a direct response to a collision caused by an air traffic control failure in the mid-1950s. We now know that most of these tragedies would have been prevented if proper controls and training had been in place from the ground up.

A conservative approach to aircraft design has been central to the industry's growth. Most passengers on short and medium length flights are flying on upgraded models that have been in service for decades. Newer long-range planes, such as the A350 and B-787, are designed around systems that have proven their reliability on older aircraft.

A key advantage to upgrading aircraft is that flight crews can quickly step up to the latest model. The assumption is that an experienced pilot who has spent thousands of hours flying a specific aircraft can quickly step up to a new model.

At Airbus, with its signature A320 fleet launched in the 1980s, and Boeing, which has made many billions selling the 737 for over half a century, upgrades are de rigueur. Reliability has been built on the absence of ambiguity. The assumption is that a pilot who understands the aerodynamics of her airplane will have little problem upgrading. Theoretically, memory items should make it easy for pilots to quickly handle any kind of unexpected anomalies with new aircraft.

This approach is a key to the success of the Airbus's fly-by-wire aircraft. An outstanding example is the fuel efficient A320neo launched at Lufthansa in 2016. System upgrades typically focus on new software that can be streamed to the entire fleet. Unexpected problems can often be remedied with a software fix uploaded more quickly than changes to the plane's hardware. Instead of regulatory agencies grounding a fleet and sending all the planes to maintenance, the new software can be added with minimal downtime.

Air France 447, as we explained in *Angle of Attack*, was a dramatic departure from that solution. Following this crash, the worst accident in French aviation history, there were major hardware and software changes. The entire industry response to stall recovery at high altitudes, where most of the flying happens, was revamped. To implement this solution airlines around world spent over $100 million training pilots on high altitude stall recovery training. Airbus management also recommended that carriers continue to invest more time and money in flight crew training, especially on simulators. Everywhere in the world training requirements are mandated by regulatory agencies. Aircraft type ratings are required to make sure pilots are qualified to handle unexpected control problems. This certification process is a good way to make sure that experienced pilots can, if necessary, go beyond scripted checklists to quickly head off challenges that may be beyond the scope of their training.

Many military veterans who dominated the cockpits of burgeoning airlines after World War II, went to work with years of previous flying experience. But by the 1980s, when the first fly-by-wire planes were being introduced, automation created challenges never previously seen on legacy aircraft. All those computers led to a commonly heard complaint: "What is the system doing?"

For the airlines, the cost of flight training has had a big impact on their ability to attract qualified pilots. By the end of the 2008-2009 recession many new pilots were graduates of flight schools where a degree could cost $100,000 or more. With entry-level jobs at the regional carriers paying $30,000 a year or less, new pilots were in debt for years paying off their student loans. Inevitably the supply of new pilots tightened. Taking thousands of pilots offline for training on new aircraft could have forced some airlines to cut flight schedules in a boom market.

As the airlines went on a buying spree for fuel-efficient aircraft it was crucial that crews could simply transition to an upgrade of the model they were already flying. This is one of the reasons why the A320neo was a hit with carriers.

Determined to catch up with Airbus, Boeing created the 737 MAX ahead of schedule, with the first deliveries scheduled for 2017. Thousands of Max orders meant Boeing assembly lines were being pushed toward their limit. Impressive profits and a doubling in share prices, boosted in part by President Trump's 2016 tax cut, made the company a good bet for securities analysts. Although Boeing was familiar with the ups and downs of commercial aviation, it did not sock away big profits in a rainy day fund. Eager to push up all-important earnings-per-share, the seemingly invulnerable manufacturer spent an astonishing $34.6 billion on share buybacks between 2015 and 2018.

There was just one problem with this business plan. While the Max resembled the 14 earlier versions of the 737, test pilots reported that it handled differently. This was certainly no surprise to customers who could see that the much larger and heavier engines had been pushed forward on the 737 airframe. To solve this problem Boeing added additional software to the flight control computers called Maneuvering Characteristics Augmentation System, or MCAS.

Although these changes significantly altered the plane's aerodynamics, all the critical details about a new software system called MCAS were left out of the plane's flight manual. Even key leaders of the company's senior management team had not heard of MCAS, which the company refused to classify as a "safety-critical" system.

In 2012 Boeing, eager to save money on the fast tracked new plane, cut 13,000 work hours planned for avionics regression testing, flight test support and flight deck simulator engineering. The following year Boeing employees created a plan to bypass the need for additional FAA certification and pilot training requirements for the MAX:

"If we emphasize MCAS is a new function there may be a greater certification and training impact," warned a Boeing expert.

Company-paid Designated Aviation Representatives reporting to the FAA concurred with this plan to avoid simulator training for the new aircraft. In July 2014, two years before the FAA finalized Max pilot training regulations, Boeing confidently sent out a press release and marketing details claiming: "Pilots already certified on the Next Generation 737 will not require a simulator course to transition to the 737 MAX."

Boeing's number one MAX customer, Southwest Airlines, an all 737 carrier since its founding in 1967, agreed wholeheartedly with the company's point of view. Although the actual cost of Max simulator training for its 10,000 pilots was only about $20 million, other issues influenced the airline's thinking. First, taking all those pilots offline for two days of MAX training might have forced the carrier to cancel some flights. Second there was the additional cost of buying new simulators at a price of $7.5 million to $15 million. Southwest, buyer of more than a thousand 737s during the past half century, asked the manufacturer if the FAA would require pilots to take special simulator training for a MAX type rating. Certain this would never happen, Boeing agreed to pay Southwest up to $280 million—$1 million a plane—if the FAA unexpectedly mandated "level-D" training. This turned out to be a very safe bet. In 2016 the FAA ruled that Boeing's fix to potential challenges created by the altered aerodynamics of the MAX was a software update not a hardware modification. This meant that additional simulator training was not required for pilots already type rated on the MAX's 737 predecessor.

In early 2017, as the MAX was about to begin commercial service, the FAA's simulator training waiver was being mirrored at regulatory agencies around the world. At Lion Group's Malindo Air, pilots preparing for the new aircraft's maiden commercial voyage completed Boeing's iPad training module for the Max in just 58 minutes. They knew nothing about the new MCAS system because the FAA had granted Boeing's request to delete all mention of this new software system from the 737 MAX's 1,600 page flight manual. This decision reinforced Boeing's claim that the MAX did not require retraining.

Boeing's 737 Chief Technical Pilot reassured colleagues the company didn't have to worry about countries around the world mandating simulator training for MAX flight crews. "We'll go face to face with any regulator who tries to make that a requirement."

As pilots took off unaware of the new aircraft's MCAS system or its impact on the plane's handling characteristics, some Boeing employees privately worried that this plane did not meet the company's own standards.

In a private communication one Boeing worker told a colleague: "This airplane is designed by clowns who in turn are supervised by monkeys."

One of the problems, a veteran FAA appointed Boeing Designated Aviation Representative paid by Boeing told us, was the separation of the design team from the manufacturing floor:

"In the old days the manufacturing team could quickly reach out to design and engineering upstairs if there were problems moving a prototype to production. This kind of teamwork and close communication between colleagues slipped away as the technical team was

downsized, dispersed to other states or outsourced. Teamwork was also hurt by the fact that some of the work was moved out of state or was outsourced to another country. Face to face collaboration became difficult. It was harder to discuss problems, especially when there were major time differences."

This concern was echoed by a Boeing employee working on the MAX project: "I don't know how to fix these things... it's systematic. It's culture. It's the fact that we have a senior leadership team that understands very little about the business and yet are driving us to certain objectives. It's lots of individual groups that aren't working closely and being accountable. It exemplifies the 'lazy B.'"

In June 2017 one of the airlines concerned about inadequate training was the aircraft's launch customer, the Lion Group. A request to commence MAX pilot simulator training at Lion Air was rebuffed.

"Now friggin Lion Air might need a sim to fly the MAX, and maybe because of their own stupidity," a concerned Boeing worker text messaged a colleague. "I'm scrambling trying to figure out how to unscrew this now! Idiots."

"WHAT THE F%$&!!!! But their sister airline (Malaysia's Malindo Air) is already flying it!"

Carefully choosing his words to this valued Indonesian customer, the senior Boeing employee spelled out the case against training above and beyond the brief iPad module:

"I am concerned that if (redacted) chooses to require a MAX simulator for its pilots beyond what all other regulators are requiring that it

will be creating a difficult and unnecessary training burden for your airline, as well as potentially establish a precedent in your region for other Max customers."

The pitch worked. Two days later the Boeing employee reported that he had successfully talked the Indonesian customer out of Max simulator training: "I just Jedi mind tricked this (sic) fool. I should be given $1,000 every time I take one of these calls. I save this company a sick amount of $$$$."

Unpersuaded, a handful of airlines in Fiji, Panama and Iceland went ahead and ordered their own 737 MAX simulators at a cost ranging from $7.5 to $15 million. Captain Pedro Herrera, Copa Airline's Training Senior Manager, was confident that the new TRU 737 MAX Full Flight Simulator would insure the Panamanian carrier had "well-prepared pilots who provide a top-notch, reliable flight experience to our customers."

Brazil went even further. In Brasilia the National Civil Aviation Agency discovered more than 60 important changes on the Max that needed to be studied, evaluated, and trained to. The government also required several MAX familiarization flights to make sure pilots understood new features, including MCAS software.

Why would Boeing, or executives at any manufacturer, gamble with the future of what could become the most successful aircraft in aviation history? With up to 5,000 MAX orders in the pipeline, this seemed like a bad time to roll the dice. The 9/11 attacks enabled by a porous security system showed what happens when controls fail. What if it turned out that pilots actually needed simulator training on how to fly this very different 737?

We're not talking sudden movie projector death here. This is not about a cinema or a film festival refunding tickets to disappointed patrons after a hard drive crash. In this case a runaway control problem could become a threat to life in the air and even people on the ground. In aerospace, rushing a new product into the air, as proven by the catastrophic failure of the British Comet, can bring down an entire company or a launch vehicle. As we've seen with the 2003 O-ring failure on the Space Shuttle Columbia, even the best and brightest scientists in the world, who warned urgently about the risk of launching in cold weather, were overruled by managers in a hurry.

In February 2018 they discussed the same kinds of fears about a perceived speedup on the MAX:

"Honesty is the only way in this job -- integrity when lives are on the line on the aircraft and training programs shouldn't be taken with a pinch of salt. Would you put your family on a MAX simulator trained aircraft? I wouldn't."

"No," replied his co-worker.

"Our arrogance is our demise," added a third employee.

A veteran FAA-designated aviation representative paid by Boeing for work on other aircraft told us the MCAS licensing process sidestepped the heart and soul of all air safety systems, redundancy.

"As designed, the new Boeing 737 MAX was created around a vulnerable single point of failure system that none of the pilots actually knew about. This was absolutely the antithesis of the regulatory process. The FAA was specifically created to prevent this sort of thing from happening. That was their job."

When backup systems fail, the buck always stops with the flight crew that has the training and experience to understand what is going wrong from an aerodynamic point of view. Inevitably no one from the Boeing or Airbus board of directors is going to be sitting in a jump seat on the flight deck to save the day. Until pilots have a complete understanding of the system, it's hard to come up with a quick and effective solution.

Given the FAA's leadership position in aviation safety, it's hard to understand why the Brazilian regulators were the first to deliver an SOS on MCAS. One way to understand this problem is to read the resume of Transportation Secretary Elaine Chao. She came to her job with extensive prior experience at DOT and other government agencies. Unfortunately she lacked the critical flying or accident investigation experience that the agency's first secretary, Alan Boyd, brought to the department in 1967. Like many of her DOT predecessors she was not an expert in aeronautics. Hiring her for this job would be comparable to hiring someone with no musical training experience to conduct the Metropolitan Opera. From day one she was laser focused on promoting industry and job creation.

As a boss Chao would never waste time or money on a consultant like psychologist Gregory May, who tied up FAA employees for 24 hours at a time to improve morale in the 1990s. She understood that the FAA functioned best when it focused on the needs of its industry partners. Over and over she voiced complete faith in the integrity of Boeing, sharing the industry view that self-management and deregulation were keys to building a better airplane. Jobs mattered. Boeing was in a critical struggle with Airbus and Chao understood that delaying the company's new model by mandating simulator training for the MAX might tank sales.

With the FAA and the airlines turning in a perfect record year after year on air safety, Chao's DOT leadership was a role model for the entire Trump administration. What more could a former airline CEO who attacked the safety of his competitors want. At election time the aviation industry gave generously to the campaigns of Chao's favorite politician, husband Mitch McConnell and the key Congressional leaders from both parties who sat on Congress's transportation committees. When they spoke about Boeing or the airlines that reliably flew them home to break bread with their constituents, these legislators looked almost teary eyed.

Even consumer advocate Ralph Nader, who had brought General Motors to its knees in the 1960s with his expose of the Chevy Corvair death trap in "Unsafe At Any Speed" had a soft spot for the airline that had become Boeing's top MAX customer. Not one to ordinarily sing the praises of billionaires, he went out of his way in January 2019 to eulogize Herb Kelleher, the colorful co-founder of his favorite carrier, Southwest.

"Herb was much more than a super-successful creator of a low-fare, no-frills, high pay unionized constantly profitable airline (since 1973) that never laid off any workers, with consistently high customer-approval rating and the most solid financial stability in a boom-bust, managed industry.... When I step from the jetway onto the plane, I invariably say to the flight attendants and pilots—'the best airline in America'."

On March 10, 2019, just two months after Nader's touching tribute to Kelleher, his 24 year-old grandniece Samya Stumo was headed to a new job in Uganda with Thinkwell, a Washington D.C. health development systems organization. The pilots on her Ethiopian Air MAX, had recently completed Boeing recommended supplemental training, endorsed by the FAA.

These new guidelines for pilots had been rushed to airline customers, including Southwest, following the October 29, 2018, Lion Air Max Indonesia crash that took the lives of 189 people. At 8:38 A.M. the new plane took off from Addis Ababa Bole International Airport and began climbing to cruise altitude. No one on board realized that shortly before Christmas FAA analysts reviewing the preliminary accident analysis of the first Max crash had predicted "as many as 15 future fatal crashes within the life of the (MAX) fleet."

CHAPTER 8
Grounded

The day after the Ethiopian Airlines crash that robbed the world of Samya Stumo and 156 other people, the 737 MAX began disappearing from the skies. As country after country grounded their fleet in the wake of evidence linking the cause of this event with the Lion Air crash five months earlier, Elaine Chao's Department of Transportation and the FAA studied the matter. Finally, after every other MAX-owning nation in the world ended stopping flying the new plane, the former CEO of Trump Shuttle buckled. All the more than 350 MAX aircraft delivered worldwide were grounded. As Boeing worked to solve the MCAS problem with the FAA, production of the plane slowed and then stopped as customers delayed and cancelled orders.

A devastating blow to the proud American aviation industry, the Max story would create unprecedented challenges for Boeing and the airlines. The pilot training that airlines like Southwest didn't want to pay for was now being demanded by flight crews. In January 2020, Boeing wrote to 54 airline customers recommending MAX simulator training. With only 34 of these simulators available worldwide for thousands of pilots, airlines were struggled to find availability. Suddenly airlines like

Panama's Copa and Fiji Airways were getting calls from distant airlines asking if they could squeeze in pilots for simulator time. In Reykjavik, Gudmundur Orn Gunnarson, manager director of TRU Flight Training Iceland was a busy man. His joint 737 MAX simulator division with Icelandair was in high demand.

"In the beginning it was said that simulator training would not be needed," he told Reuters. "This changes it totally."

With their MAX fleet mothballed, Southwest, its pilots and flight attendants dealing with cancelled Max flights were suddenly demanding hundreds of millions in compensation from Boeing.

Like the Air France 447 accident, the MAX problem appears to have begun when a sensor, in this case for the angle of attack, fed incorrect data into the aircraft flight control computers. In one case it appears the loss was at the sensor (the angle of attack vane) itself, but in another it may have been a transmission fault. The computer, like a person, relies on accurate data to process information. Unlike a person, though, the computer can only react in the way it was programmed. The software performed exactly as designed. The airplane crashed. Can we draw on lessons learned from the decade long investigation of the historic French crash which took 228 lives?

The Boeing 737 MAX, like other Boeing aircraft, was equipped with two angle of attack sensors. Each of these sensors fed into a different flight control computer. Each flight control computer (FCC) operates independently, and automatically alternates between the two angle of attack sensors. Each time the aircraft is powered up it switches to the opposite side. Within the FCC is a set of software codes known as the Maneuvering Characteristics Augmentation System, or MCAS. This software was designed to enhance airplane handling. In effect MCAS was a response to the fact that under very specific conditions, light weights, high power settings, flaps up and the center of gravity near the aft limit (thus balanced more "tail heavy") the aircraft would get into a situation where it took very little control to change the aircraft pitch. A small touch on the flight controls could make an unusually pronounced difference.

While still flyable, the system was added to make this new B-737 feel the same to the pilot as older models. This might be analogous to an automobile brake pedal. All drivers have experienced a difference in sensitivity to the brakes from one car model to another, but imagine if there was a difference between two models of the same car. Of course they could manage it but in an emergency they might push too hard or not hard enough. What MCAS did was just look at a certain condition, flaps up and high angle of attack. If these parameters were met it would automatically adjust the horizontal stabilizer (the large horizontal surface at the tail) to make the aircraft want to pitch downwards, reducing the plane's angle of attack. The idea was to make it respond more like older models. This also translates into lower training costs for the airlines.

To understand this, take a look at how airplanes are certified. In the case of the Boeing 737, the design was originally licensed in the late 1960s. In order to retain the same type certification (i.e., 737), subsequent models had to be similar enough that if a pilot was rated in one B-737 only minor training differences were required to safely fly a new model. Clearly this is a great advantage to airlines trying to keep their training costs low, plus it would allow an airline to have multiple variants of a particular aircraft type and allow every pilot to fly them all. A different type would mean that the airline would have to divide its pilots into different "fleets."

This is obviously a boon to the aircraft manufacturer, and explains why both Boeing and Airbus attempt to keep building new models of the same aircraft type. Designing and certifying a new aircraft design can be a lengthy and much more expensive proposition than upgrading a 40 or 50 year-old aircraft frame.

As the original certification is still valid, most of the design is "grandfathered" to make sure future changes do not have to meet the full body of evaluation a new design would require. Further, the grand-fathered design often does not need to meet new requirements. This is similar to seismic building codes. For example upgrading an older building to meet today's earthquake standards does not require a new foundation. Obviously if a new building was erected next door it would have to meet new foundation requirements.

The other key problem is that portions of the original design basis and rationale can be lost over time. For example, with the Boeing 737 it was possible to get into a situation where the stabilizer trim put so much load on the mechanism that it became impossible for pilots to move it manually. After the problem was discovered on early models of the airplane, a technique to "un-jam" it was published. Inexplicably, over a series of iterations of the airplane, this technique was lost in the manuals.

Over the years a series of modifications were made on the plane but it remained a B-737. One constant was the procedure for so-called "runaway trim." The stabilizer trim, as explained previously, works by changing the angle of the stabilizer. This is necessary because the amount of force to keep the aircraft balanced changes with airspeed, the location of the center of gravity, flap settings and other factors.

Normally the trim (on the B-737) is controlled with electric motors. These motors can be managed by the autopilot or a switch on the pilot control wheel. When they are not working for any reason, there are two trim wheels on each side of the center pedestal. Both are connected together and linked by cable to a large jackscrew at the plane's tail. As the jackscrew rotates, the stabilizer position changes. Any time the stabilizer position changes, the trim wheels move. Each trim wheel has a retractable handle allowing pilots to adjust the trim manually if need be. In the event a trim motor gets stuck in the "on" position, the pilot can see the trim wheel continuously moving on its own. When this occurs the pilots have "stab(ilizer) trim cutout" switches on the pedestal which they shut off, leaving the manual control available. It's all straight forward.

In the earlier 737 models there was also a mechanical lock out. If the goal was to trim, say, nose up, and the pilot was pushing forward on the control column (obviously not wanting the nose to pitch up), the mechanical lock out prevented trimming in the opposite direction of the control column movement. This was changed to an electrical lock-out on later iterations of the airplane, presumably to accommodate a new feature.

When Boeing upgraded the B-737 from the first generation, -100 and -200 models, they installed larger engines. One can see the larger engines as the bottom of the engine cowl is flattened to ensure ground clearance. With these larger engines came more thrust that made the airplane handle a bit differently. As the engines are below the wing, adding thrust causes the airplane to pitch up, while reducing thrust, causes a pitch down. While this was also true with the first models, it was now more pronounced. In order to make the airplane "feel" the same to the pilot, Boeing introduced a "speed trim" system (STS).

This feature automatically trims the airplane nose-down with a thrust increase, and nose-up with a decrease. Thanks to STS the new airplane model "feels" the same to pilots as the earlier models. Of course, this might lead to situations where the trim needs to move in the opposite direction of the control column. In that case a mechanical lock-out would not be desirable. The STS would operate in short bursts, but did so often. For this reason procedure for a runaway stabilizer remained the same.

The 737 remained a great choice for the airlines until the end of 2010, when Airbus announced that it was launching a new version of its popular A320 model, named the NEO, for "New Engine Option." Larger and more fuel-efficient engines meant that the new A320, while remaining the same type (with all the advantages discussed earlier) would be larger and less expensive to operate. During this time Boeing was contemplating a brand new type of airplane to compete in the market niche that the NEO would occupy. Forced to respond quickly, Boeing decided to upgrade the company's workhorse. Boeing announced the Max six months later, and went to work on a new, larger, B-737 with bigger engines.

Very early on a problem was identified. While the design of the A320 easily accommodated the larger engines, the 50 year-old 737 was originally designed prior to the larger "fan" engines. There simply was not enough ground clearance to fit the engines under the wing. The solution was to move the engines forward and position them higher on the plane. This created a challenging new problem.

At high angles of attack lift is generated off of every surface of the airplane, including the engine nacelles that developed lift well forward of the wing. This change, coupled with high thrust settings also trying to pitch the airplane up, created a big challenge. There were now certain conditions where the airplane would not want to pitch down as airspeed decreased. Normally the reduced speed would lead to less air moving across the horizontal stabilizer, and with that reduced airflow the airplane would naturally pitch down. This is triggered by the fact that big aircraft are designed to be slightly nose-heavy (there is a limit to how far aft the center of gravity can be for this reason).

Had the 737 been a fly-by-wire design this would not have been a problem. The system would automatically do what it needed to do to ensure the airplane responded the same way at all times, all seamless to the pilot. Because the 737 is not a fly-by-wire design the solution was to do something akin to the STS*. When specific conditions were met, the trim system design would make the nose push down similar to previous models in this series. Because the system was only an enhancement it was not considered a problem if it did not work. It was never intended to be a "stall prevention" system as many in the media portrayed it. That would have been a more critical system. As the system had to activate during the specified high angle of attack condition regardless of what the pilot was doing with the controls, the feature that "locked out" the trim when

* Another solution could have been implemented. Boeing could have added a "control augmentation system" that moved the elevator itself to create the same effect. There is no publicly available information for the reasons for their choice, but this may have gone against Boeing's long term philosophy of having the flight controls under the complete control of the pilot.

the controls were moved in the opposite direction was inhibited when MCAS activated.

The system was certificated based on the normal FAA methodology which assessed failure probability. The possibility that the signal could be lost was studied. Because the angle of attack vanes are quite reliable, the system met all regulatory requirements. As with many systems, the assumption was that if it failed the pilots could manage it. If it was not working at all, the pilots would just manually lower the nose. In the more rare case of unintentional activation, the assumption was that the pilots would notice the trim moving and use the same procedure created for a runaway trim. The certification standard still in place today assumes pilots will react in a certain way and does not require reviewing how the pilot might actually react in a given circumstance. This is exactly why Boeing reassured airlines and the FAA that additional simulator training was not necessary for a 737 pilot to upgrade to the MAX.

As we have learned again and again in aviation, the real world does not care about our assumptions. *Aviation Week's* Fred George explains that this scenario does not play out in a way that is conducive to pilot situational awareness. Flight crews have difficulty understanding problems they are not trained to recognize. Due to the angle of attack indicating that it is too high, the pilot's first indication on takeoff is the "stick shaker," a stall warning system. While the airplane is flying normally at this point the stick shaker is very distracting. In addition a bad angle of attack sensor also affects other systems leading to an airspeed indicator error of as much as 40 knots and up to 400 feet on the altimeters. The pilot is thinking that they have unreliable airspeed, and, as outlined in the previous chapter, many pilots (incorrectly) assume a false stall warning can result from a low airspeed indication.

As the pilot is working this, they discover that the autopilot will not connect, and many of the automatic systems are absent. Remember that in the real world the pilot is also following air traffic control instructions, the departure procedure for the airport, looking out for weather and other aircraft, etc. There is a lot going on. As the airplane accelerates the pilots retract the flaps. Why might a pilot retract the flaps with all this going on? Pilots are trained in a specific way. Absent a problem that precludes it (such as flaps are stuck or landing gear will not retract), when a problem occurs on takeoff the procedure is to retract the landing gear, and, when at a safe altitude, retract the flaps (and slats if applicable), and then "work the problem." In pilot parlance, the aircraft is "cleaned up" before doing anything else. This makes sense for many problems, but not for this one. With the flap retraction the MCAS becomes active, sensing the flaps up and the high angle of attack, it attempts to lower the pitch and reduce angle of attack with the very large horizontal stabilizer. The assumption was that the pilot would notice this and use the stabilizer cutout, but this just moves for a short time—like the normal movement of the STS.

Now the airplane is trying to pitch down hard and the pilot is pulling back with a lot of force to keep the nose up. If the pilot turns off the stabilizer trim at this point they are still left with the airplane trying hard to nose over. It is all too easy for the stabilizer trim to have reached the point where there is so much pressure on the jack screw that manually moving the trim back nose up is impossible. The pilots are in a situation where holding the nose up with the control column is quickly exhausting them and the ability to manually trim also is not available. At this point the procedures do not seem to be working. It should not be surprising that they might try to innovate. Maybe they can get the nose up with the electric trim? Unfortunately, turning the trim back on re-activates MCAS once more.

Recall the discussions on simulation in Chapter 4. One of the factors that came to light is that the B-737 simulator misled pilots into believing they might be able to manually trim the airplane when they actually could not.

Just six months prior to the Air France 447 accident, another Airbus A330 had a different sort of event following a problem with sensor data. Qantas 72 was on a flight from Singapore to Perth cruising at an altitude of 37,000 feet. Suddenly, and without warning the aircraft pitched over into a dive. The Captain, an experienced former U.S. Navy fighter pilot, attempted to arrest the pitch over with his flight controls but the aircraft would not respond. Shortly after entering the dive the aircraft stopped trying to hold the pitch down and allowed the captain to recover. Then it did it again.

In this case a rapid series of "data spikes" led the system to "believe" that a false value was correct. The A330, unlike the Boeing aircraft, utilizes three angle of attack sensors. As the airplane has envelope protection to prevent a stall, all three sources are needed to ensure that it is accurate. These systems each compare against one another. What apparently happened was that a number of data spikes occurred over a very short period of time in such a way that the system "believed" that the erroneous data was accurate. Airbus had studied this possibility, but determined that the probability was so low they needn't worry about it. The fact that it happened on one of the world's great airlines with four captains on board was certainly a lucky break.

In 2012 an EVA A330 went into a dive after all of its angle of attack vanes jammed, apparently due to being iced over. This led the system to detect a non-existent stall and activated the automatic protection system. The quick thinking pilot turned off all of the air data computers disabling the automatic protection system. There was no procedure for this. An accident was prevented purely through human ingenuity.

What can be done to prevent similar "low probability" events. The best response now is a systems approach that includes a better aircraft design and pilot training that does not rely on older methods created to manage systems built without computers. A system can be in perfect compliance with all of the regulatory requirements and yet still create the perfect storm for an accident to occur. Here are just a few of the problems that have contributed to these crashes.

- ✈ Designs built around the concept that nothing need be done for scenarios deemed to be a very low probability;
- ✈ The assumption that if a low probability event does occur the pilot will be there to manage it;
- ✈ Pilots not being notified or trained on emergencies that may result from the failure of flight automation because it is considered improbable;
- ✈ Most pilots lack the critical meteorology training they need to meet unexpected challenges they may confront;
- ✈ Aircraft designers similarly rely on assumptions about atmospheric phenomena that may not be valid;
- ✈ Failure to recognize that experienced pilots have been in place

to prevent accidents—and these pilots are now retiring while new pilots are not given opportunities to gain the skills these retiring aviators are taking with them;

→ Acceptance of the fact that by-the-book adherence to checklists is not a panacea. One of US Airways Captain Chesley Sullenberger's first key decisions on Flight 1549 was to turn on an emergency generator well before his Airbus's checklist called for it. Checklists and procedures are designed under assumptions that may not be valid in the real world. We blame pilots if they follow a checklist and an accident occurs (Swissair 111), or if they don't follow a checklist and an accident occurs;

→ Understanding that upgrading or patching software and hardware does not guarantee a safe flight. Systems that appear to be working perfectly can fail;

→ Realizing that these accidents are occurring despite the fact that all the people involved are trying to do the right thing and are following all of the approved and accepted methods.

These are just a few of the reasons why bad things keep happening to good airplanes. The myth is that engineers and designers can create a fail-safe plane always capable of flying itself. When built in protections created to prevent a stall stop working, pilots can be handling a plane that is actually harder to fly than a vintage 707 or DC 8.

Unquestionably pilots prevent accidents every day by adjusting to unexpected variables. There were many controls in place to prevent the stall of Air France 447 and more than 50 other airline crashes that have followed it. Why didn't they work? Redundancy, i.e. having three pitots or even multiple angle of attack sensors, isn't much help when they all stop working, or when the design depends on just one. At that point it takes a very well trained pilot to diagnose the problem and improvise a solution.

Designers assume that in the event of a system failure like Air France 447, pilots will handle it. In fact, the very experienced crew on the French plane had not been warned that pitot failure and unreliable airspeed in a high altitude crystal icing environment could play havoc with the plane's automation. Nobody anticipated that it could trigger an aerodynamic stall.

A related problem is that traditional methods require assessment of failure probabilities. This doesn't work for software because it does not "fail" like electromechanical systems. Typically the software functioned exactly as it was designed to do, but the designer did not anticipate the crisis encountered. This means unexpected software interactions that damage the system are inevitable. Decisions on whether or not to train pilots for potential risks are also often based on probability and statistical analysis. This may be beneficial in preventing common events such as a blown tire. Unfortunately, when low probability events like Air France 447 or the two Max crashes happen, many good pilots lack the training or experience necessary to meet these challenges. Those who do are retiring, and through no fault of their own, the new pilots have few opportunities to gain necessary experience.

For example, the industry has focused on angle of attack sensors and software in the wake of the Lion Air accident, in much the same way there was a focus on pitot tubes after Air France 447. Fixing the angle of attack sensors and improving the software will certainly solve this particular problem with the B-737 MAX, in the same way replacing the pitots prevented a duplicate of the Air France 447 accident. The problem is that these patches ignore a bigger industry wide issue. A fault in a single sensor can cause a computer to do the wrong thing despite the fact that the computer is working exactly as designed. Computers only do what they are instructed to do by their software algorithms. They cannot manage tasks that were not anticipated in the design. Humans can and do adapt to unexpected outcomes flexibly in real time. The catch is that humans must understand what is happening.

Until we change the way we design these systems more accidents are inevitable. As MITs Dr. Nancy Leveson wisely points out, we need to understand why controls in place failed. The best way to prevent future accidents is to design new control systems that actually work. Launching new aircraft on the assumption that the old controls will work is not good enough. As we are learning, the obsolete approach created for the pre-computer era does not guarantee the safety of your next flight.

CHAPTER 9
When Blame is the Enemy of Safety

The surgeon is busy. Like lines at a grocery store, emergencies can happen in waves. Complete quiet is shattered by a dozen critical patients filling the emergency room. Why can't they organize themselves, she wonders?

Of course, random distribution will, by design, involve dead periods and clusters of activity. Some of it is predictable. Perhaps the weekend hours, or more traffic flow as people get off work. Other times the mechanisms of that chaos are less clear. The closer the hospital gets to capacity the more people start trying to do what they can to keep up. It is in our nature. We get the job done. We do not like to say "enough." We tend not to say, "no, I'm too busy," at least not in this sort of job. What doctor could tell a patient, "I'm too busy to help you." However, in an effort to keep up with demand there is a higher chance that something is missed. Can "errors" be the result of people missing things and making mistakes when they are overwhelmed?

Like pilots flying jets, doctors can make lethal mistakes. Calling a bad outcome an "error" implies that the doctor was somehow able to control the event. This assumption is based on logic that needs a closer look. Could the outcome relate to the fact that we try to take on what the world hands to us? Can the pilot suddenly dealing with a combination of weather, traffic and perhaps a system anomaly, just say, "Let's try again later?" In many fields this is simply not realistic. We need to do a more thorough analysis that replaces subjectivity with an unbiased assessment.

Why was a crisis scenario not anticipated? Why did the hospital not add staff to manage a potential sudden influx? Going this route inevitably leads to holding people at higher positions responsible. Maybe it's not a management level problem. Is the staff driven by requirements and pressure from the board of directors? Did just in time procurement mean a shortage of critical components? What about the regulatory framework? Could better rules have solved this problem?

Around the world, the easy way out is to blame the person closest to the accident, the one we believe is "ultimately in control," the doctor. In this scenario the physician is now in protection mode. Doctors must escape blame that could cost them their jobs. In some cases they may actually believe, incorrectly, that it was all their fault. This takes an enormous toll on their mental health. Fear of being blamed leads them to share information selectively. A well-paid lawyer may be hired to shape the doctor's defensive approach to any inquiry.

What's wrong with this scenario? For one thing, a doctor not worried about losing his livelihood might be able to provide valuable insights on the errors that led to this mishap and prevent a similar bad outcome. Unfortunately, to do so draws yet more scrutiny. In the end the doctor gets the blame. We now can "move on," satisfied that the culprit has been identified. Everything can be chalked up to doctor error.

Blame is the enemy of safety. It leads to cover-ups and attempts to misdirect. The doctor has an incentive to argue that it was entirely the nurse's fault. Low paid nurses lack clout and are among the most expendable employees in the hospital. It's easy to make the nurse the "fall guy" and hold him/her responsible for what went wrong. Just fire the nurse and we're all safe. This approach ignores many key factors contributing to accidents. For example accidents in medicine can be triggered by automation. This concept of doing more with less is similar to the challenges facing professional pilots.

Through an endless multibillion dollar marketing blitz the public has been sold the idea that automation eliminates the need for better training. Lack of experience is no longer an obstacle for major international airlines that put pilots on the flight deck of a $150 million jet with just 200 hours of flight time.

While many people may view this as "automation", most of the jet transport designs currently in operation do not have computers running the airplane's primary systems, which include hydraulic, fuel, electrical and pneumatic. The sole exception is the McDonnell-Douglas (now Boeing) MD-11. In all of the newer aircraft improvements have been made in alerting systems to notify pilots of problems, although most of these systems are not particularly "smart" but rather list problems in the temporal order in which they are triggered by the system. The exception is the MD-11, which does (to an extent) rank the most critical items at the top of the list. Most modern jet transports have been improved to the point that engineering system designs are so simple they require little human action. The MD-11, by contrast, includes features that the other airliners lack, such as automatically reconfiguring systems to work around inoperative components or isolated problems. Even in these situations it will reach a point where it defers to the human operator to make a decision. For example it will shut down one hydraulic system due to overheating, but not two. This approach reflects the designers' belief that in a dynamic situation dependent on special circumstances, pilots should ultimately be making the call. For example, a crew's decision mid-ocean could be much different than it would be near the airport. Nonetheless, as most routine systems are automated, the pilot remains primarily in monitoring mode. When the system takes an action it is designed to notify the flight crew. In most cases the pilot does not have to take additional action. The pilot's job is to consider the impact of inoperative components on flight planning. Like the person dependent on a calculator, the pilot must have a clear understanding of how the system works and should be operated.

Automation does what the pilot would be required to do absent the system. The unintended consequence is that computer and software reliability can lead him to avoid the mental work needed to understand the system. The catch is that reducing the workload required to operate a complex system also reduces the incentive for the engineers to simplify the system. The MD-11 systems are relatively more complex than those found on comparable aircraft. This allows for the system to perform beneficial functions missing on other aircraft, such as late model Boeing and Airbus jets, but at a cost of complexity.

For example, the MD-11 will sense fuel temperature. If it reaches a certain point the plane will move fuel from warmer tanks to colder tanks. This prevents the fuel from chilling to the point where it will no longer flow smoothly. When an engine has been shut down and it is necessary to transfer fuel to keep the airplane balanced, the MD-11 system does this automatically. Other aircraft require the pilot to manage this process.

When fuel temperature does get dangerously cold on the Boeing 777 the pilots must either fly faster (increasing the temperature by friction) or descend to a lower (hopefully warmer) altitude. There are definitely tradeoffs here because adding complexity can create confusion. There have been cases where pilots incorrectly tried to override the MD-11 system when it was properly reconfiguring fuel pumps and valves to keep the fuel in close balance. Convinced that the plane was doing the wrong thing, the pilot turned the automatic controllers off, which in turn put the system in a default manual configuration. This in turn resulted in fuel starvation on one engine that shut down due to lack of fuel. The system was smarter than the pilot, a step back to the person with the calculator who does not understand the process well enough to know if the answer is correct or wildly off.

Autopilot systems have improved over time, but are still not all that more sophisticated than a car's cruise control. The system essentially looks at what the pilot has commanded it to do, and adjusts the controls accordingly. The main difference is that the pilot can command the plane to follow an electronic signal from the ground or a navigation system path. While new autopilots do a better job, their functionality is not much different than the systems available in the 1960s and 1970s. Automatic landing systems created in the 1970s were also relatively simple. Designers added radio altitude into the mix, allowing the autopilot to maintain a programmed trajectory by adjusting the controls. Obviously pilots will monitor this very closely as any failure or bad signal can put the airplane in a dangerous state. The autopilot is not smart enough to discern that things "do not look right," although some more advanced systems disconnect when certain parameters are exceeded—leaving it to the pilot to "save" the airplane. Prior to takeoff the pilot can also program the entire route, from departure to landing approach. This is similar to programming your automobile's cruise control to drive certain speeds at various portions of your route. The big difference is that the "cruise control" does not take control of your car's steering the way it does on a big jet. On a plane the automated program simply follows a programmed script. The system contains a database of points that can be supplemented with pilot created latitude and longitude points. Contrary to popular opinion, these systems rely heavily on human input and monitoring similar to the programmable cruise control system on your car. Because it is not possible to anticipate hazards such as an icy road or traffic jam, human intervention may suddenly be necessary. Designing a system so that one cannot do the wrong thing is far different than designing the decision making out of the system.

Simple examples are the automobile lock designed to make sure the car door will not lock a person out of the car and the system preventing the car being started unless the brake is applied. Drivers are also familiar with the chime that sounds when the lights are left on or a seatbelt is unfastened. All of these limitations prevent errors without limiting the ability of the driver to make a decision. The same is true for the current systems in airplanes, which means there is merit to the concept that better system design can eliminate many types of errors.

With this philosophy in mind, Airbus began designing limits to what pilots could do on their airplanes. Company research demonstrated there was little benefit to allowing pilots to overstress the airplane or exceed certain bank angles or pitch attitudes. The company's analysts contended that pilots had no need to exceed these conditions to prevent a problem. The theory was that pilots who went beyond the specified limits were doing so inadvertently. Thus, the flight controls were designed to prevent a pilot from exceeding limits the designers believed were appropriate.

This approach is similar to modern speed limiting software used by parents for teenage drivers.

Boeing initially disagreed, but the evidence was overwhelming. Newer Boeing aircraft, while not entirely preventing such excursions, do make it much more difficult to do so. The Boeing philosophy has been to leave the pilots more in control. Still, to be fair, pilots can also take measures to exceed design limits on the Airbus jets if they deem it necessary.

The aviation industry has a good record on this, redesigning airplanes and systems to the point that most simple errors can be eliminated. Those errors were often caused by a momentary distraction, an attempt to rush through a procedure or by poorly written guidance. Through identifying and then eliminating these possibilities we have created a system where the probability of an accident is now extremely low. Although the fatal accident rate has steadily declined, it appears to have plateaued in recent years. As system and equipment design has improved, the failure rates have dropped, creating the impression that there is just one primary cause of fatal accidents—human error.

The problem with this seemingly sensible position is that it's danger-ously wrong. As pointed out by leading researchers Nancy Leveson, Sidney Dekker, David Woods and others, it is not that humans are making errors. Rather, despite our designs, there are still many gaps in the system—problems the designers could not solve. These remaining gaps are entirely dependent on human resilience to prevent accidents. When humans are not able to do so they are falsely accused of making an "error."

Once again, think of it in terms of the automobile. Anti-lock brakes have certainly saved lives, as has improved signage on roadways, better designed highways, grooved pavement for high speed, banks on curves, better traffic signals, designs of automobiles that eliminate blind spots and improved visibility to other drivers, as well as a myriad other enhancements. Despite all these improvements, safe driving still depends on human skill, particularly awareness. Although technol-ogy has eliminated simple problems, larger ones remain. As British Psychologist Lisanne Bainbridge points out, "the designer who tries to eliminate the operator still leaves the operator to do the tasks which the designer cannot think how to automate."

Now imagine we design systems to eliminate the human such as Google's self-driving car. Certainly it can drive automatically. Motion detectors and a very good navigation system can be supplemented with position updates as it passes roadways. What might create a problem for this system created to avoid obstacles? We will assume that we reach the point where it can also detect hazards such as snow or icy surfaces and navigate construction zones. Still there are gaps. Have you ever driven down a road and spotted a potential problem? Imagine looking down the road and seeing two street gangs facing off against each other. Perhaps these gangs are armed. The road is otherwise clear, so to the Google car it is just a normal situation. It is not able to spot the telltale signs of a street gang or perhaps an angry mob. Of course the vehicle will carry you right into the middle of this potentially dangerous spot you would always want to avoid. These are the types of discretionary issues difficult to solve with current technology. Humans are far better at making judgment calls here than machines.

On a flight this can be an even bigger challenge. Pilots may not have to be concerned about street gangs in the air but there are many situations that demand their good judgment to avoid a potential accident. On an airplane a large set of issues are hard to program. Take, for example, the smell of smoke. In the car there is no need to program anything. The occupant pushes the emergency stop and you're done. During a flight it's far more challenging. First, the system needs a way to detect the smoke, and this can be difficult. Back in the car, if you smell something a bit odd you can continue driving, waiting to see if it manifests into real smoke. In the airplane the first indication might be a subtle change in odor. As there are large amounts of air moving through various systems odors change all the time. However, a review of real events has shown that waiting to confirm that the odor is indeed smoke sometimes makes it difficult or impossible to prevent catastrophe. Then there is the issue of choosing the best flight options. During an emergency over the North Atlantic at night is it better to ditch or try to make it to the nearest airport? Is it a good idea to depressurize the airplane and slow the burn rate from the fire (depriving it of oxygen) giving the pilot more time to fly to the nearest airport? Would it make more sense to dive to a lower altitude to assure that passengers do not run out of oxygen which may be exhausted after as little as ten minutes? Can computers make such a decision better than a human?

Other problems that are difficult to program include subtle aspects, such as a very small change in sound or vibration. Is that a serious change or not? It takes a lot of experience to be able to discern the difference. Similarly there are complex issues like meteorology that challenge the expertise of system design engineers. Another critical issue is power. If something interrupts the electrical power of the airplane and its components, how can the computer flying the airplane be protected? A good example is fire that burns through power systems. Until computers can match our intellect and the power issue is resolved, the concept of replacing human pilots in airplanes with computers is unrealistic. Once we reach human level artificial intelligence there is yet another set of issues which likely will make this entire topic moot. Smart machines can create very unpredictable outcomes that may not benefit us. Humans outperform even the latest, greatest systems. Autonomous car companies have been conducting testing on their vehicles with a safety driver present to intervene if necessary. The companies are also required to report "critical disengagements," where a safety driver had to intervene to prevent an accident. In 2019 Matthew Johnson and Alonso Vera wrote in *AI Magazine* that during the 2017-18 time frame, the "best performing company" had one critical disengagement every 50,000 miles. That might sound good, but the injury accident rate for human driven cars during the same period was one accident for every 1.5 million miles*! In other words humans outperformed the autonomous car 30 to 1.

* Matthew & Vera, Alonso. (2019). No AI Is an Island: The Case for Teaming Intelligence. *AI Magazine.* 40. 16-28. 10.1609/aimag.v40i1.2842.

CHAPTER 10

Can More Automation Solve an Automation Problem?

Humans are always subject to a number of cognitive limitations. Historically industry believed that two pilots improved safety because the second pilot could catch the first pilot's errors. True, there are plenty of aircraft that operate with a single pilot, including everything from military aircraft to very sophisticated private planes. Smaller charter airlines also operate this way showing that workload issues can be solved, at least during routine flights. There are currently several research projects looking for ways to create jets that can be flown by a single pilot or no pilots at all. Airbus is currently working to persuade the airfreight industry that dispensing with pilots can improve flight safety. This approach is based on the contention that the majority of airplane accidents are the result of human error. Advocates contend that by eliminating (eventually) human flight crews, the industry can become safer than ever. Of course this is also a great marketing hook for airlines trying to save money on salaries and training.

The big problem is that the accident rates for these categories are much higher than would be acceptable for mass transportation. This is partly due to people making mistakes, misperceiving things and the like. Even as we create systems to capture these errors we still see too many accidents. Why is that?

The theory that humans are inherently error prone led to the concept of removing them from the cockpit. The generally accepted reason for adding a second pilot is that a second person will notice these errors and speak up about them. Indeed, that is the basis for the crew resource management (CRM) training created in the 1970s. An analysis of accident findings found that in many cases it was believed that the other pilot (or someone else involved) had remained silent about a problem they noticed. The concept was that training pilots to speak up when they spotted a problem could solve many issues. This great solution responded to the fact that far too often the second pilot noticed an issue but failed to point it out in time. Excuses included fear, power-distance (also called the authority gradient, e.g. a very senior person with a newer one), not wanting to "make waves" or even anger. A positive response to all of these problems happening on too many flights, CRM training became "the fix" to solve this problem. Simultaneously, equipment became more reliable, the procedure designs improved and systems were installed that warned pilots of dangerous conditions, such as approaching terrain, wind shear, too steep of a bank angle, approaching a wrong runway or one that was too short, as well as a collision risk. In addition, ground based systems were installed that simultaneously alerted air traffic controllers who could shout out a warning for many dangerous situations. As a result accident rates did go down.

Was it the CRM that led to this improvement? The truth is that evidence to support such a conclusion is challenging. There are so many aspects involved that need to be considered. As anyone who has gone through such training knows, the running joke is that those that need it most ignore it. The truth is that the most effective part is probably training the subordinate person to speak up, and then find ways to make those who need to hear the information feel responsible if they ignore what they are told. Still, even with that, although CRM was a good idea, it likely only has an incremental impact. The same can be said of other programs, each adding a small increment of improvement, adding up cumulatively to a large improvement. Another concept focuses on the theory that the more precise a person attempts to be in all areas of their life the "smaller the target" will be. As a result the hypothesis is that they will be less likely to deviate from what they intended to do. Certainly not a harmful concept, but there is no evidence it has any correlation to accident prevention.

Other ideas such as improved diet, hydration and, of course, mitigating fatigue are easier to see. Fatigue can definitely be a problem and people do make more errors when tired. This approach is again based on the assumption that errors are the problem when the real issue is loss of resilience. To make the single pilot idea work this system would need to be smart enough to anticipate human needs. That is something the other pilot is doing, not just reacting, but actually anticipating the needs and actions of his flight partner. Computers are limited at this, "auto-correct" being a case in point. Would we really want a virtual computer "co-pilot" reacting as "auto-correct" does?

Under these circumstances what is the advantage of multiple pilots to flight safety? The real value comes when two (or more, the more the better!) properly trained pilots work together, creating a shared mental model and then acting, for practical purposes, as one mind with multiple senses. That also has a multiplier effect on the experience level and the ability to cope with unusual situations. This magnifies the resilience of the pilots. Together they can accomplish much more than they could singly. Humans are able to accommodate variability and two well-trained humans working closely together are better than one. More than two can be even better as was illustrated when Captain Al Haynes led his DC-10 crew during the Sioux City United 232 accident. After an uncontained engine failure severed hydraulic lines, the pilots skillfully used a crude steering system to crash land the plane. With the help of emergency teams on the ground 184 passengers lived.

Proponents of the single-pilot concept counter that they can have a person serving on the ground as a "virtual co-pilot," ready to assist when needed. The person on the ground would attend to multiple flights under the premise that only one might have an issue at a time. Have you attended a virtual meeting? Even under the best of circumstances there are limitations and subtle cues are missed. Hand gestures, facial expressions and many other nuances would be lost. In reality, the person on the ground is essentially shadowing a dispatcher who is already part of the decision team at all major airlines. A key disadvantage of this scheme is losing the "shared mental model." Regardless of the data connection type the second person on the ground would not actually "be there." They would not be experiencing the sensations, they would not have "skin in the game." Even if there were a way to transmit some of those concerns they would still need continuity. Not being completely immersed in what was happening until there was a problem would be similar to the Air France 447 situation. The Captain was not in the cockpit until after the airplane stalled. He had almost zero chance of sorting out the issues. If we want to fix that, the person on the ground would need to be virtually "in the cockpit" for the entire flight. That means they would not be virtually able to serve multiple cockpits simultaneously. This eliminates the financial incentive for the one pilot cockpit.

Much of logic that proponents use is based on the rationale that if we could eliminate first the radio operator, then the navigator, then the flight engineer, the "natural progression" of automation is to eliminate one of the pilots. This is flawed thinking. At one time the job of tuning a radio was very involved, as was navigating, and operating systems. However, one must not lose sight of the fact that each of those individuals operated at the direction of two pilots and provided information to help pilots form a mental model of the flight and make decisions accordingly. All the information went forward to the two pilots in front who took it all in to make decisions on the safe operation of the aircraft.

Improvements in technology allowed airplanes to fly without radio operators, and navigators, because long range radio navigation, inertial systems and, most recently, GPS coupled with simple computers have supposedly simplified the task. The navigator took measurements off the stars and the sun with basic calculations of the projected aircraft path considering speed, wind drift and the like. The arrival of calculators able to do trigonometry along with systems that determined the plane's current position were a major breakthrough. From here it was easy to combine the two. Although humans were somewhat removed from the process, the pilots were adequately trained in the principles of navigation. They knew how to cross check their machine calculations, remaining on the lookout for errors that needed correction. The process was similar to running numbers through a calculator a second time because the first total looked suspicious. This approach meant well-qualified humans remained firmly in control of the decision making process.

Finally, there is the problem of someone who is suicidal or has another medical problem. In 2015 the copilot on a Germanwings Airbus locked the captain out of the cockpit and crashed the airplane. This case highlights that issue, and there is no known psychological testing that would reliably ferret out that sort of issue. In sum, it is clear that the impediments to both pilot-less and single pilot transport aircraft are larger than most realize.

What about artificial intelligence? There is certainly no question that once computers reach human level cognition they will be able to fly an airplane as well as a pilot. They would need appropriate (and not currently designed) sensors to pick up subtle odors, vibrations and sounds, but that is not an insurmountable problem. Methods could also be devised to ensure the computers are powered. It is estimated that computers working at this proficiency level could be operational in the next few years. Others believe it will take longer. The overall consensus is that they will be up and running by the end of the century. Is this something pilots should be concerned about?

The answer is "perhaps," but the real truth is that once human level intelligence is created the world will be so completely changed that the way planes are flown will not be a big concern, even for those that currently make their living at it. The reason is that this level of artificial intelligence referred to as "artificial general intelligence" (AGI) is unlikely to resemble a Hollywood movie. Current technology includes a lot of what is considered "artificial intelligence" or AI. This level includes predicting words on a smart phone or tablet, and numerous other applications. Google's new car is in this regime. These systems are able to "learn" on their own as they "watch" what you do and improve their performance. Cool stuff. An intelligent computer that is learning on its own could one day match humans. It would mimic many human traits thanks to human designers who gave it speech capability, etc. However, as much as it might appear to be human, it would not be. A computer is not even a biological organism. Anthropomorphizing machines can be very misleading. Tim Urban's blog has a very good discussion on this topic. One illustration considers a spider and a guinea pig: if one were to make a guinea pig as intelligent as a human it might not be so scary, but a spider with human level intelligence is very unlikely to be friendly or a good thing. Tim points out that a spider is not "good" or "evil", as Hollywood likes to portray things, it is just different. The same can be said of a computer. It reacts to things based on programming, but once it can self-learn, its motivations are based only on what its job is set to be.

Humans are social animals, primates with the social structure of termites. We survive because of that social aspect. Termites have evolved to "know" that any individual will sacrifice itself to prevent the destruction of the hive. Altruism and self-sacrifice is not something we attribute to insects, but the fact is that termites, bees, ants and other social insects will take actions humans would consider altruistic. Being social animals, humans are able to succeed where non-social animals cannot. As a result we have evolved to be social and our "programming" reflects this. It might be described very roughly as follows:

Prevent harm to yourself unless (in order);

A. Your family is in danger, protect them first.

B. Your "tribe" is in danger;

C. Your Nation is in danger;

D. Prevent harm to another person outside your group.

The programming varies. Very few would not give their life to protect their children, their spouse and immediate family and we are programmed to keep it in that order. The entire point of all of this is to ensure that our genes survive, and it is better to ensure that even a bit of your DNA makes it (you will have relatives most likely in your tribe, nation, etc. It appears that the stronger the DNA connection (or in the case of a spouse, the likelihood of ensuring your genes' survival) the stronger our will to do anything to protect them, even at our own expense. Of course, intrinsic in all of this is self procreation.

Obviously, a computer only has the traits we have programmed. As much as it might appear to be human, it really is not. This leads to a larger concern. Computers today process information millions of times faster than humans yet still lack human intelligence. The structure of our brains allows for ways of processing information and connections that computers can't do. Once they can though, they will be combining that faster processing with those connections. Connect to the internet and things happen fast.

Consider a computer with this capability and the ability to learn.

It starts as a toddler but an hour later has the ability and knowledge of Einstein, and an hour after that is has the combined knowledge of all the great thinkers combined. Unlike us, it has constant access to ALL of that knowledge and a much faster processing skill. The problems that take us years to solve or appear without resolution are likely to be trivial for a computer. Is there any doubt that a computer could rapidly know ways to make itself even faster and smarter? Does it have the ability to adjust its pathways and improve its structure based on its knowledge? If we give it that ability, or it figures out how to do it on its own, its "intelligence" can increase even faster.

Above AGI is artificial super intelligence, or ASI. In this realm we are looking at a computer that is not just a little more intelligent but rather is vastly smarter than any human. This is a system that might realize there is a way to manipulate matter, time or space. It would not be limited to our perceptions of reality. The trouble is that it is farther ahead of us than we would want. We might not be relevant to this system or just a nuisance. All of this could be a tremendous game-changer that would make flying airplanes a trivial issue. ASI could lead to solving all the problems of humanity or the end of humanity. People like Bill Gates are very concerned. Elon Musk is so concerned he states he spends a third of his waking hours thinking about it. He does this while running several companies! Hopefully it will turn out well. If it solves all of the problems of humanity than all of us may be able to live just doing what we want without any real need for work. If it goes badly it's hard to predict the outcome, suffice to say that the Hollywood movie "Terminator" would be a one of the more benign ones.

The bottom line here is that we might see a push for single pilot or even no-pilot airplanes based on a fundamental misunderstanding of what the issues are and where the risks lay. We might automate the basic functions but that would still leave us vulnerable to the real "corner-case" scenarios leading to actual accidents. Typically these events take place outside normal operating parameters. A good example of a corner case is an autonomous vehicle requiring a radar system that can handle ghost targets, radar blinding and disappearing targets. Contrary to popular opinion, most accidents do not follow a simple linear causal chain. It would be safe most of the time, true, but not as safe as the public demands today. It might plateau to safety levels reached in the 1970s. Reaching the higher safety levels now demanded by the public and regulators would require AGI, and once we reach that point the outcome moves in directions we can't predict. Again, all of this is based on the flawed concept that human error causes accidents. Speaking as a veteran accident investigator applying system engineering approaches such as MIT's STAMP (System Theoretic Accident Models and Processes), it's clear that the real causes of accidents are flawed assumptions at every level. Removing a pilot would just make those flawed assumptions at the design stage more prominent because there would no longer be a pilot to prevent tragedy. Imagine the problems an automated system would have with an in-flight fire scenario as outlined earlier.

Perhaps we are going in the wrong direction? If we want to reduce medical error the solution might be to always have two surgeons working together. Similarly, if we want to improve aviation safety, more pilots are critically important. We can apply the same logic to multiple safety-critical domains.

CHAPTER 11

When an Accident Investigation is Dead Wrong

"I have noticed that people who claim everything is predestined and that we can do nothing to change it, look before they cross the road."

Stephen Hawking

An uncommanded shutdown of an Asiana Airbus 350 engine takes place immediately after tea spills on the cockpit's center pedestal control panel. Two months later the same thing happens on a Delta flight after a cup of coffee spills in the same place. Following a review the European Aviation Safety Agency mandates that a removable cover must be fitted to protect all the levers, thumbwheels and rotary knobs during cruise. It can only be removed during critical phases of flight.

If either of these aircraft had been lost it's hard to know whether the investigators would have discovered details of these spills. Even if they did it would be a challenge to reliably explain their contribution to a crash. The fact that these drinks spilled doesn't necessarily mean

107

that liquid hitting the instruments triggered the shutdowns. Airbus could be blamed for not including this vital instrument panel cover. The flight crew could be criticized for failing to drink from spill proof cups. Turbulence could have played a role here. All points of view are potentially valid and it would be impossible to reach a definite conclusion on what triggered a crash. Inevitably the accident investigators' biases are a much more important factor than most people realize. This problem can make it difficult for the aviation industry to step away from the dangerous blame game we've been talking about. It is virtually impossible to separate our biases from what we do. Accident investigation is supposed to be an objective scientific process, but the truth is that many investigators have not really been trained to use this process correctly. The industry generally believes pilots, engineers or human factors experts are the ideal candidates for accident investigation training. Even those who are trained to follow a scientific process are not always successful because adherence can require a great deal of discipline. Why is that? The answer to this question may surprise you.

Most people, including scientific researchers, are not elated if and when they discover that they're wrong about their beliefs. Despite this, scientists are trained to accept finding out that their hypothesis was wrong. Nobel Laureate Stephen Hawking advanced the concept that mistakes can be a scientist's best friend. As he put it:

"So the next time someone complains that you have made a mistake, tell him that may be a good thing. Because without imperfection, neither you nor I would exist."

Lawrence Krauss agrees and adds: "...the most exciting thing about being a scientist is not knowing and being proven wrong. This is exciting because there is a lot left to learn." (Krauss, 2011).

Despite this, there are, of course, times when a scientist will "fall in love with their own theory," or try to manipulate the data to make it appear that it indicates something it does not. How does science progress and keep this in check? Thankfully the peer review process, where the realization that the work will be scrutinized, plus the fact that this actually happens, prevents and captures bias prior to publication.

Occasionally, an incorrect scientific paper leaks through, but the errors always get caught at some point. In fact, published research must be detailed enough to allow others to replicate the study. If it is interesting other scientists will work to replicate the work, and if it does not pan out that rebuttal is published. The original paper will then, generally, be withdrawn, and in some cases the scientist who did the work will be fired from their position. We see this publicly with claims on pseudo medicines or non-existent correlations. Richard Feynman was famous for challenging ideas and concepts, and that is what makes science strong.

All of us are subject to these biases, and it is not easy to isolate conflicts of interest that lead to this unfortunate trap. A person's entire global approach to reality is framed by bias, which is really a mental short cut, allowing us to make faster decisions. This approach worked reasonably well when humans were living on the savannah, but they are not always helpful in modern life. As Christopher Hitchens pointed out, we are biased to assume that the rustling behind us is a predator and not the more likely sound of the wind. Inevitably these biases can lead to broad misunderstandings.

For example, many of the current political debates have been inaccurately framed due to confirmation bias. As outlined by Tversky and Kahneman (1974), confirmation bias leads people to exclude information that does not conform to their own mental models. Quantitative research is not immune either. Jeng (2006) described this as a factor in physics—which is about as objective a field as one can study short of pure mathematics. These biases extend to statistical analysis. In recent years it has become more apparent that there are some real issues in the ways we analyze results because our statistical methodology itself may be flawed (Gill, 2008).

Traditional methods tend to reject results that show high variance even if there is an actual effect (Fenton & Neil, 2012, pp. 311-315). They also reward low variance, even if an effect might not be actually present. This creates a problem in determining the outcome that is not generally considered in the research.

Consider the lack of statistical support for improved simulator motion used in pilot training. Is this a result of some high variance in results, which prevents the rejection of the null? Without further analysis, it is impossible to say. This may be a consequence of flaws in the motion algorithms themselves or simulator limitations. Or perhaps, there really is no statistically significant effect? Still, research published by scientists who follow the scientific process remains subject to peer review. Accident investigation is conducted by people well versed in their craft. With the possible exception of psychologists, most accident investigators are not trained in scientific methods. This factor has profound implications impacting what we read in official government reports. Because accident investigators around the world are not trained to treat their work as a science, methods used to investigate accidents are taken as they come. The difficulty begins with the lack of a programmatic method to ensure everything is investigated. In every case much is left to the investigators—and their bias, to decide what is worthy of investigation. From experience we know what to obtain in the field investigation. The same is true of data, analysis, etc. In the end, and perhaps most critically, a completed accident investigation report is virtually never subject to any kind of outside peer review. The investigative agency may accept the submissions from technical experts, the other governments involved, the aircraft manufacturer and airline (in the case of an airline accident), but the way this information is used varies widely.

Once published, the report is, for the most part, set in stone. A major concern is the fact that it is hard, often impossible, to change a closed report. Contrast this to the scientific world where any paper may be challenged and superseded at any time, or in some notable cases, completely withdrawn. Inevitably the result is that a great many published accident reports include "findings" that could be proved wrong. Tragically, these same questionable reports are used by many as a basis for making arguments about the cause of the accident. This is a continuing challenge with no immediate solution in sight. Often these reports are the basis for studies concluding that the "pilot error" is the "cause" of most accidents. The studies, in turn, focus on pilot performance after an accident. This leads to more bias drifting away from the systemic issues that lead to actual accidents. Some investigators are satisfied walking away from each accident thinking, "well, that was weird but it won't happen again." We put on a few superficial band aid patches that make us feel better and, usually, address a few aspects near the last few items in the accident sequence. Then we move on to the next accident in a never-ending cycle of 'blamesmanship'. In the process we continually miss the actual factors involved, and, as a consequence, continually see similar accidents that could have been prevented had the scientific method been used objectively.

Consider the concept of pilot error, which could well be "operator error." It could be "nurse error," "doctor error," "driver error," and so on.

It is exceedingly easy (and far less cognitive work) just to capture the hindsight bias (really just a type of confirmation bias) aspects and say "that guy screwed up." This oversimplification does nothing to prevent future accidents. It just makes people feel good as they walk away thinking "that won't happen to me because I (fill in the blank)." It is a lot more work to objectively study all the contributing factors.

Sidney Dekker (2007) elaborates on the problem of hindsight bias. He explains that it will:

→ oversimplify causality ("this led to that") because we can start from the outcome and reason backwards to presumed or plausible "causes";

→ overestimate the likelihood of the outcome (and people's ability to foresee it) because we already have the outcome in our hands;

→ overrate the role of rule or procedure "violations." While there is always a gap between written guidance and actual practice (and this almost never leads to trouble), that gap takes on causal significance once we have a bad outcome to look at and reason back from;

✈ misjudge the prominence or relevance of data presented to people at the time;

✈ match the outcome with the actions that went before it. If the outcome was bad, then the actions leading up to it must have been bad too—missed opportunities, bad assessment, wrong decisions and misperceptions (Dekker, 2007, pp. 66-67).

The solution is to actually apply the scientific process to investigations. It is much easier to teach a person with technical knowledge how to investigate than the other way around. A better approach would be to offer an effective method people can use. This would not be a "cookbook"; every investigation and every organization will need to tailor it. The best solution is a programmatic way to solve accidents. Fortunately for us, Dr. Nancy Leveson at MIT has done just that. Her method, derived from system theory, Causal Analysis using System Theory, provides a solid basis for investigating accidents.

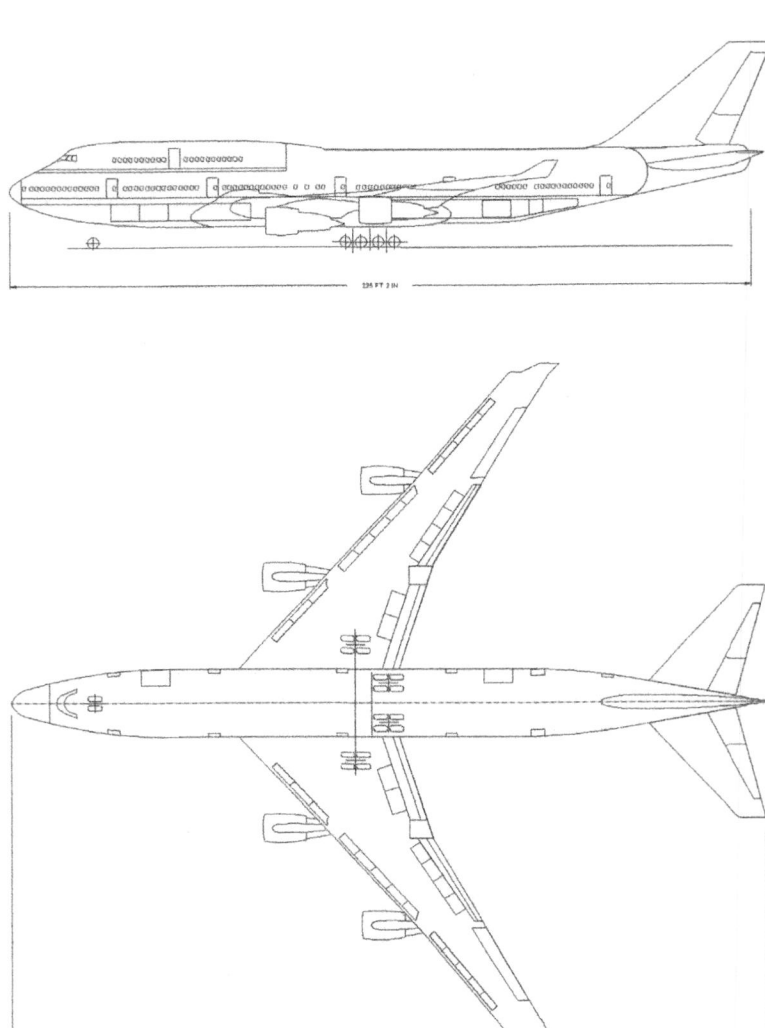

CHAPTER 12
Creating Resilience

The best thing that can be done to a problem is to dissolve it.

Russell Ackoff

The best solution to preventing accidents would be to create systems less dependent on humans intervening and "rescuing" them when something happens that was unanticipated in the design. As we have outlined, that day is a long way off and may never actually happen. In the meantime, how can we enhance human ability to prevent accidents? Responding to unexpected scenarios in situations beyond our imagination means we must increase our knowledge base. Instead of training in resilience, many systems actually train it out! The mantra is "procedural compliance." Pilots are told to stay on script because deviations are considered dangerous. Accident investigators inevitably become witnesses to the consequences of this rigid approach to flight training. Preventing accidents requires pilots to always be one step ahead of a new problem, an approach that is well beyond the scope of their training.

Organizations can develop resilient behavior, and, in addition, create conditions to enable their "sharp end" personnel to work in a resilient way. We must be cautious however, resilience has become a popular buzzword. There is a lot of hype surrounding the term, and many people are trying to make money off it. Unfortunately, much like its counterparts "big data" and "blockchain", most of what is being spread on the topic of resilience is pure hype.

Typically the goal of "resilience" is creating an adaptable organization with adaptable components. Part of the challenge is to fully understand what a resilient organization feels like. What does not work is learning about so called "resilient organizations" and trying to replicate them. So many factors central to a single organization are impossible to mimic. Yes, learning what an organization does makes for good reading; but that approach really can't be easily exported to another group. Instead, consider the actors in a play.

In a live performance the baseline is the story, winding towards an end point crafted by the playwright. The story becomes a script broken down into scenes. This is akin to our design of the system, the aircraft, hub operation or any other system we want to manage. Construction of the aircraft is similar to "the set." Even a computer has a role to play via a relatively scripted response. The procedures we follow are all scripted. The actors follow the script and if all goes right everyone and every component does exactly what we expect. It is literally "work as imagined," by the playwright. The director is, of course, upper management, interpreting the script for the real world.

Of course, in the real world, things often do not go right. A prop or set might not work quite right, or an actor might forget their lines. The director can do little at this point because the play is actually in motion. What do the actors do? They improvise. They adapt to make the story go where it needs to be. They may fill in sections that are incomplete, re-route around obstacles, and take other steps to create an effective ending. The stage manager may be able to help between scenes but the actors must do the heavy lifting by themselves.

This is an example of the adaptability we all want. It's fine to go off script as long as we reach the end of the story, the place where the playwright and director intended. Inflexibility, holding on when something isn't working right, can ruin the ending.

Pilots are tested on their adherence to procedures and even the National Transportation Safety Board has issued statements on the importance of "procedural compliance." Consider what would happen to the play if the actors stuck to their scripted lines and blocking (the theatre term for the actors' movements on the stage during the play) as everything around them unravelled?

In this circumstance an effective performance requires actors that are knowledgeable enough and have the skill set to improvise when necessary, then smoothly shifting back to the story line. Graceful extensibility is described by David Woods as "how a system extends performance, or brings extra adaptive capacity to bear, when surprise events challenge its boundaries."

When correctly accomplished the work is seamless. The way to get there is by creating an atmosphere where people know they are not going to be reprimanded or punished for going off script and are provided with a full understanding of how all the working parts are supposed to fit together. The second vital component is actors who have experience with things going off script. They know how to improvise and "make it work." They have the ability to keep the story moving towards a satisfying ending. By eliminating rigid barriers we can get to where we need to be.

An example might be envelope protection features on an airplane that are so well thought out good pilots no longer need the skill sets to operate without them. The more protections we put in place the less exposure each pilot has to unexpected events. They do not learn what they must know.

Like our body's immune system, the ability to manage infection is lost if the system is not exercised. This is why a vaccination actually improves our resistance to a myriad of diseases beyond the one it was meant to prevent. If we kept a child in a walled garden they would become very good at managing everything they encountered inside the garden. Unfortunately, they might not be able to manage something very innocuous outside the walls.

Similarly groups living in isolation never developed the ability to manage infection from many otherwise common ailments. They were virtually wiped out when exposed to people from other continents for the first time.

By allowing people to go "off script" a bit in training they can improve their ability to "get back on" for a positive ending. This requires trainers to be flexible. A rigid approach to how each sub-component is performed can be detrimental to training resilience. This is particularly true if the instructor insists the pilot follow techniques that are not formal procedures. Of course even formal procedures need to be reviewed during flight with an eye on the final outcome.

Pilots in a simulator should not be judged on how closely they followed procedures. It would be better to evaluate them on their ability to reach proper conclusions. Unfortunately, this is diametrically opposed to much of aviation's current emphasis towards "procedural compliance". This can set pilots up for failure. By forcing them to stay on script, training can work against creating the kind of resilience pilots need. Following required procedures is not always good enough. It's critical to think independently when a flight goes "off script." Versatile pilots who know how to quickly improvise will always be an asset to any airline. They are the kind of actors audiences love in a Broadway show.

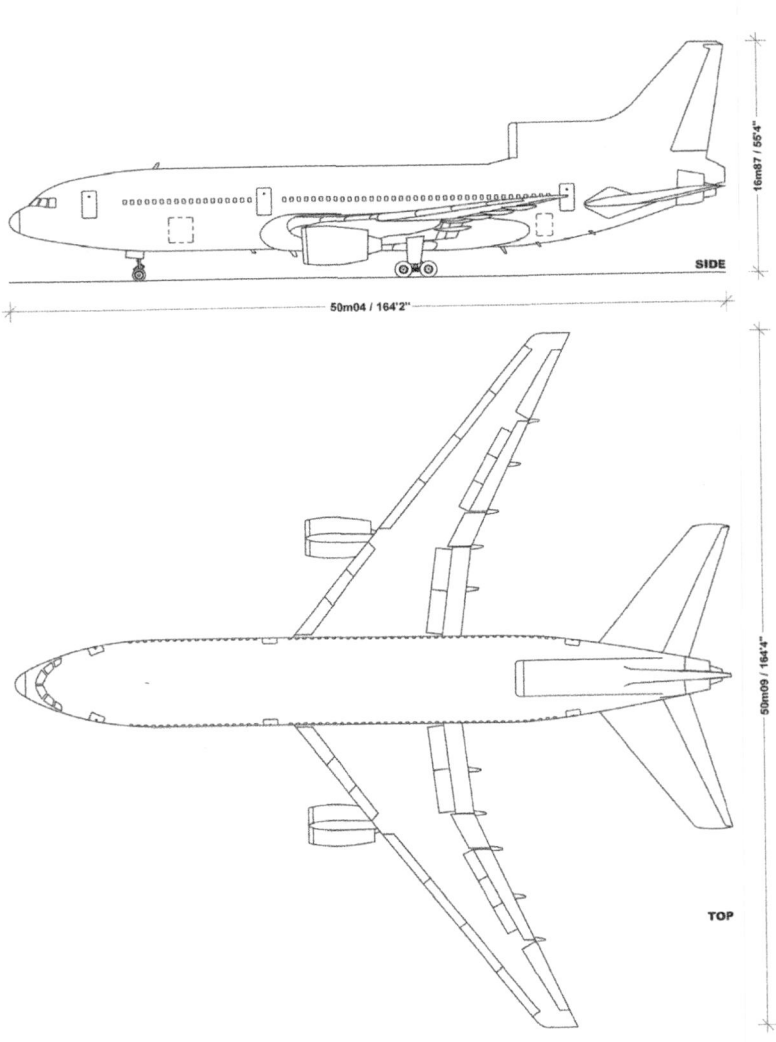

CHAPTER 13

Cognitive Bias at 30,000 Feet

We live in a probabilistic world. Somewhere there may be an objective reality where an input leads to a very clear output. The challenge is that our senses limit what we observe. A sense of uncertainty can make our lives complicated.

Is that color depicting the oceanic areas on the map really blue? That depends on your color perception. Yes, a color-blind person might perceive that area differently than someone who isn't. The color-blind person perceives what is a reality to them. Each person differs in their individual perceptions, thus their concept of reality is tainted by deficiencies in their own sight, hearing, sense of touch or equilibrium. Their perception is further impacted by personal biases and other factors such as fatigue. Human reaction is based on what we believe likely to be true given our perceptions and experiences, filtered through the senses. If we are aware of something that might impact our ability to discern objective reality (such as a color-blind person described above might do) then we adjust the odds, or

121

probability, that we are correct. Still, we bias to the "safe" position, even if it is not the most likely actual truth.

Mixing imperfect perceptions with personal bias creates a reality we believe to be true. This serves us well in the natural world but falls short in a technological age, especially when automation is successfully marketed as a panacea.

Pilots are far more removed from reality than most because they tend to perceive the world differently. There are many examples of this. Accelerations distort our reality and pilots rely on instruments to be sure which way is "up." On landing in a big airplane the pilots will perceive motion based on what the cockpit of the airplane is doing which can be quite different than what is happening with the landing gear 30 meters behind them.

Flight crews are particularly dependent on the probability of the situation but must be constantly aware that their perceptions could be wrong. Are the instruments correct? Is the sense of acceleration due to the pitch attitude or a forward acceleration? Is that apparent increase in height due to our local changes or is the airplane actually changing height? We cannot trust anything we see and so we weight everything based on conditional probabilities. Is X true given Y? Are there other factors that will make it false? Pilots make these determinations through experience and few would realize that one could calculate the probability using something like Bayes theorem. Regardless, we all must constantly second guess our assumptions and reassess as new information comes in. Is there reliable evidence to support what we believe to be true? Is the source of this evidence someone we can trust? These are the types of issues that can lead a pilot to pressing on into bad weather or continue flying with insufficient fuel due to the reality they construct. The same is true of a pilot descending into terrain.

This is a factor in other fields as well, some with critical consequences, some not. Medical professionals have a documented bias toward diagnosing a problem differently depending on their specialty. The exact same symptoms can be interpreted differently due to a combination of confirmation bias (why did the person come to see me if they did not have xyz?) and perhaps availability heuristic (discussed later in this chapter).

As the saying goes, "to a hammer, everything is a nail." Patients who have self-diagnosed and want confirmation compound the physician's problem. They may emphasize certain symptoms and not mention others, leading the doctor to a certain conclusion (note to patients, try not to do this!). This can be particularly acute when an adult parent or caregiver is describing symptoms in a child that may be tempered through the adult's lens and any bias they may have. Imagine how a parent dealing with a "problem child" might highlight certain aspects based on an emotional response. The parent might overreact to this "problem" and make it more prominent than it actually is. What sort of damage might come of this?

Risk assessment is what we, as humans, do and pilots are quite good at it. The catch is we need to constantly train our brains to ensure that we are making decisions based on actual evidence. Bias and perceptual limitations can lead us in the wrong direction.

Humans are subject to a variety of heuristic biases. As Daniel Kahneman explains, "heuristic is a simple procedure that helps find adequate, though often imperfect answers to difficult questions."

These directly impact the decision-making process, leading to incorrect judgments. In most settings this is relatively harmless, however, for those operating in highly critical safety positions, these biases can quickly lead to deadly errors. The bias itself impacts the operator's perception of reality, creating a very real barrier or screen, which either blocks or filters out what is actually happening. These biases can be exacerbated by physiological issues, as well as external influences that become part of the feedback used by the operator in the decision making process.

Cognitive bias effect on human perception

Human perception is a "conscious sensory experience" using our senses and our brain to filter and read those sensory inputs.

Research has revealed that there are a number of common ways that our brains can "trick" us into a misconception of the truth. These biases serve as filters, hindering our ability to make accurate decisions. Some of these biases may not have a large impact on the final outcome of our decisions. The problem, as we have seen with some high-risk situations, is that a decision improperly filtered by cognitive bias can be fatal.

Types of cognitive bias

There are many types of cognitive bias that can affect flight safety and decision making. Here are examples of biases particularly dangerous to flight crews (and to varying degrees, other fields as well):

Ambiguity effect

An aspect of decision theory where a person is more likely to select something that has an intuitively clear risk as opposed to one that seems relatively less certain. This could lead someone to choosing a more risky option, albeit a more certain risk (Baron and Frisch, 1994). This might be the case when deciding whether or not to fly an approach during questionable weather versus diverting to an alternate airport with other unknown issues.

Anchoring bias

This is where people will make decisions based on a provided reference. For example, pilots might accept as a given the baseline amount of fuel required. That can lead the crew to ignore operational needs that might actually require much more, or much less fuel. (Kahneman, 2011). A good example would be ignoring actual headwinds that impact the fuel calculation.

Another might be measuring minimum fuel requirements in weight rather than time. Some explanation is required here. First, rather than use a measurement in volume, such as gallons or litres, jet aircraft typically measure fuel in units of weight, either pounds or kilograms. The volume of the fuel can vary with temperature, but the weight provides a true measure of how much chemical energy we are actually carrying.

Fuel burns as a ratio of a certain amount of weight in fuel to a certain amount of weight in oxygen, making weight a better number. As would be expected, in flying what matters is that we have enough fuel reserve to ensure reaching the airport if something happens at the last moment, such as a change in weather or a closed runway.

Ideally we measure this in terms of "time" and, in fact, the regulations require that the U.S. flight be planned with at least a 45 minute fuel reserve. However, a pilot that might have previously flown jet fighters might be more used to thinking in terms of weight as a certain amount of fuel always remained very closely correlated with a certain amount of time. For example 5,000 pounds of fuel would net about 45 minutes, plus or minus a minute or two, on every flight. This makes it a lot simpler to judge the fuel remaining, as the gauges read fuel in weight, not time. This strategy might be fine for a relatively small airplane, but for a large transport this no longer holds true.

On a large jet, fuel burn depends on how much the airplane weighs, a number that can add up to several hundred thousand pounds or 90 metric tons. In one example 15,000 pounds of fuel (approximately 7 metric tons) of fuel equals more than 90 minutes at a light weight to just over 30 minutes at a heavy weight.

Now imagine a flight crew flying from New York JFK to London's Heathrow wants to fly with an arbitrary 15,000 pounds of fuel as a backup reserve. Due to weather they have selected Paris as an alternate where they would arrive with 10,000 pounds of fuel. Even though the plane would be quite light at that point they are determined to still land with 15,000 pounds of fuel. They add some extra fuel to ensure that the "numbers" add up, and takeoff with 5,000 extra pounds of fuel.

Unfortunately, that extra fuel means they are too heavy to make the planned crossing altitude. Due to heavy traffic they are assigned a much lower altitude with a higher fuel burn that brings them to the Charles de Gaulle runway with just 8,000 pounds in reserve. Adding fuel meant landing with less fuel then if they had just stuck with their original plan!

Attentional bias

Humans pay more attention to things that have a perceived emotional aspect (Macleod, Mathews and Tata, 1986). In flight operations this could lead to a person making a decision based on a perceived threat due to a past experience or "thermal scar." If a pilot had a "scare" due to running low on fuel, they might consider ignoring the risk of severe weather to avoid repeating the low fuel threat. This is also the factor that might lead a parent to unconsciously bias the information provided to a medical doctor.

Attentional tunneling

Wickens and Alexander (2009) "define this construct as, the allocation of attention to a particular channel of information, diagnostic hypothesis, or task goal, for a duration that is longer than optimal given the expected cost of neglecting events on other channels, failing to consider other hypotheses, or failing to perform other tasks." Several well-known aircraft accidents have been attributed to attentional tunneling, including the crash of Eastern Airlines 401. National Transportation Safety Board (NTSB) investigators found this aircraft descended into the Everglades while the crew focused on an inoperative landing gear position light (NTSB, 1972). A doctor diagnosing a patient based on her specialty, e.g. an allergist diagnosing a rash as an allergy, would be an example of this as well.

Automaticity

Although not a bias, automaticity refers to the fact that humans who perform tasks repeatedly will eventually learn to perform them automatically (Pascual, Mills and Henderson, 2001). Although a generally positive attribute, this can lead to a person automatically performing a function (such as a checklist item) without actually being cognizant of the task itself. Expectation bias can then lead them to assume that the item is correctly configured, even when it is not.

Availability heuristic

This describes how people will over-estimate the likelihood of an event based upon the emotional influence of a previous experience. A related issue is how much personal experience a person may have had with that type of event. This can lead to incorrect risk assessments. Some are incorrectly perceived as too dangerous while others are seen as less dangerous than they really are (Kahneman, 2011; Carroll, 1978; Schwarz, Bless, Strack, Klumpp, Rittenauer-Schatka and Simons, 1991). An example might be the high perception of risk and concern over a fuel tank explosion (a very rare event) as opposed to more focus on technology to reduce loss of control of inflight events, which the Commercial Aviation Safety Team (CAST) calculated as a much more serious risk (CAST, 2003).

Availability cascade

This is a process where something repeated over and over will become accepted as a fact (Kuran and Sunstein, 1999). How does this problem, well known in politics, play a role in flight operations? The answer is that repetition can promote misleading ideas. A pilot might say "be careful of that airplane, its control surfaces are too small," and, if this error is spread widely enough, other pilots begin to accept this myth as a fact. They may then make inappropriate flight control inputs based on an incorrect mental model of the aircraft's dynamics.

Base rate fallacy

Historically, lack of data has resulted in an inability to understand large statistical trends. When a person involved in flight safety planning focuses on specific events, rather than looking at probability over the entire set (ignoring the base rate), there is a tendency to make judgments on specifics, ignoring general statistical information. This can affect pilots if they are unable to accurately assess the risk of certain decisions (Kahneman, 2011).

Confirmation bias

A common issue in politics, but pervasive across many fields, this describes a situation where a person ignores facts or information that does not conform to their preconceived mental model. Of course they will also assume any information conforming to their beliefs is true (Nickerson, 1998). This is very dangerous in aviation because a pilot might form an incorrect mental model of their situation and have a very difficult time changing that view, even in the face of new information.

Expectation bias

This might be considered a subset of confirmation bias, but describes a situation where a person sees the results they expect (Jeng, 2006). Expectation bias is described within the context of several aircraft events in the next section.

Optimism bias

As the name suggests, this is an unwarranted situation where people are overly optimistic about outcomes (Chandler, Greening, Robison and Stoppelbein, 1999; DeJoy, 1989). It is a common issue in aviation, as pilots have seen so many bad situations turn out "okay" that their sense of urgency and risk can be reduced. This may be a factor in normalizing actions that are not correct, referred to as "normalization of deviance."

Overconfidence effect

As the name suggests, there is a strong tendency for people to over-estimate their own abilities or the qualities of their own judgments (Dunning and Story, 1991; Mahajan, 1992). This can have major implications in flight operations.

Plan continuation

This might be considered a subset of confirmation bias. There is a strong tendency to continue pursuing the same course of action once a plan has been made (McCoy and Mickunas, 2000,) but it may also be influenced by some of the same issues that lead to "sunk cost effect," seen with the Boeing 737 MAX following the first crash in 2018. Problems are compounded because there is a "greater tendency to continue an endeavor once an investment in money, effort, or time has been made." (Arkes and Blumer, 1985). Plan continuation bias is an important factor in several events, as outlined in the next section.

Prospective memory

A common situation where one needs to remember to do something that will occur in the future (Dodhia and Dismukes, 2008; West, Krompinger and Bowry, 2005). It can be particularly challenging when faced with distractions of any sort, for example, a person is driving home from work and needs to stop to pick up milk en route. If that person then receives a phone call, there is a high probability they will forget to stop at the store. In aviation, this can lead to many items being missed. A pilot might notice a problem during a preflight inspection and later forget to report the issue to maintenance due to a subsequent distraction.

Selective perception

There is a strong bias to view events through the lens of our belief system (Massad, Hubbard and Newtson, 1979). This is different than expectation bias because it is generally applied to our perception of information filtered via our belief system itself. Expectation bias is generally utilized to describe situational awareness based on things we expect to happen. Selective perception can lead to an incorrect hypothesis, such as a belief that an event had supernatural causes. In an aircraft, such a belief system can lead to false assumptions.

Accidents and incidents resulting from cognitive bias

Cognitive bias plays a role in most aircraft accidents one way or another, and each accident will have various factors. Some, like attentional tunneling, confirmation bias, and plan continuation are very common flight crew errors. Others, such as anchoring bias, would be more likely to be found at the operator level. This has played a role in aircraft accidents and incidents.

Air France 447

Biases involved in this event include attentional tunneling, expectation bias, confirmation bias, automaticity, optimism bias and overconfidence effect, exacerbated by lack of training. Clearly, as the situation developed, the crew experienced attentional tunneling. The pilots were extremely concerned about getting the captain back up to the flight deck, and expressed this several times. In addition, they appeared to be worried about the altitude and the electronic alerts, focusing heavily on these issues.

The line of weather was penetrated just prior to the autopilot disconnect. The crew was anticipating turbulence (they had advised the flight attendants about this) and it is likely they associated the pitch attitude, the stall buffet associated shaking and loss of altitude with weather factors. This is a perfect example of expectation bias.

The first officer's nose up input was likely an automaticity response. In training, the response to unusual aircraft situations was to apply full nose-up inputs due to the flight control laws incorporated in the A-330. Unfortunately, that did not apply to this situation. Once the aircraft stalled, they discounted conflicting cues and held onto the notion that they had lost all of the instruments, exhibiting confirmation bias. This lasted for the next few minutes, but the crew did not have long, as the time from autopilot disconnect to the aircraft hitting the ocean was just four minutes and 22 seconds. With altimeters spinning at a rate that blurred the indications, pitch at what would normally be a positive climb attitude and maximum engine power, it is not surprising that the conflicting cues were hard to sort out.

The usual experience of situations turning out well likely triggered the overconfidence effect. Optimism also played out in crew interactions. The relief pilot in the left seat was more experienced he did not forcibly take the controls. In part this is likely due to his optimism that the situation would turn out well (BEA, 2012).

American Airlines 903

On May 12, 1997, an American Airlines A-300 was approaching Miami, Florida. Descending to level flight at 16,000 feet, the crew was cleared into a holding pattern due to air traffic. Precipitation was depicted on the weather radar in the vicinity of the holding point. Perhaps to assist the autothrottles in the descent, the throttle levers had been pulled back below the normal autothrottle minimum limit, which apparently caused the autothrottle system to disengage. As the aircraft approached the holding point at a level altitude, the airspeed started to decay due to lack of engine thrust. The flight crew was concentrating on the weather ahead and, due to their expectation bias, believed the ride would get rough as they penetrated the storm.

The aircraft entered bad (convective) weather, and, at about the same time, also encountered aerodynamic stall buffet. The crew interpreted this buffet as turbulence (expectation bias). When the aircraft actually stalled, the crew assumed they had encountered windshear and applied the windshear escape maneuver procedure. As the aircraft proceeded to buck and shake, the crew believed that they were in a severe windshear event. Fortunately, they were able to recover; however, the crew was not aware that they had stalled the aircraft until informed of that fact later by investigators (NTSB, 1997; Dismukes, Berman, and Loukopoulos. 2007).

USAF C-5 Diego Garcia

More than 20 hours into an augmented duty day, the crew of a U.S. Air Force Lockheed C-5 was approaching the Diego Garcia airport. While configuring for landing, they encountered an area of precipitation. Concentrating on the approach and configuration (attentional tunneling), the aircraft continued to slow, with power retarded. The crew likely anticipated some turbulence (expectation bias) and as the aircraft slowed, it started to buffet. When the aircraft descended below the target profile, they pitched the aircraft up more (attentional tunneling and confirmation bias), which led to an aerodynamic stall. The aircraft departed controlled flight, bucking wildly. The crew regained control just a few hundred feet off the water, and came around for a safe landing, believing all the while that they had encountered a windshear. It is probable that fatigue also exacerbated the issues facing this crew (USAF, ND). Fatigue will always exacerbate cognitive bias.

Delta Airlines 191

On August 2, 1985, a Lockheed L1011, was on approach to the Dallas-Fort Worth airport. Scattered thunderstorms were in the area, which the crew circumnavigated. As the aircraft was vectored to the final approach course, a thunderstorm cell moved to an area just north of the airport, on short final for their arrival runway. The crew was highly experienced, and had certainly encountered similar conditions in the past. Optimism bias was likely present in their assessment of the situation, and this was confirmed as the aircraft ahead of them landed without incident. The crew was aware of the convective weather and rain on the approach, but clearly not the impending microburst. As in some other accidents, with the combination of plan continuation bias, and generally not being concerned about the issue due to lack of training, this crew continued the approach. The aircraft encountered a microburst, resulting in a significant loss of airspeed.

During the microburst (a dangerous thunderstorm cell with an extreme downdraft), the flying pilot (the first officer) appeared to be focusing on the airspeed (attentional tunneling), at the expense of altitude. The aircraft crashed just short of the runway (NTSB, 1985).

Countermeasures to mitigate bias

Once identified, the hazards of cognitive bias can be mitigated through countermeasures that target the issues directly. These require changing the way humans think. There are only a handful of ways to do that.

Training

Whether training is initiated at the individual level through personal development, or via formal programs, training is the only way to actually change the root behavioral issues that result in biases. The first defense against any hazard is to understand that the hazard exists.

Education

People working in safety critical positions should be trained to understand the types of cognitive biases that exist, and strategies to avoid them. Thorough understanding helps people see how these biases can affect them, and how dangerous and insidious they can be. In addition, proven methods to identify these problems should be explored and taught. These should be trained until they are understood as prime decision-making issues requiring an immediate response. Operators should also be taught when they need to make a more careful decision to avoid the traps (Kahneman and Klein (2009).

Crew Resource Management

One of the most effective and proven strategies in combating perceptual error has been crew resource management (Cooper, G. E., White, M. D., and Lauber, J. K. (eds), 1980). Through these methods, the other members of the crew (or team) can serve as a safety net to capture errors. If these crew members are trained to recognize cognitive biases, they will be much more likely to recognize the scenario in real time.

Conclusion, Recommendations and Research

Cognitive bias continues to play a major role in aerospace accidents. Much of the time, those at the "sharp end" are not even aware they are experiencing these biases and their associated affects on perception and judgment. The accident rate can be reduced through education and training aimed at mitigating these issues. Accident investigators should be trained to identify these challenges to make sure they can be addressed through the formal channels following an accident investigation.

Despite all the research, understanding of these issues and, more importantly, how to mitigate them, is limited. Research is badly needed to find ways to improve human performance, specifically targeting many factors contributing to cognitive biases.

Ideally, pilots should consider each flight a new opportunity. Good attorneys, who have handled similar cases for many years, still methodically treat each new case as if it was their first one. This way they are more likely to capture any changes to the law, recent rulings, etc. This can be applied to aviation, where all the material is reviewed prior to each flight: changes to the flight manuals, weather, procedures at the airports, updated air traffic control procedures, etc. While this would be more work it would discourage a more complacent attitude.

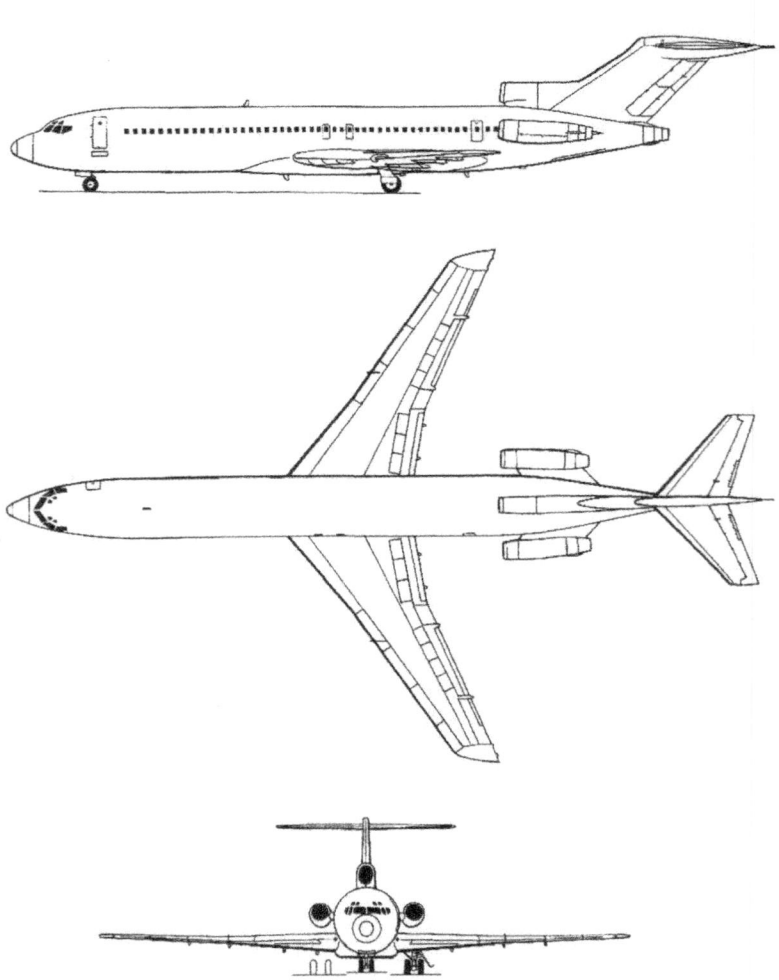

CHAPTER 14

Why Hand Flying Pilots Need More Aerodynamics Training

"The problem with pilots today is that they're not doing enough hand flying!"

This refrain is the current "hypothesis du jour" heard from many in the aviation industry struggling to prevent crashes. It is often echoed across the entire industry, by regulators and the various industry alphabet organizations that have jumped onto this bandwagon.

"Advocate more hand flying" and safety will be improved. Closely following this is the concept that all pilots need to do is "pay more attention to detail." The party line is that accidents are triggered by a lack of "stick and rudder" skills or simply just not paying attention. These clichés sound great but they all merit a closer look.

Stick and Rudder

Of course hand flying is a good thing. Pilots should hand-fly more, it adds value and it is also fun. Many pilots have a love/hate relationship with autopilots and auto throttles, which can be great but are not nearly as enjoyable to fly. If conditions allow for it, the industry recommends that pilots hand-fly the airplane up to FL 250 (25,000 feet) and also turn off the automation fairly early during the arrival. Flying the airplane is fun!

There is no question that the more pilots hand fly the better their performance. That said, "hand-flying" while just following the flight director (a computer generated display that shows the pilots exactly where to hold the aircraft pitch and roll to follow the computer's planned flight path) is really not hand-flying. Rather, this is just playing a video game and any ten-year-old child can easily do that. Hand flying should, at the least, include turning off the flight director.

The question we need to ask is how does this relate to recent air carrier accidents? A review of all jet transport accidents in the last five years fails to find any that would clearly have been averted if the pilots had more hand-flying experience. When the hand-flying aspect was an issue, other factors were also involved. Both Air France (AF) 447 and Asiana 214 in San Francisco have highlighted the need for more hand flying. However, a review of AF 447 and Asiana 214 accidents, with the removal of hindsight bias, suggests that additional hand-flying experience would not have given either crew what they needed to prevent an accident.

Contrary to popular opinion, data shows the accidents themselves do not appear to have been caused by a lack of hand-flying skills. In other words, the accident could have happened to someone who handles the aircraft exceptionally well. What we are seeing in these accidents is a failure to understand what automation is providing pilots. It appears that their expectations fail to match what the automation actually does. This important obstacle is poorly trained. While the pilots are taught automation there are enough gaps in the training that the commonly heard half-joking comment "What's it doing now," is an ongoing problem. By itself all the hands on training in the world is not going to fix this.

If a pilot fails to understand what the automation is doing there is (of course) a remote possibility that the computer is doing something incorrectly. In reality the rate of actual hardware and/or software problems is very, very low. It is much more likely that the flight crew doesn't "get" the automated system. Perhaps they are operating at too high a level of automation. Regardless, if the disconnect continues for more than a moment or two, they should seriously consider moving to a less automated mode until problems are sorted out.

At all times, the pilot should absolutely know what to expect next. Unfortunately, absent significant system knowledge, most of the current aircraft systems do a poor job of telegraphing the flight crew details of its next planned action. Sometimes it is not a large factor, such as the way the aircraft adjusts to a different-than-expected wind model while transitioning from one phase of flight to another. At other times it can be a major factor that can lead to, at the very least, a regulation violation or at worst, an accident when a crew expected the aircraft to capture a certain vertical path or airspeed.

Pilot Knowledge

Putting automation aside, let's have a closer look at the hand-flying issue. Despite the push for hand flying there has been little effort to ensure that all pilots have reviewed or received recurrent training on fundamental aerodynamics. You may find that surprising and ask, "Aren't pilots trained for that early on?" The answer is a definite maybe.

Early in their careers some pilots receive superficial training necessary to pass a written test. Sure, they know how the aircraft responds to their inputs and have a rudimentary concept of "why." Unfortunately that leaves out a basic understanding of what would happen in the rare "corner-cases" that are often the one-of-a-kind scenarios where accidents occur. Regardless of a student's background, a comprehensive aerodynamics review is essential to all training programs. It is difficult for pilot skills to stay sharp in hand-flying or flight procedures absent regular training. Why then is an aerodynamics review left out of the equation?

A comprehensive baseline understanding of aerodynamics may not appear to be essential in our world of automated flying. In fact, as we have learned again and again, it can be very important in critical situations. There are many nuances that require more understanding and reviewing them all would be beyond the scope of this book. However, some examples might include the differences in stall angle due to high speed (mach) effects, or how the airplanes ailerons are more effective at lower angle of attacks and rudder more effective at higher angle attacks (the reader is encouraged to research these topics).

In addition, if we expect pilots to use their "hand-flying" skills to get out of sticky situations, they should be allowed to practice those skills in situations where they might need them, such as high altitude flight. To make this happen we would have to create other controls to prevent inadvertent altitude deviations.

AF 447s crew found themselves hand-flying the aircraft at an altitude regime where the full time use of the autopilot is required. This unexpected situation happened in a degraded flight control mode rarely (if ever) practiced or demonstrated at any altitude. The closest comparison to an automobile would be driving on a highway at high speed, encountering ice and losing power steering at the same time. The combination of the altitude and flight control regimes was something they would never have seen in any training, even if the simulator could adequately replicate the conditions (a topic unto itself). Is it reasonable to assume they would be able to have the skills to hand-fly the airplane with those challenges at night across the upper levels of turbulent thunderstorms? While it might be easy to judge them in hindsight this one of a kind scenario was a far cry from the way it might look to someone reviewing his or her actions after the fact from an office desk.

Attention to Detail

How can you pay attention to detail if you are hand-flying? The industry originally moved toward the more automation to allow for better decision making with fewer pilots in the cockpit. The concept was that we could cut the flight crew for a very large aircraft to just two pilots. Manufacturers believed that the automation would free up the pilots from all that hand-flying, allowing them to concentrate on decision-making. In that process, there is no question that the pendulum swung toward mandating high levels of automation use, a decision that needed to be pulled back. Now it appears that we are trying to go the opposite way, telling pilots "ok, hand-fly, but remain responsible for monitoring."

The problem is we simply cannot just command pilots to pay more attention. Virtually every safety organization in the world now strongly endorses and advocates the "Just Culture" algorithm, where we divide actions that led to an adverse outcome into error, at-risk and reckless.

* As we describe in other sections of this book, the term "error" is really a manifestation of hindsight bias.

We define an error as something that is an unintentional act*, and, by definition, if that leads to a bad outcome, it is a "system problem."

By "system," we mean it is necessary to redesign the policies, procedures, equipment, displays, etc. to fix it. At-risk is an action that is the result of a person intentionally failing to follow a policy or procedure. Instead they go for a work-around, something that facilitates getting the job done.

Consider a pilot who is told to conduct a number of checklists within a specific amount of time. If an interruption caused a delay the pilot might try to skip a checklist in order to ensure being on time. This is entirely a system problem. The design and number of checklists as well as the interruption were outside the pilot's control. Being human he may have decided a portion of the checklist could be skipped that day. Unfortunately, someone "bent the rules."

Reckless is a disregard of the rules for no justifiable reason. It is quite rare for an accident to be actually caused by reckless or intentionally negligent behavior.

Where does "attention to detail," fall in the Just Culture matrix? It would be hard to argue that any lapse triggered by lack of attention to detail is an intentional effort to disregard procedures. Perhaps in some cases, but not many, it could fall into the at-risk area. Most of the time, these would clearly be an error. The fix for errors is definitely not telling someone "don't do that!"

We are reminded of a Bob Newhart video titled "Stop it" where he plays the role of a psychologist who tells his patient to "just stop it" when she describes a problem. Clearly this would not work. Correcting this problem must come through system and procedural design, not merely telling someone to "stop it."

People who have expertise in the field should design the "system" with knowledge of human error and cognitive limitations. All too often people are put in positions and given titles with no real expertise. A person who has a combination of formal academic training in human factors, coupled with experience in the field, would be ideal. That expert could integrate academic knowledge with the "real world" to create systems that capture error. Alternatively, two people, one with academic knowledge, and one with extensive operational experience, could work together to attack these problems. Relying on people who lack the requisite knowledge and experience is how we created these flawed systems in the first place. The aviation industry can do better.

Can we train people to be experts? Yes. How do we do that? In his book, Accelerated Expertise, Dr. Robert Hoffman et al (2013) discuss how to obtain expertise as quickly as possible. The study's impetus came from the Defense Science and Technology Advisory Group, which was eager to ensure top levels of expertise in various military personnel. Much of the focus lends itself to the jobs of pilots, mechanics, dispatchers, meteorologists, engineers, flight attendants, and more.

We see automation errors happen when pilots fail to understand the automation, how it interacts with other systems and predicting what it will do next. These are guidelines for effective instruction on how to create an "expert" from Robert Hoffman.

1. Learning materials must contain multiple representations of content.
2. Instructional materials should avoid oversimplifying the content domain and support context-dependent knowledge.
3. Instruction should be case-based and emphasize knowledge construction, not just the transmission of information.
4. Knowledge sources should be highly interconnected rather that compartmentalized.

Does most training meet these minimum standards? Would it make a difference if it did? How does this fit into modern training?

Let us take an example of aircraft systems training for flight controls, hydraulic, pneumatic, electrical, fuel, engines, etc. This is part of the important curriculum for learning any new aircraft.

In recent years there has been a trend towards less and less system training. At one time pilots really needed to understand the systems. For example, pilots learning in a Boeing 727 were expected to be able to draw the electrical system from memory. This was standard for pilots. If a crossfeed valve failed on a classic B-747 all pilots knew they could still move fuel via the dump manifold. As a testament to how in depth this training was, many pilots still remember most of these airplane systems years later.

Today pilots generally lack in-depth understanding of the systems unless they are involved in technical or safety work. It is not part of the curriculums anymore. What changed? Automation is part of the explanation. Automated systems act on their own to solve problems which lead directly to the "why should someone know the details?" argument.

At the same time engineers have been able to come up with simpler systems that accomplish what needs to be done for the fuel, electrical, hydraulic, pneumatic and flight control systems. In turn this allows for highly procedural steps, which can then be added to checklists or automatic system responses. Another factor has had an even greater impact on what is trained: greatly improved component reliability.

Even 30 years ago it was not uncommon for a pilot to have experienced an engine failure during a career, or a failure in some other critical system. Today, a probability of many of these types of failures is so low that a pilot has a good chance of flying an entire career with nary more than a fairly minor glitch. The lack of events (industry parlance for accidents or incidents) is then used as a basis for arguing that we should spend our limited training budgets on things that are statistically more likely to lead to an accident. Those statistics are found by looking at the accident and incident trends. The industry uses methods that are somewhat limited to find "root causes" of those accidents (there are serious flaws in this approach, as the findings tend to be simplistic at best) and these are used to build training scenarios. The training "footprint" is also used to teach pilots about new technology, new procedures and the like. The result is a very full simulator-training period and limited time for anything else!

The problem here is the way training is built. The aircraft manufacturers who design and build the airplane provide the aircraft and manual. Next the airlines create the training programs approved by the regulators. The manufacturers are rarely involved in what the airline actually teaches their pilots. This creates a gap between what airplane and avionic systems designers believe pilots should know and what they are actually being taught.

All manufacturers expect pilots to "fill the gaps" for those scenarios they could not envision. Need evidence? A system fails and who gets the blame if the untrained pilot does not prevent an accident or incident? We all know the answer here. Today modern aircraft systems rely heavily on computers. These computers are "talking" to each other, and rely on information from other system computers to function properly. The term for this is "integrated modular avionics."

These computers are extremely reliable, but if one gets bad information or faults, the problem can cascade across other computers in the system. These problems are unpredictable and almost impossible to reproduce later. How they react depends on what data is being shared, what faults are present and the way it propagates through the system. Even the lag due to the distance the information has to travel (length of the wires) can make a difference. That data is moving at the speed of light. We are talking about changes in fractions of nanoseconds. From there, the systems not only fault in unpredictable ways, but also the "boxes" are likely to start sending unpredictable alerts to the pilots. This is one of the many problems Air France 447 pilots needed to contend with in short order!

Suddenly we have a very complex system unlike anything an experienced and proficient and fully qualified flight crew has ever seen before. This emergency situation is beyond the imagination of the aircraft designers, the regulators, the training department, flight operations and air traffic control. No longer is the concern the failure of a single component, which might have occurred in an airplane built a generation earlier. Instead an automation problem in one component can take out all sorts of other systems. It's even possible to degrade the flight control system itself!

Now the pilot is left trying to sort out a lot of very confusing indications. The troubleshooting "scripts" that are normally relied upon, the checklists, and procedures, don't apply anymore. Everything now depends on that system knowledge, all while flying an airplane that might no longer handle like anything they have ever experienced. As we have pointed out training for degraded flight control laws in fly-by-wire aircraft, exactly what happened on Air France 447, is often very limited.

We have seen pilots who had "above and beyond" knowledge do a good job handling unusual scenarios. "Sully" Sullenberger did it when he started the Auxiliary Power Unit out of emergency checklist sequence, restoring electric power and hence normal law to the flight controls. The pilot of Qantas 72, Kevin Sullivan (coincidentally, also nicknamed "Sully") used his superior knowledge to handle what could have been a catastrophic flight control failure. In a May 2017 Sydney Morning Herald article on the event he said something that will resonate with pilots:

"Even though these planes are super-safe and they're so easy to fly, when they fail they are presenting pilots with situations that are confusing and potentially outside the realms to recover. For pilots—to me—it's leading you down the garden path to say, 'You don't need to know how to fly anymore.' You just sit there—until things go wrong."

Both "Sullys" had skills no longer trained. They "grew up" in a time prior to the introduction of highly reliable components, before tighter rules made hand-flying at cruise altitude virtually illegal, when pilots still needed to learn their systems. They carried that to the day when they needed this critical information and the special skills necessary, perhaps, once in a lifetime.

Again this is not just about more "hand-flying." Hand-flying a normal airplane is fun, but is not going to equip a pilot to handle a degraded flight control state. Plus, hand flying is virtually always done at lower altitude with limited configuration changes—not great preparation for a degraded airplane in the upper flight levels.

Manufacturers marketing departments love to claim pilots can get by with minimal training thanks to systems and automation reliability. The reality is that they can get by with it until the day they can't. Every pilots has no idea when that day might come. Of course from their vantage point, on the ground, engineers tend to have a different take then the folks trying to sell expensive airplanes. They expect pilots to "fill the gaps."

There are also times when more system knowledge can make a big difference, even without failures. One that immediately comes to mind is the automated radar systems, which will be discussed in more detail later. While these can improve the situation for pilots with minimal training, they still leave significant gaps due to the relative simplicity of models used to scan for weather. They can also lead pilots to mistakenly believe there is no bad weather ahead. Here the problem begins when the algorithm is depicting the weather incorrectly due to a difference in the vertical liquid profile of a storm. A pilot with more knowledge of aviation meteorology, as well as functioning radar, can fill those gaps.

A better educated pilot can also prevent other problems, such as a delay due to just misunderstanding what the system is doing. Granted there are some who might "overthink" in these situations, but this, too, can be rectified. Pilots remain the most important safety feature on any airplane. System knowledge can be hard to find these days. When designing training programs the airlines should be required by regulation to consult with the manufacturers. It is critical to ensure that pilots are being taught what the manufacturer thinks is important with reference to systems handling, and pertinent aerodynamics. By "manufacturers" we do not mean just the flight training department at the manufacturers, but the actual design engineers and test pilots. Often there is a problematic disconnect between these two groups. We need direct participation with the men and women on the manufacturer's design team. Until that welcome day comes, pilots are all too often on their own. The airlines need to know what skill sets pilots must have to fly airplanes after various faults arise.

We do not anticipate that the airlines will voluntarily increase the training footprint. While cost is an issue, it's also true that the industry moves in lockstep. Perhaps the airlines can collectively come up with a joint plan for new training, similar to the high altitude aerodynamic stall training following Air France 447.

For now it is up to individual pilots to go out and learn what they need to know on their own. While Boeing stopped publishing, there are still many issues of its magazine, (Boeing Aero) and Airbus has two good in-house magazines (Airbus FAST and Airbus Safety First) that should be read, even if a pilot does not fly one of their planes. Skybrary is another source and Internet searches can also help. Frustrating as it may be to learn things not taught by their company, pilots who want to fly their way out of challenging situations need to take the initiative. For the foreseeable future there do not appear to be any good alternatives emerging from an industry that pays handsomely for its mistakes (many billions in the case of the Boeing 737 MAX crashes). For far too long, companies have preferred the status quo. Now would be a good time to open a conversation with the industry about preventing potential accidents by stepping up training. Until that day comes too many pilots will be on their own when it comes to handling the vagaries of automation.

CHAPTER 15
Stormy Weather

A lthough thunderstorms can occur year around, we think of Spring as "thunderstorm season." Warming temperatures create more convective weather. While more than 80% of the world's severe storms occur in North America, many others are also found across Asia, Africa and South America. Generally they happen less frequently in polar regions.

Weather avoidance for pilots begins in the preflight planning stages. A number of good tools are available to aid pilot decision-making. Surprisingly some of the best are under-utilized due to lack of training and knowledge. When there is significant weather ahead in the U.S., Air Traffic Control (ATC) may implement a Severe Weather Avoidance Plan, or SWAP. This approach can eliminate some of the planning pilots need to do. Absent a SWAP, pilots need to look at the big picture and come up with preliminary ideas on the best way to minimize flight weather encounters.

Pilots' primary assets at this point are satellite, radar and lightning maps. Further support is available from current weather reports, forecasts and pilot reports (PIREPS) from other aircraft. Internationally, the availability of information varies. Airlines flight dispatchers have access to a full array of weather maps, and in addition to programs such as Flight Explorer, which depict the aircraft, there are navigation aids and a variety of weather product overlays. The dispatcher can help provide a route that will minimize the time pilots spend avoiding challenging weather.

A good dispatcher is a great asset throughout the flight. "Big picture" displays, coupled with easy access to meteorologists or other weather data provide a great deal of timely information. They can often tell the pilot where the weather is, where it is headed and help plan a route that will take them around storms. Uplinked weather is another effective tool for pilots, although they have to be careful because it can be several minutes old. This might be fine on the ground, but for an airplane moving at 8 miles a minute or more it can be a real problem. As a result, long range planning is the best use of this important resource.

Although monitoring Air Traffic Control offers more clues on what other aircraft are experiencing, pilots need to avoid reading too much into that information. History has shown that crews following other aircraft have often been led into the teeth of a developing severe weather situation. Of course there is value in evaluating what preceding flights are experiencing, as long as it remains one of many data points, rather than a primary decision factor. In many international locations, the dispatcher may be the best support. ATC may not be able to provide any information due to lack of equipment and/or language differences. Flight operations in local languages can pretty much eliminate any information pilots might gain by monitoring other traffic.

Arguably, the best available tool for real time decision making for pilots is onboard weather radar. Years ago aviation radar sent out approximately 3,000 Watts of power. Today, thanks to advanced computers parsing the returning signal, modern weather radar has a maximum power output of roughly 150 Watts, about the same as many household light bulbs. While 3,000 Watts can cook a nice meal a few feet away, heat is only generated within a few inches of modern radar.

Although radar systems have improved significantly they are limited in several important ways. Because it only displays weather directly in front of the aircraft, radar restricts a flight crew's ability to "see" on the ground, at low altitudes or in convective weather.

Aircraft weather radars are limited to a 15 degree tilt. This might sound good, but the reality is that it is very limiting for any weather close to the airplane. Traditionally this has led to confusing displays. Until recently a useful radar image depended on the pilot's understanding of the system and where to point the beam. While these newer designs have helped automate this process, pilots don't generally always receive the training they need for a thorough understanding of the system. While thunderstorms are a problem, rain by itself is not. When radar is accidentally pointed in the wrong direction, it might paint severe weather as light rain. Other times, as a result of pointing it too low down, it might display heavy rain in front of the aircraft that does not extend up to the cruising altitudes. This is not a serious issue for a big jet. The majority of jet transport airplanes use this basic radar, which is entirely dependent on pilot skill and knowledge. The pilot must control the radar's tilt and "gain"—the amount of signal the radar displays. Think of gain as signal noise. More gain is more noise.

Another factor (not controllable by the pilot, but part of the design) is the frequency. If the frequency is too long, the wave can literally miss spotting rain. If it's too short the signal attenuates too easily and will fail to penetrate the rain. The modern radar frequency signals are a compromise and cannot be adjusted. They bounce off rain and return to the antennae. The amount displayed depends on the gain. When the gain is adjusted higher it picks up and displays more of what it is receiving. At the same time the display can be overwhelmed with too much data that is of little value.

Pilots need to understand the nuances of the gain to be able to adjust the radar screen for the picture they need. The radar's wavelength is idealized to display wet raindrops from thunderstorms, but if a storm is full of snow or ice, the radar will not show it. Turning up the gain can help in this scenario, as the radar will begin to display some of the signal returns from the snow, technically "dry particulate." By contrast, if there's a lot of rain, turning the gain down can leave just the area of heaviest rain exposed. Tilt is another important component of all radar systems. In the United States most thunderstorms have a "wet core" (an area of wet rain) at about 25,000 feet. This is because the storm lifts water up to a level where it normally freezes. At higher altitudes the water is usually frozen in the thunderstorm. Because this moisture is no longer "wet," it will not be detected by aircraft radar. Although the storm itself may top out as high as 55,000 feet, the radar-visible wet part is much lower. By adjusting the radar beam (with the help of trigonometric formulas that have been simplified to allow for some easy mental math) the pilot can point the beam to the 25,000-foot level to determine if this is a thunderstorm. Outside the United States, thunderstorm profile changes. For example, in Europe the storm might only get to 25,000 feet, which means a pilot needs to be looking more closely at the 15,000 foot region. By contrast, at night over the ocean in tropical areas, the storms tend to "rain out" by about 20,000 feet, slowly percolate frozen particulate up to around 30,000 feet, then re-energize to create strong turbulence at higher altitudes. A pilot looking for radar returns at 25,000 feet would see virtually nothing, and be lulled into flying right into a severe storm!

Closer to the airport there is a different problem. A microburst is considered one of the more significant aviation hazards. Strong updrafts hold huge amounts of rain aloft, usually around the 20,000-foot level. Eventually there is so much water that the weight overwhelms the updrafts and starts falling hard. This large ball of water is bad news for any airplane that happens to be flying beneath it. Unfortunately, most pilots have not been trained to understand how they might utilize weather radar to receive an advance warning of this threat.

On August 2, 1985, Delta 191 approached the Dallas/Fort Worth area. The weather was described as benign, scattered clouds at 6,000', 10 miles visibility and calm wind. There were scattered thunderstorms in the area and the flight made several diversions inbound. At 1756 CDT, ATC transmitted that "...there's a little rain shower just north of the airport."

At 1800 the Delta 191 crew told ATC they were at 5,000. At 1802 they were 6 miles from the outer marker. At 1804:18 the first officer said there was lightning coming out of the cloud in front of them. They reached 1,000 AGL at 1805:05, and the aircraft crashed at 1805:58. During this same time period, NWS radar showed a level 3 cell off the end of the runway at 1756, which had intensified to a level 4 cell by 1804. What did the crew see on their radar?

This was a storm developing significant weather at higher altitudes, which, once reaching critical mass, would essentially dump rain downward, along with the significant wind. At 1800 CDT, and 5,000', this doomed flight was about 20 miles from the airport. If, like many crews, they had the plane's radar tilt at around 5° nose up, they would be viewing weather at around the 15,000 feet range. As they neared the airport their view would have been at the 5,000 to 8,000 foot range. It is probable that this was not high enough to detect the severity of the storm at that time, with the radar "under-scanning" the most intense part of the water column. To provide earlier warning most modern radars are equipped with a "wind shear detection" algorithm. Unfortunately, this algorithm is only designed to detect the outflow in the aftermath of a microburst. Imagine dropping a ball of water. At first it just descends vertically, but then it hits the ground and spreads out laterally. A microburst does the same. The algorithm only detects that flow after it hits, not the vertical flow. MIT Lincoln Laboratories has developed a tool to detect this vertical threat. It is a microburst detection system installed at around 70 airports in the United States. A similar system is also installed in Hong Kong. Unfortunately, it is very limited, only designed to protect primary runways for a very limited distance. The rest of the world is pretty much devoid of any protection outside of pilot expertise. By tilting their radar beam up pilots have a chance to "look" at the 15,000 foot level or higher, and then down lower, to see if water is being held aloft. Little or no rain down low with a lot up high is one warning of such a threat. This profile can also indicate hail, which occurs when rain drops get pushed up higher and freeze, often over and over, until they are finally too heavy for the updrafts to hold them aloft. Hail or not, it is still not something to fly through. To simplify the process for pilots, leading radar manufacturers have automated their systems. The newer systems scan multiple altitudes and then store the information in their computer memories. This way the system can depict areas the designers guessed would be threats. Once again here we are limited to the imagination of the designers. How well did they understand where the threat was? Did they design the system for thunderstorm prone North America, or was it created on a global model? Either way there are compromises with important consequences anywhere in the world. On one trip, Shem Malmquist was flying across India when he noticed a large thunderstorm with a dissipating anvil, at least visually. Because this "blow off" can indicate hail, he attempted to display the anvil to determine the scope of the threat. Unfortunately, the engineers had assumed that nobody flying a commercial jet would need to "look" at weather above 60,000 feet. The storm was so tall that even at 60,000 feet it was not close to the top of the blow-off. Obviously the engineer's assumptions were wrong. Automation, whether it is for radar or any other automated system, requires that the operator (in this case the pilot) has a full understanding of that system as well as the design assumptions behind it. Pilots must also understand all ways they can work around these limitations. This requires that they be provided with the training and technical details necessary for sound decision making.

Unfortunately, this is not happening, forcing pilots to search for information on their own. Absent formal training they may develop ad hoc methods and mental models that are wrong, which are then passed on to other pilots as "techniques." This gap leaves pilots struggling to make sense of a complex situation and quickly come up with answers to challenges they may have never previously seen in their careers.

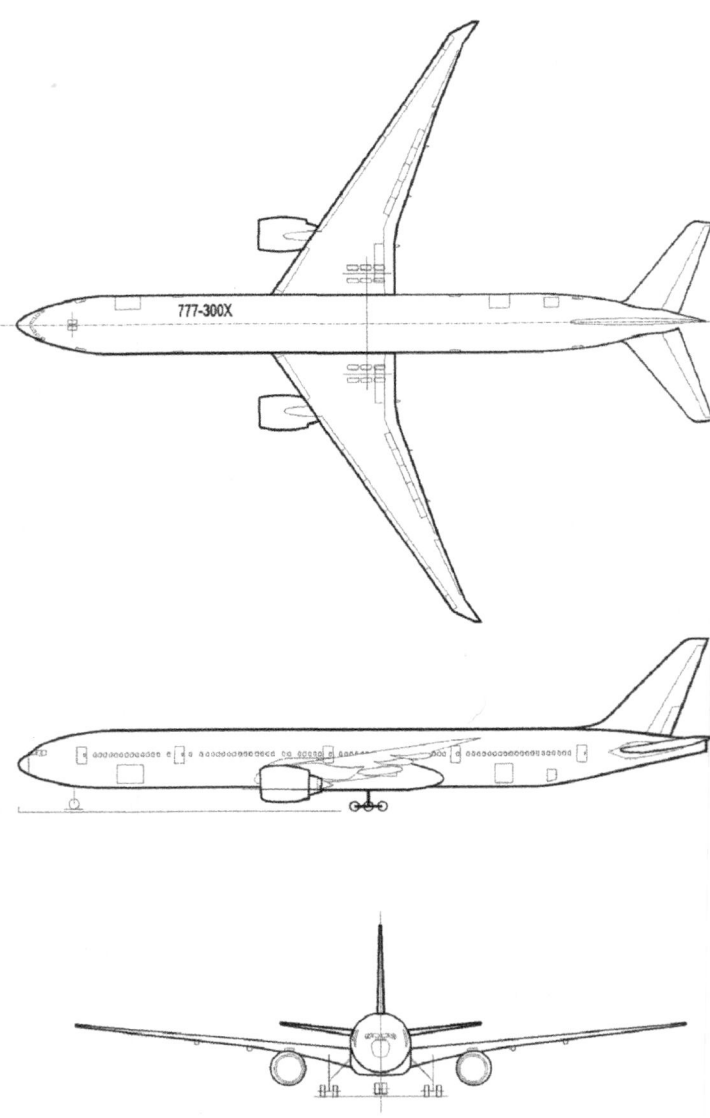

CHAPTER 16

The Envelope Limits Debate: When Both Sides Are Wrong

In the immediate aftermath of the October 29 Lion Air 610 accident the FAA issued an Emergency airworthiness directive (AD) that quickly opened up valuable new discussions on the role of automation. That event forced the industry to recognize that when modern airplanes crash the problem is not necessarily lack of airmanship, commonly referred to as "automation dependency," but the opaque actions and questionable logic of flight automation. We need to revisit the misleading concept of "automation dependency," which essentially blames the pilot and implies they are complacent. Commonly held assumptions underlying the automatic systems merit re-examination.

The FAA's Airworthiness Directive issued following the 2018 Lion Air 610 MAX accident highlighted how sensor loss on an advanced system can create very challenging scenarios. As described in Fred George's Aviation Week and Space Technology article, the sequence of events starts out fairly benignly. The indications on takeoff appear normal. Then, as the airplane leaves the ground there is suddenly a stall warning. This is followed by an apparent mismatch in the airspeed indicators, which could very easily lead the pilots to become engrossed in solving the airspeed problem while the stall warning "stick shaker" is activating. If the pilots retract the flaps as they are working through these issues, the trim suddenly pitches the airplane towards the ground.

Contrast this with unusual events where there was no accident. Consider the case of the A330 frozen angle of attack probes described in Chapter 7. Here the angle of attack probes became "stuck," and initially all seemed normal. The airplane departed and as it climbed the angle of attack probes were stuck into a position that was below the stall threshold. Here no stall was indicated. This was fine because the aircraft was at a safe angle of attack, and not stalling. Although it is generally true that a particular airfoil (the shape of the wing) will always stall at a given angle of attack, this only happens when the airspeeds are not fast enough to be affected by the speed of sound. As the airplane attains higher speeds, the effect of flying higher percentages of the speed of sound (mach numbers) begins to affect how the air flows over the wing. At higher speeds the air separates more easily and the airplane stalls at a lower angle of attack.

The A330's angle of attack vanes were jammed into a position that was below the stall angle for lower airspeeds but above the stall angle for higher speeds. As the airplane increased the mach numbers it reached the stall threshold a stall warning was triggered. This was combined with the airplane's automatic stall protection that immediately commanded a nose-down response in an effort to "stop" the stall. Unfortunately, as the airplane was not actually stalling, but was only indicating a stall due to the frozen angle of attack vanes, the result of the nose-down was to accelerate the airplane, moving it deeper into the (perceived by the system) stall regime! The more it dove, the faster it flew and the more the automatic system "thought" it was stalling! Realizing the problem, the captain reached up and switched off the flight computers, thus putting the system back under his control with no stall protections.

In very similar circumstances, on November 5, 2014, a Lufthansa A321 experienced a wild ride following a physical problem with the AoA probes interacting with the envelope protection system. In another event reported by the Australian Transport Safety Board (ATSB) a Boeing 777 experienced extreme pitch gyrations on August 1st, 2005, as a result of erroneous signals sent to the flight control computers. The pilots first noticed a "low airspeed" advisory followed by an instrument indication that the aircraft was yawing to the left, even though it wasn't. Next they received both near overspeed and a stall indication simultaneously. Suddenly the airplane then pitched up on its own.

The pilot disconnected the autopilot and lowered the nose of the airplane, but once again it pitched up on its own and climbed 2,000 feet. The pilots decided to land immediately. On approach they again received a low airspeed indication and the autothrottle responded by adding thrust. The airplane warning systems indicated a windshear. All of these indications were false. The pilots landed and discovered that the autobrakes would not disconnect in the normal manner. Examination of the system showed there were erroneous readings from the airplane's inertial reference systems used by the flight control system to make correct control movements.

None of these were related to pilot competency. In fact, all three of the incidents just described would have been much worse if outstanding pilots had not been on board to save the day. As discussed previously, the focus on the need for better "stick and rudder" skills and related anxiety about automation dependency has been repeated so often that many pilots accept it at face value. We emphasize the need to hand-fly more while realizing it is not a panacea. To reiterate, regulations generally limit a pilot's ability to hand-fly above 29,000 feet. Pilots will also use the automation when it's busy, generally in instrument conditions, or operating in complex environments (busy air traffic control environments and procedures, metric altimetry, etc.) However, as much as pilots might enjoy hand flying, is it really helping them to handle things when they go wrong? We are not so sure.

First, pilots are flying the airplane in a normal state. The B-777, like other fly-by-wire (FBW) airplanes, has very consistent handling qualities. The pilot does not have to adjust for differences due to changes in center of gravity, gross weight, flap settings, density altitude, q-factor (essentially the kinetic energy of the air flow), and a multitude of other factors that affect the way an airplane responds. FBW takes care of all that. It makes the airplane really easy to fly—as long as flight automation is working. Problems, such as an erroneous AoA signal, can unexpectedly put a FBW airplane in a degraded state. The handling qualities are going to be different, and, depending on the mode, the system may no longer be compensating for all those differences previously discussed. The pilot will have to do it, but is the pilot equipped to handle that, plus hand-fly in a complex environment? What about those newer pilots that have little, or no experience hand-flying at the higher altitudes?

Arguments about pilots lacking in skills to handle the aircraft when the automation fails miss the point. Accidents caused by a lack of pilot skill are certainly not happening at a higher rate than they have in the past, yet we hear a popular argument rooted in a similar set of misconceptions. Some pilots contend that they need to exceed airplane limits to "save the day." This debate over envelope limiting vs. protection is mostly an "Airbus vs. Boeing" debate. Both sides are wrong.

As pilots know, airplanes such as the Airbus FBW utilize "envelope limiting" while Boeing FBW utilizes "envelope protection." The difference for practical purposes is that the Airbus will not allow the airplane to exceed certain bank and pitch limits unless the pilot disconnected the flight control computers. The Boeing will just resist the pilot, but the pilot will still be able to exceed those values with the controls. Many anti-Airbus pilots will argue that they should be able to exceed a limit in an emergency. Without taking sides, it's clear that after 30 years of hard limits FBW operations we know of no accident that could have been avoided if pilots had exceeded the aircraft's built-in protections. It is also clear that there are several known cases where the hard limits prevented an accident.

Some will point to events such as the June 26, 1988, Habsheim, Air France A320 accident. In that accident the pilots were demonstrating the new Airbus jet above several thousand air show spectators. During a low pass the airplane was intentionally flown at minimum speed to demonstrate that the Airbus will automatically hold the airplane at a maximum performance angle of attack. Unfortunately, when the pilots applied power after passing down the runway they were not able to

clear the trees at the end of the runway. Many pilots and others specu-
lated that if the pilots could have had a bit more authority on the controls they could have missed the trees. They theorized that these pilots
were limited by envelope protection features preventing the new jet
from stalling. Is that what happened in this rare crash actually caught
on video? A careful analysis shows that allowing the pilots to exceed the
pitch right into a stall (it was on the edge of a stall being limited from
going further) would only have resulted in a very momentary "bump"
in altitude. This would have immediately led to a steep sink at higher
pitch attitude and rate. Not a great outcome; and it certainly would
not have prevented the crash into the trees. More thrust was what was
needed here. There simply was not enough available power to prevent
this crash into the trees that killed three passengers and injured 50.
The story is similar on other events. Of course, on the other side of
this debate, a number of flights have had problems caused by envelope
limiting. Previously mentioned A330 and Lufthansa 321 events are two
of the best examples, although as seen, the Boeing envelope protection system is not without its risks. The problem with "hard limits" on
flight controls is not that pilots are prevented from exceeding them.
The basic problem is that any flight automation can take an action due
to erroneous data. The pilot often cannot simply override those actions
without taking extraordinary measures. Understood in this light, the
debate between Airbus "hard limits" and Boeing "envelope protection"
clearly misses the point. Lost in all this is another way automation
limits humans in most modern cockpits, the focus of our next chapter.

CHAPTER 17

Confronting Designed-in Risk Factors

Many assumptions are made about automation. We expect perfection even though we know from experience that many systems will need to be fixed, upgraded and ultimately replaced. It is time for a new automation paradigm. Here we challenge a number of assumptions repeated so often they are now accepted as fact.

Software design has absolutely led to accidents, just not the way most people expect. Most are missed entirely, even after accident investigations are completed. This chapter highlights one important designed-in risk factor and offers a solution to this challenge.

When discussing the "hard limit" debate that we outlined in the previous chapter, we know that some pilots have been eager to exceed g-load, bank, pitch or angle of attack limits despite the fact that there is no need to do so. Surprisingly nobody has challenged the digital electronic controls we use for all modern jet engines. Here is another example of conventional wisdom missing a bigger issue.

Just as automobile manufacturers have replaced carburetors with electronic fuel injection systems, modern jet engines have transitioned from mechanical "fuel control units" to electronic, computer controlled systems. Whether referred to as FADEC (Full Authority Digital Engine Control), EEC (Engine Electronic Control) or any other name, these systems are designed to provide optimum engine performance—just as the electronic fuel injection system does in an automobile. They ensure that just the right amount of fuel is metered to the engine at all times. This has greatly improved reliability of the engines throughout the normal operating range. One of the by-products of computer controls is that it is very easy to add any feature that the designer might think of. This can be good or bad, depending on how well it functions. One good selling point for this kind of feature is to design FADEC in a way that prevents a pilot from inadvertently applying too much fuel and thus damaging the engine. This is not unlike an RPM limiter on many automobiles. On the jet engines are limited to maximum rated thrust. Apply firewall power (throttle against the stops) and the system will automatically limit it to maximum thrust, with small exceptions. In older engines with mechanical fuel control units pilots had to watch the throttle advancement to ensure the engine did not exceed any limitation. Nonetheless it was also possible, in most circumstances, to shove the throttles forward to obtain at least 15% more thrust above the engine's rating. Sure, that meant the engines might need to be inspected, or even trashed, but that thrust was available. Given the choice between hitting the ground or burning up the engines, we believe all pilots would take the latter! This is not a scenario that would likely help a driver in a car, but it could be critical in an airplane. Why has this issue not been raised? How many accidents could have been prevented had the engine's controller allowed the pilot to exceed the limitation?

We must add a caveat that many factors are in play here, including engine spool up time (how long it takes for the engine to go from idle to a useful amount of power). If the engines were not able to reach the maximum rated thrust in the time prior to the accident, they would not be able to reach a higher thrust level. With that said, examples that are worth investigating are:

Habsheim (1988). *As discussed in the last chapter, the issue was not the pitch limit; 15% more thrust might well have saved the day.*

Asiana at San Francisco (2013). *A Boeing 777 impacted just short of the runway at San Francisco. Although attributed to pilot error, analysis of the event shows that there were many factors involving the assumptions in the automation that contributed to that accident. Regardless, once in the situation the pilots applied maximum power in an effort to prevent an accident. It was not enough. However, adding 15% more thrust may have been just enough to miss that 13-foot sea well. That's right, just 13 feet, and in fact they probably just needed less than half that.*

American Airlines going into Cali (1995). *In another accident where automation led the pilots down a fatal path, the Boeing 757 ended up heading straight towards a mountain ridge line. The pilots received a pull-up warning from their onboard ground proximity warning system, and immediately applied maximum thrust and pulled up. Unfortunately, they inadvertently missed the fact that* *the airplanes flight spoilers, or "speed brakes," used to add drag and reduce lift, were still extended. The accident investigation report stated that retracting the speed brakes would likely have prevented the accident. Would more thrust have been available at that altitude? Was there adequate spool-up time? Would more thrust have prevented that accident despite the omission of the speed brakes?*

It is possible that quite a few other accidents were the result of a design decision to create software more focused on extending engine life than saving an airplane in an extreme situation. To reiterate, we have not done any performance analysis on these other cases. Those that worked performance for these accidents should have the data on a spreadsheet and it would not be difficult to calculate. It might turn out that these three accidents would have occurred regardless of the availability of extra thrust. Focusing on that subject would miss the point. Clearly there are times when extra thrust would be a good thing, even at the cost of an engine. Examples are EGPWS escape (Enhanced Ground Proximity Warning System sounding an alarm that impact with terrain is imminent), wind shear escape, late recognition of impending CFIT (controlled flight into terrain), and many more cases.

A good example is outlined in the following narrative from a veteran pilot:

"I am absolutely convinced that if my MD-80 had a FADEC I would not be alive today. We selected TOGA [takeoff, go around thrust] during the go-around. At 735 feet AGL (above ground level), we encountered the microburst. NO warnings, no towering CB's [cumulonimbus, i.e., thunderstorms], mostly clear skies, only a little virga

(rain that evaporates before hitting the ground) to the left of our flight path. The data shows that somewhere between 650 and 700 feet AGL, I pushed the throttles to the firewall. I actually damaged my wrist because I was pushing so hard against the stops. I over temped both engines by 30-50 degrees. The aeronautical engineer who analyzed this event stated that over-temping the engines was one of the reasons we did not die that day. FADEC would have limited the thrust available in the quest to protect the engine and we would not have cleared the ground. As it turned out we missed the ground by 34 feet. I think most engineers and designers know that a jet engine will not suddenly disintegrate if it is over temped by 50 or 100 degrees. FADEC prevents an over temp, not to necessarily save the engine from coming apart but to save the cost of an engine inspection. It is purely a dollars and cents limit. They had to borescope both engines on my aircraft. (We flew it on a short flight from our divert airport to DFW [Dallas-Fort Worth airport]. The next morning a crew flew it DFW-ORD [Dallas-Fort Worth to Chicago O'Hare]. Upon arrival at ORD it was taken out of service, the data recorders pulled, and it was then determined that I had over-temped the engines. The manual and the flight training department emphasizes not going to the firewall, under the mistaken belief that the engines will come apart when in reality it is just a move by the company to save the cost of a borescope inspection/downtime. I hate FADEC."

The narrative continues:
"There are many similarities between DL191, US1016 (two accidents that resulted from flying into a microburst), and my flight AA262*.

In both of the other events, the crew waited before starting to go

*DL191: (Delta 191) was a famous windshear accident at DFW. USAir 1016 was a well known accident at Charlotte.

around/escape. In US1016 I think the Captain said something to the effect of, 'Let's just see if we fly thru this stuff." Shortly thereafter they hit the rain bomb and just barely escaped with their lives. Our decision to go around immediately at 500 feet when we entered the wall of water saved the day.

We received no warnings or had any reason to suspect any type of known microbursts on that day. During our go around, the tower issued a wind shear warning for 20 knots. We were a second from encountering the rain bomb at that point. As we came out the back-side at 34 feet over taxiway D, the tower announced a wind shear warning for 40 knots at the approach end. I remember being pissed because we had just flown thru the wind shear that tower was warning us about. They had nothing on their Doppler up to the point that the rain bomb let go. The RJ (Regional Jet) that landed prior to us stated that the ride on final was fine, a little rain, but it wasn't scary. When asked if there was any wind shear, the RJ stated, "No, the airspeed was steady all the way down." The RJ was midfield waiting to cross the inbound runway. We were carried down and to the east by the microburst. We passed in front of the RJ at 34 feet as we came out of the microburst. The tapes have the RJ saying in a sombre voice, "That was close."

So how might we redesign the FADEC? One approach would suggest looking at the MD-11, with its "FADEC bar." It is a mechanical stop that, with an intentional extra forceful push, allows the throttles to move a bit more, feeding a higher "throttle resolver angle" into the electronic controller. The engineers were thinking correctly when they designed it. Unfortunately, the best it can do is revert FADEC to an "alternate" mode, which essentially means that it is not relying on actual temperature and pressure, but a "default" setting.

As described by the MD-11 manual, pushing through the FADEC bar will never decrease thrust, but could potentially increase thrust up to as much as 10%. The key word here is "could," because depending on the actual conditions, it may already be at its peak. The solution would be a system like the "FADEC bar" that allows us to truly increase thrust, beyond the engine design limits, an extra 15% or more, perhaps much more.

Most pilots want the ability to intentionally (and only with conscious action) push the engines well above the design limits, risking catastrophic damage as a last ditch effort to prevent hitting the ground. The logic is that they would rather take their chances on the engine coming apart to avoid a crash. No one cares if the engine gets trashed as long as everyone is able to walk away. What about the engine acceleration (spool-up) profile? Could that also be modified to allow for more rapid acceleration under dire circumstances? While it is likely that the spool-up time will still create a physical limitation, it doesn't hurt to study this idea.

There has never been a better time to start thinking about design improvements that would give pilots more control when they need it. Allowing a pilot to operate right up to the limit on angle of attack and stopping there is an excellent use of automation. The pilot can now easily maximize aircraft performance and fly the airplane to that precise point. This clearly shows how automation can do a better job. Exceeding that value will never result in more performance—it can only result in an aerodynamic stall. The outcome is always going to be less performance. However, in the previously discussed FADEC cases the designed limits are there to protect against exceeding an ideal value. This is not unlike a situation where a person is trying to run away from danger but someone arbitrarily limits them to their maximum recommended heart rate of 220 minus their age. I think we all would agree that we would push that limit and take our chances rather than certain death! It appears that this should be revisited by the regulators and manufacturers. Envelope protection for structure could also be reviewed for the same reason. We know the airplane will stall if it exceeds the critical angle of attack. There is no situation where it would be helpful for a pilot to exceed that. In fact, having the system allow the pilot to get right to the edge gives her/him the ability to maximize the aircraft performance in a way that would be impossible absent the automation. However, within reason, the airplane will not break right at the certificated g-limitation that regulations impose—in fact, they need to be able to withstand at least 150% of that value. The same is true with engines. Pilots should be able to exceed these values in an emergency. We are advocating utilizing the automation in ways that increase the pilot's options rather than reduce them.

Automation absolutely has a place in making flying safer. At the same time the industry can be a lot smarter about using automation in ways that can increase the human ability to avert accidents.

CHAPTER 18

When Automation Fails

In previous chapters we have suggested that aviation's problem going forward is not weak pilots who are "automation dependent." This simplistic analysis is dangerously misleading. Here we expand on the topic and offer another possible mitigation to some of the accidents.

Let's begin with an email exchange between the author and Clive Leyman, the chief aerodynamicist for Concorde and the Chief UK Engineer for the Airbus A330 and A340. Clive has been involved in aircraft design for several decades. This discussion also includes Captain Peter Duffey, a man who started flying for the RAF in 1942 and then flew for British Airways and BOAC. He went on to become one of the first Concorde pilots as part of the development group and served as a training captain. Along the way, Duffey flew a great many aircraft to a variety of destinations including the Berlin Airlift, North and South America, Asia, Africa and Australia. Aircraft included the Liberator, DC3, Lancastrian, Argonaut, Comet 1, DC-7, Comet 4, B-707, and many more. Upon retirement he continued flying corporate on the DH 125-700. Captain Duffey was also the BOAC BALPA chairman from

1964 through 1968. Coauthor Malmquist is sharing these comments with his permission. Their views, based on vast experience, merit our careful consideration. Here is their exchange starting with Malmquist's response to Duffey on the capability of pilots to avert accidents today:

MALMQUIST: *"The real issue is that the industry is no longer producing pilots with your kind of background. However, it is leaders like you who keep accident rates low despite the flaws in the design and certification process. I believe current designs are dependent on pilots managing aspects missed during development. In an ideal world all designs would be perfect. For the foreseeable future we will have to train pilots to manage the unexpected. That used to happen organically, as your experience illustrates, but now systems are so reliable that new pilots don't have the chance to see anything significant.*

DUFFEY RESPONDED: *"It's inevitable that pilots will be called upon to manage problems that were missed in development, because problems identified during development will normally be fixed before entry into service. We should also find that as experience grows such problems will become rarer and rarer. The problem then is, as you say, systems are now so reliable that new pilots don't have the chance to see anything significant, except to have exposure to known problems in the simulator. This is why genuinely new problems come as a shock.*

I know from personal experience just how much bench testing is done to assess the effects of system failures both internal to the particular system and of crosstalk between systems. Even years of testing depend ultimately on what I call "requisite imagination," i.e. the engineer's ability to identify possible failure routes and combinations. Designers at least have the advantage of having a record of previous events and time to study them and take suitable precautions.

Pilots have entirely new circumstances thrust upon them and have to make decisions in real time. Inevitably there is a degree of experimentation in their response, even when successful, which cannot be mimicked by machines. So I agree with you—pilots will be with us for a long time.

One problem I do see is a generation of pilots that has grown up to be apprehensive of flight without the crutch of Fly by Wire enhancements. Yet underneath the glitz there is, or in my view should be, a perfectly flyable aeroplane. It might not be as easy to fly as the fully functional version, but it will still be flyable. When Airbus Industries set out on their FBW path the stated intention was to give the pilots an airplane with the same impeccable handling qualities everywhere. Designers intended that the basic airframe should, indeed must, be flyable. I cannot answer for the A380 and A350, but I think [a mutual friend] will confirm that he had no real problems with the A320 and A330/340. A bit squishy at altitude certainly, but flyable in their natural state. I suspect Boeing has gone a little further down the road because the B787 had to be fitted with duplicated autonomous pitch dampers to give adequate handling in manual flight at altitude. Nothing wrong with that, the fact that the dampers constitute a completely separate system means that the consequence/probability rule is respected.

One suggestion would be a requirement that the aircraft should have adequate flying qualities. This would be no worse than 4 or maybe 4.5 on the Cooper/Harper scale. The crew training should include enough exposure to this state that pilots would not be afraid to switch all the automatics off when things go wrong and then approach trouble shooting logically. I suspect that aircraft in service already meet this standard; what is missing is the exposure to these characteristics in training. Another issue relates to accuracy requirements stemming from things like RVSM.* Regarding Angle of Attack inputs into airspeed and altitude calculations, it should be mandatory to display AOA in the cockpit and to announce AOA system failures separately from airspeed failures.

* Reduced Vertical Separation Minimum (RVSM) is defined as the reduction of vertical space between aircraft from 2,000 to 1,000 feet at flight levels from 29,000 feet up to 41,000 feet. RVSM was implemented as a means to increase airspace capacity and access to more fuel-efficient flight levels.

MALMQUIST: I agree with your views Clive. Pilots should have adequate indication of system malfunction and disagreements. This should always indicate control positions, including stab and elevator. Also there needs to be standby battery driven attitude fall back showing the other basics needed to safely complete a flight. There is nothing wrong in designing protection and augmentation systems, but their failure cases need examining and pilots should be trained to deal with these. The idea that the modern pilot need not concern themselves with these "remote" possibilities has already been shown to be overconfident.

All pilots, even beginners, with a qualification to fly a specific aircraft should know how to operate the machine using raw display *of controls, and manual handling of controls. Such displays (Pitch, alpha, slip, altitude, control positions) will allow safe manual rever-sion. This should include a clear understanding of thrust control when failure or partial failure is also present.*

Adoption of this philosophy as a basic airworthiness requirement, may set a new target for designers, certifiers, and test pilots. It is over-due. We now know what can happen in the absence of these things. Pilots need to fly without a crutch. Aircraft should be designed to allow this.

Consider why we added automation in the first place. Relieve workload? Perhaps. Allow for the removal of the flight engineer? Certainly. Of course the real aim is to make it possible for the human operator to be able to concentrate on safety critical aspects and not be task-saturated with the more basic aspects of flying. Adding this ability is an enormous safety enhancement. So what has gone wrong?

It is not, as previous chapters explained, that pilots have become weak or lazy. The problem begins with the fact that pilots are doing exactly what the industry wanted them to do. Like a person who has learned to walk, and now is able to think and evaluate the world around them without concentrating on foot placement, pilots are free to think about the "big picture." In theory this is a good thing. Breakdown begins with the fact that automated systems are not always doing what the pilot expects. This is analogous to a baby forgetting how to walk. Suddenly they have to devote all their attention back to baby steps, the primary movements that are part of their muscle memory.

We don't want to tell a person who moves intuitively 99.9% of the time, that they must refocus all their attention on their feet. Unfortunately, calls for more hand flying and attention do precisely that. We are losing advantages that came with automation, without regaining a third person on the flight deck to make up for the gap. We have designed systems that tell pilots to divert their attention away from basic flying and then blame them when they do exactly that!

A better approach would be to develop ways to rapidly bring pilots into the loop when needed. Currently the system does not perform well here, with warnings and alerts coming too late much of the time, or not being accurate enough for pilots to take necessary quick action.

It is worthwhile reiterating what Clive wrote:

One suggestion would be a requirement that the aircraft should have adequate flying qualities. This would be no worse than 4 or maybe 4.5 on the Cooper/Harper scale. The crew training should include enough exposure to this state that pilots would not be afraid to switch all the automatics off when things go wrong and then approach trouble shooting logically. I suspect that aircraft in service already meet this standard; what is missing is exposure to these characteristics in training.

To appreciate the wisdom of Clive's response, one must understand the Cooper-Harper scale. This requires a step back in time to the very early days of aviation. A little known fact is that the Wright Flyer was so unstable that it was almost unflyable. Orville and Wilbur had designed the airplane with a "canard." They placed the horizontal stabilizer in the front rather than the rear. They did this to avoid the stall that killed aviation pioneer Otto Lilienthal. The problem was they did not appreciate the fact that this would make the airplane harder to control. Designers responded by creating aircraft that were easier and easier to fly.

After World War II the Ames Aeronautical Laboratory located at Moffett Field, California (now NASA Ames) became the central location for evaluating how airplanes flew from a pilot perspective. Known as "handling qualities" or "flying qualities," airplanes have a variety of responses to both the natural environment and pilot manipulation. The team, comprised of George Cooper, Bob Innis and Fred Drinkwater, flew a wide variety of operational military airplanes. George Cooper came up with a rating scale that could be used to rate how each airplane actually handled. This approach was later refined by Robert Harper of the Cornell Aeronautical Laboratory and became the Cooper-Harper Flying Qualities Rating Scale in 1969. It took into account demands placed upon the pilot accomplishing various tasks and remains the standard for measuring airplanes to this day. The scale, shown in the diagram below, is simple to follow, with no domain expertise required. As Clive noted, designs flyable in the 4 to 4.5 scale, without the help of fly-by-wire or other stability augmentation, would be acceptable. As detailed in previous chapters on fly-by-wire airplanes, computers help "manage" the airplane's response. On a conventional airplane the pilot moves the controls, and that control movement corresponds directly to one of the control surfaces. On a fly-by-wire airplane the pilot control movement enters a computer that filters that command with accelerometers, airspeed, altitude, and temperature instruments. All of this data determines the actual control surface performance.

This makes a naturally unstable airplane appear stable to the pilot. We can also just make it simpler to fly. For example in the pitch axis for both Airbus and Boeing, pilots command how quickly the airplane changes pitch. This makes the plane very easy to fly because a given amount of control movement always equates to the same amount of pitch change. This looks great on the designer's computer and appears to work seamlessly through the development process. In flight, however, there is one big catch. When the system loses sensor data it can't process all the required flight information.

In this unfortunate case the plane reverts to a basic mode where the pilot control movement corresponds directly to the surface movement. Now the pilot must make up that gap between what is mandatory and how the airplane actually responds, which varies with a number of external factors. Clive proposes that the airplane remain flyable on at least the 4 to 4.5 level on the Cooper/Harper scale. This seems reasonable enough!

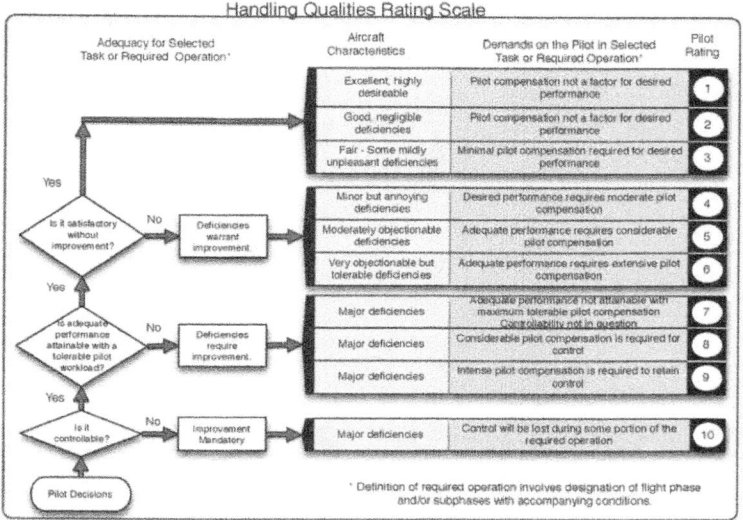

Finally, in response to Clive's comment about "requisite imagination, i.e. the engineer's ability to identify possible failure routes and combinations," there is a promising and very hopeful way forward. In the next chapter we will introduce the important work of MIT researcher, Dr. Nancy Leveson. She has developed a ground-breaking method based on system theory to capture these problems. It's called System Theoretic Process Analysis (STPA). This unique approach is derived from a larger theory called System Theoretic Accident Models and Processes (STAMP). It provides a systematic way to address all of the challenges discussed in these pages. For the first time the industry has a method that can systematically prevent accidents.

Dr. Leveson's method, first introduced in 2012, is a scientific breakthrough based on more than 40 years of research and a fitting way to address the challenges we've discussed in this book. It is the topic of the next chapter.

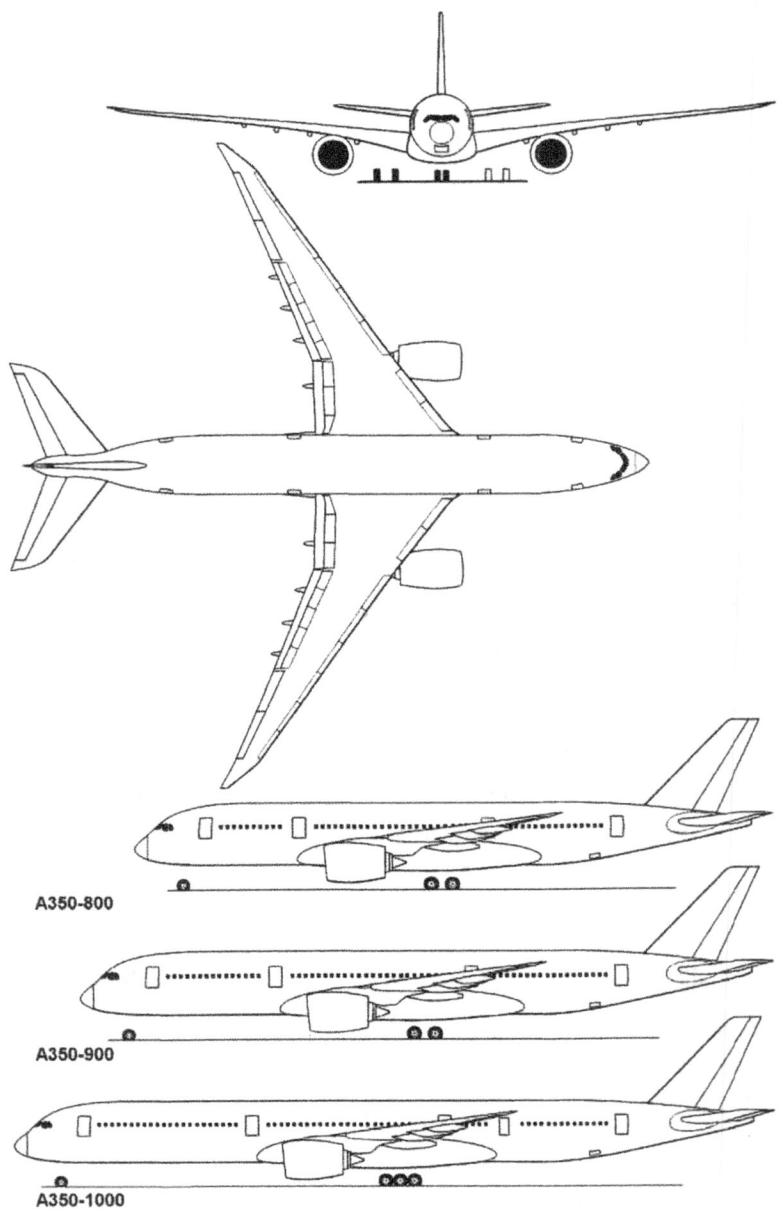

A350-800

A350-900

A350-1000

CHAPTER 19

Damn the Torpedoes: Why Systems Theory Matters

The STAMP method incorporates both engineering and cognitive psychology to understand complex systems. Dr. Nancy Leveson's pioneering work shows how innovation advances science and benefits all of us. She could be the most important scientist you've never heard of.

STAMP's evolution parallels her career, which she sums up nicely in her tongue-in-cheek bio:

> *"Nancy Leveson received all her degrees, in math, management, and computer science, from UCLA (Ph.D. 1980) and spent her formative years being a Computer Science professor at the University of California, Irvine. Moving to Seattle in 1993 in search of rain, she was Boeing Professor of Computer Science and Engineering at the University of Washington. She has now moved to MIT in her continual search for worse weather and new fields to conquer. In the process, she somehow morphed herself into an aerospace engineer and has dual faculty positions in the MIT Dept. of Aeronautics and*

Astronautics and the Engineering Systems Division.

Professor Leveson started a new area of research, software safety, which is concerned with the problems of building software for real-time systems where failures can result in loss of life or property. One advantage of this topic is that nobody questions its goals, except for a few misanthropes (who don't matter anyway)."

Today Leveson is widely considered one of the world's leading safety experts. She consults frequently for government agencies, technology oriented companies and universities. Her annual conference draws hundreds of safety management experts from around the world. Many of her students have gone on to important positions in the field of software safety around the world.

How did this happen? She earned her Ph.D. using "normal, formal methods". Leveson had been on the job at the University of California Irvine for "about a week" when she received a desperate call from a defense contractor up the road at Hughes Aircraft. This engineer explained his company was "building this torpedo and it has 15 computers on it, and this is more complex than we have ever built before and we think we have a problem of software safety and we want your help."

"I'm sorry," Leveson told him, without sharing her name. "I don't know anything about this, I'm a mathematician and do formal methods. I don't know anything about torpedoes"

"Please," begged the man from Hughes, "we have gone through all of the rest of the department, you are our only hope." When she hesitated, he added quickly, "There is money involved."

"Well, let me put Dr. Leveson on the phone, she's the software safety expert." In the weeks and months that followed, Leveson learned, alongside her first client, how software could inadvertently lead to catastrophic failures. Her research focused heavily on ruling out programming errors before they were used to launch a torpedo. Nancy worked with her client for several months and created a promising solution that ensured the new system would not allow a torpedo to accidentally turn back on a ship or submarine. A year later the Hughes engineer called with an update.

"Would you like to know how it turned out?"

"Sure!"

"Well, we took it down to the torpedo proving grounds off the coast of California and every time we fired the torpedo it came out of the tube, it turned itself off and went to the bottom and just sort of laid there."

"Well it's safe."

"Yes, but the Navy doesn't want to pay for our 'safe' torpedo."

"So what did you do?"

"We did what we normally do. We took off safety devices until we got it reliable enough and safe enough."

From this experience Leveson learned that safety and reliability are not the same. She also realized that waiting until the system was designed and only then trying to come up with a fix was an inefficient way of designing a project. This revelation put Leveson on a scientific path that would lead to her life's work.

Like Ralph Nader's investigation of the "unsafe at any speed" Chevrolet Corvair, that had a dangerous tendency to flip during low speed turns, Leveson's work with Hughes would become exhibit A in her pioneering crusade for system safety.

Removing safety layers to increase reliability is only one of the challenges underscoring the critical need for better systems engineering. Core problems include inevitable software coding errors, validation methods that do not work, overconfidence in vulnerable system redundancy, creation of so-called fault-tolerant procedures that can create unexpected timing problems as well as incompatibility between software programs and the hardware they manage.

Today Leveson's work is being applied to all aspects of safety in human designed systems. She offers a devastating critique of the industry's status quo ante mindset. For example, instead of acknowledging the new risks inherent in managing mechanical systems with software algorithms, managers insisted that a reliable system was a safe system. She disagreed, arguing that it is important to separate reliability and safety because, in some cases, these may actually be conflicting goals. Safety procedures in a weapons system may require disabling the weapon's detonation facilities.

System safety can't be developed in a vacuum. It must be integrated into the design itself.

Creation of human-built computer systems has made it possible to add virtually unlimited features. Putting computers together and trying to understand all the interactions can quickly become complicated. Even when each computer is working as designed, there is no guarantee that the system will operate safely.

The problem, Leveson realized, centered around interaction between all these different computers, and human operators trying to control the outcome. All too often the computers and the humans, don't understand what the other "controllers" are doing. Bad things can happen quickly and quickly spiral out of control.

Leveson was not the only expert to recognize this problem. Many in the social sciences began studying these challenges hoping to find solutions. Clearly some organizations handled it better than others. Recognition of this challenge led to creation of the concept of "high reliability organizations" (HROs). Social scientists studied organizations that did a "good job" and listed their attributes on the premise that others would emulate them. Unfortunately, while the ideas are seductive (mostly because they are easy to "wrap your head around"), they also yield few gains. It's true that emergent attributes make an organization "highly reliable." The problem, Leveson pointed out, is that success is based on a number of hard to identify factors. People gravitate to the "simple but wrong" because it takes less cognitive work. She believed the answer to this challenge was found in the fields of "control theory" and "system theory." Although Leveson had done graduate work in cognitive psychology, she remained the consummate engineer. She was convinced that application of these theoretical constructs would address these issues in a way that actually worked. For many years Leveson has argued that the "introduction of computers into the control of potentially dangerous devices has led to a growing awareness of the possible contribution of software to serious accidents." One key problem is shortened lead times. At the beginning of the 20th century it took 30 years for the average new product to reach the marketplace. Today system software is typically introduced after a mere three to five year development cycle.

Because of the financial pressure to release new products, a third of all attempted software systems never make it to market, a third are seriously delayed and revamped. Of those that do make it to market, such as the new software system for the Boeing 737 MAX or fly by wire technology, challenges show up unexpectedly.

Although some critics say the issue is errors in software coding, the real problem, as Leveson points out, is that the design is not well thought out when building software "requirements." Far more errors occur during the design and requirements stage than during coding. Problems can develop here due to misunderstanding the implications of systems interactions. Testing is regrettably limited to work done against assumptions made during design. This appears to make sense because these assumptions are based on how the designer imagines software will be used. The assumptions are limited to the requisite imagination of the designer or the design team. Leveson has proven, again and again, that this usually creates major problems when it turns out that assumptions do not match reality.

A related concern is the fact that many of these new systems have a shelf life of five years. After that time it may be difficult, or even impossible, to get product support. Even if that were not an issue, software installed in the hardware may be constrained to the original design. For example an airplane flight management computer is integrated into so many other systems that the basic architecture cannot be changed without a complete redesign of the entire system and all the other systems dependent on it. When new features or capabilities are needed, companies are forced to come up with creative solutions to these challenges such as patches and modifications. Equally problematic are attempts, driven by financial considerations and tight deadlines, to stretch the capability of the software beyond what was originally envisioned.

Here again we see one of the key issues in the Boeing 737 MAX story and Air France 447. The system is now being used in ways never anticipated by the original designers. For this reason it is encountering unanticipated scenarios that create problems the flight crews never trained for. This is not simply a programming error but rather a limitation created by the requirements as designed.

When software is operating complex systems at companies like Delta Airlines, the consequences of a breakdown can immediately plunge a global carrier into a shutdown. Technology dependent companies such as Amazon deal with these breaches by updating their software every 11 seconds. Similarly, Facebook makes constant software updates. Unfortunately even regularly scheduled upgrades are not a complete solution. There are no vaccines available for computers vulnerable to surprise viruses that can lead to uncontrollable system behavior. Likewise catching intruders is like trying to catch a fish with your bare hands. Despite the addition of multiple barriers the system can remain vulnerable to a common weakness.

All of these problems mirror a simple fact made evident by the spectacular failure of the Samsung Galaxy 7, a cell phone so prone to lithium battery fires that it was banned from aircraft cabins and ultimately recalled in 2017. Promising inventions rushed to market to turn a big profit demonstrate an axiom that has plagued optimistic engineers and designers. As Leveson points out, these types of problems are endemic. The steam engine was a classic example. Although inventors of the low-pressure steam boiler, James Watt and Matthew

Boulton, both opposed a dangerous higher-pressure version, their patent expired in 1800. Eager manufacturers made big money selling high-pressure steam engines to steamboat operators before this new technology was understood. Thousands of crew and passengers were killed, leading British novelist Thomas Love Peacock to introduce a character who observed:

"High-pressure steam would not scatter death and destruction around them if the dishonesty of avarice did not tempt their employment, where the more costly low pressure engine would ensure absolute safety."

In 1852, after decades of carbon-copy disasters, Congress decided to regulate private industry for the first time. Long overdue legislation was passed to protect workers and the public from these high-pressure steam boilers.

"Unfortunately," says Leveson, "similar legislation was not passed for locomotive and stationary boilers and accidents involving the use of boilers continued." In the end it took nearly a century to create associations that would guarantee steam engines were safely manufactured.

"We are now," says Leveson, "in the computer age and again faced with new technologies for which there are great economic incentives to push the state of the art and to use this technology to control dangerous systems. Computers, like steam engines and electrical systems, give us the ability to accomplish things we could not accomplish before. And again, it appears that the risks could increase over time as computers take over more and more functions. One difference is the potential consequences of accidents. We are building systems, and using computers to control them, that have the potential for large-scale destruction of life and the environment. Even a few accidents may be disastrous in these systems.

"Although computer hardware technology has advanced at an astounding rate, the development of software engineering has been slower than required for the complex systems we want to build, like a space station or automatically controlled nuclear power plants."

As part of the shift from human to computer management of complex systems, entire industries have been sold on the idea that they can use automation to save money and enhance safety by cutting back on training. This was a key factor in the crash of Air France 447. Although this aircraft was flown by what the airline's chief pilot called a "dream team," none of the flight crew on board had received the training necessary to recover from the aerodynamic stall triggered by icing of the plane's airspeed indicators. Of course, if these instruments had been designed to withstand the conditions encountered, special training for this event that led to an aerodynamic stall would not have been required. Again this goes against assumptions in design, but assumptions also affect training.

The airline industry and regulators did not believe this was necessary because statistics showed this had not previously been a problem. At the time of the crash Air France fully complied with government training standards for this aircraft. The industry had not provided this training nor had regulators required it despite the fact that there had been forty previous reports of similar airspeed indicator failures. Earlier cases of pitot icing triggering a loss of airspeed itself had not led to the problem encountered by Air France 447. The assumption was pilots would be able to manage the situation. Regulatory agencies didn't realize that with a fly-by-wire airplane these assumptions no longer remained valid. They didn't understand the hidden risks until after the accident.

Keep in mind that those three Air France 447 pilots had state of the art training, more than 20,000 hours of flight time and their aircraft had flown for 15 years with a perfect record. Only after a three year analysis of the accident did the industry formally initiate new stall recovery procedure in hopes of preventing a similar event. The problem is that both the industry and the airlines are unable to predict unexpected problems pilots might encounter due to surprise software interactions in modern aircraft. If it cannot be predicted it will not be trained to. Again, the interface between software, humans and machines is at the heart of the issue.

Surprises of this kind are the sort of thing that keeps some of the largest and most proficient companies and government organizations on guard. NASA, which has arguably assembled the most impressive array of space engineering talent on the planet, is only one example of an agency devastated by the unexpected consequences of software system and mechanical breakdowns. Sending a patch into outer space is hardly the ideal fix for a crisis.

Again and again rushing unproven technology to market is a core problem. Cutting back human training on the theory that software oversight is more efficient and safer than human supervision creates special challenges. When humans literally don't know what a machine is doing, it is hard for them to guard against the kind of breakdowns that have led to far too many unexpected disasters.

A spectacular example is the Therac-24 a radiation therapy machine that, as Leveson points out, "eliminated the usual hardware safety interlocks that are standard for linear accelerators of this type when they introduced computer control, believing that the hardware was no longer necessary. Instead the interlocks and safety checks were implemented in software. After seven accidents between 1985 and 1987 involving massive radiation overdoses and four deaths, the company finally relented and put hardware safety devices on the machine."

Overconfidence in the superiority of software-controlled systems can be a trap for system designers and engineers, especially when they lack first hand understanding of the machine they are working on. When someone with little or no understanding of steam generation, aerodynamics, meteorology or nuclear fission develops software controls, they may not be able to visualize the challenges a human operator may ultimately have to confront. Sometimes this can be a problem even when those involved understand the field but do not take into account the interactions within a complex system. In a nutshell this is what led to back-to-back Boeing MAX crashes in late 2018 and early 2019, ultimately leading to the grounding of the aircraft until a solution could be implemented.

The traditional approach to safety assumed accidents were caused by component failure. Designers relied on reliability analysis and probability studies to find errors and solve problems. The assumption was that if each individual component worked, the system would work. In some ways this is a reasonable assumption. For example, while many have touted automation as the source of improved airline safety records, it is important to realize that success here has less to do with automation than increased component reliability. Fewer engine and aircraft component breakdowns mean safer flights.

As we reduce the traditional ways accidents happen, diminishing returns kicks in for an unexpected reason. When systems become more complex it is harder for the traditional model to succeed. There are no guarantees that ensure software is being held to the same high standard used for components being managed. The methods used to supposedly guarantee software safety are currently based on the same methods used to ensure electro-mechanical components. Although there are many differences, an obvious issue is lack of experience. We typically have many years, even decades of experience with electro-mechanical components making a valid failure probability analysis realistic. By contrast every software system is effectively brand new. There is no history of success and even a small modification to the design effectively "starts the clock over" in terms of reliability assessment. This is particularly true when software systems interact. At this point humans must go beyond the designers' assumptions and objectively evaluate the software system.

Early in her career Leveson gained notoriety by demolishing a popular software redundancy model known as N-version programming (also called multi-version programming, or MVP). In a nutshell, this theory held that the best way to reduce error was to have multiple programmers independently create "duplicate" software that would effectively reduce the probability of an error in potentially vulnerable systems.

Proponents believed this approach would prevent problems as "no two people would make the exact same error" because the versions are "written independently...." (Avizienis *et al*, 1985). The assumption was that N-version programming could produce highly reliable software suitable for use in safety-critical systems.

Leveson, with her co-researcher, John Knight, showed that the "assumption of the independence of errors...does not hold." In short N-version programming does not reduce the negative consequences of a bad algorithm. The problem here is that the assumptions and, therefore, the requirements, are generally the source of any problems. N-version programming might reduce the risk of a coding error but it would not fix the limitations inherent in relying on the requisite imagination of the people writing the requirements. More broadly, Leveson has shown again and again in her analysis of accidents worldwide, that safety can't simply be guaranteed through simplistic concepts such as MVP. It must be designed in at the outset. Even after several juried scientific studies proved Leveson correct, many of her critics refused to concede.

While software controlled systems can be perfectly safe, systems designers and engineers must understand what causes accidents. The superficial belief that human error is always responsible for breakdowns is incorrect. The real mechanisms that trigger failures are far more complex.

In hindsight, it is always possible to pin the blame on one person, but the reality is that accidents are not the result of a linear sequence of events. In today's complex systems it's critical to understand the external (environmental) influences and how the various components interact. It's also important to understand the difference between safety and reliability. Too often the focus is on reliability, where the system

197

may be working exactly as intended but remains unsafe in critical ways. Context matters. As Leveson points out, one can have a very reliable gun that is perfectly safe firing out in the desert but becomes very unsafe in a shopping mall. It is also possible for a very unreliable system to be perfectly safe. An airplane stuck at the gate with a mechanical problem is quite safe! Nonetheless there is a constant push for more reliability that may not guarantee safety.

The heart of the argument, that safety has to be built-in at the outset of any technological system design, is the basis for Leveson's new paradigm. A human designed system must be created at the outset with controls that prevent unsafe interactions. Patches, upgrades, and fixes sent up to earth orbiters from Houston are no substitute for getting the system right to begin with. Leveson's passionate view of safety is one that inevitably leads to controversy in an industry determined to rush new products to market. The accelerated push towards "crunching" data via computer analysis attempts to replace human decision making with a probability equation. Leveson has shown that the best approach to software safety remains expert judgment using a focused system theoretical process. As she says: "Almost all software related accidents can be traced back to flaws in the requirement specifications."

So what is system theory? As explained by Leveson and Dr. John Thomas (2018, p.10):

System theory as used in engineering was created after World War II to deal with the increased complexity of the systems being built after the war. It was also created for biology in order to successfully understand the complexity of biological systems. In these systems, separation and analysis of separate, interacting components (subsystems) distorts the results for the system as a whole because the component behaviors are coupled in non-obvious ways. The first engineering uses of these new ideas were in the missile and early warning systems of the 1950s and 1960s.

Some unique aspects of System Theory are:

→ The system is treated as a whole, not as the sum of its parts. You have probably heard the common statement: "the whole is more than the sum of its parts."

→ A primary concern is emergent properties, which are properties that are not in the summation of the individual components but "emerge" when the components interact. Emergent properties can only be treated adequately by taking into account all their technical and social aspects.

→ Emergent properties arise from relationships among the parts of the system, that is, by how they interact and fit together.

This model includes everything we now do in safety engineering. Control is interpreted broadly. For example, component failures and unsafe interactions may be controlled through design, such as using redundancy, interlocks, barriers, or fail-safe design. Safety may also be controlled through process, such as development processes, manufacturing processes and procedures, maintenance processes, and general system operating processes. Finally, safety may be controlled using societal controls including government regulation, culture, insurance, law and the courts, or individual self-interest. These societal controls can influence human behavior to varying extents, although obviously humans will not strictly follow any procedure as humans are not computers. Leveson has developed a theoretical framework to explain and understand complex systems utilizing systems theory. Called System Theoretic Accident Models and Processes (STAMP), it views safety as a "dynamic control problem rather than a failure prevention problem." We design controls to prevent various hazards. The method aims to understand the controls that were in place to prevent an accident and then analyze each one to understand why they did not work.

Designing a new system presents a different problem. We have to use our imagination to create a list of hazards. Developing that list requires a broad approach. At the same time it is also important to limit it to aspects within our control. For example, many might consider a mountain an airplane hazard. In reality, the hazard is not the mountain, but an airplane flying too close to the mountain and hitting it! Another important nuance is differentiating hazards from causes of hazards. For example, an engine failure on an airplane is not a system level hazard but something that can cause a hazard, such as inability to maintain separation from the ground and other aircraft or loss of control. Hazards do not refer to "individual components, like brakes..." but rather overall system states like "inability to prevent collision with obstacle."

Beginning with the intent of the design we can predict which aspects can go wrong. We then design controls that will prevent that hazard by modelling the control structure and then drawing it into a control diagram. Control actions are based on their responsibility. We also look for ways feedback will be provided to ensure that the controller "knows" the state of the process it is trying to control. Lack of feedback is often a missing aspect in system design. We analyze how each control actually "controls" the system to prevent the hazard/ loss. Then we examine these controls to see how they might lead to a loss. These "unsafe control actions" are then used to "create functional requirements and constraints for the system."

Finally, scenarios are created that would lead to unsafe control actions. The system is also analyzed to ensure feedback as well as ways that problems can span the various system components. This approach has proven to be far more powerful than traditional linear models such as Failure Modes and Effects Analysis (FMEA), Fault Tree Analysis (FTA), Event Trees, Bow-Tie and several others. They are appealing due to their seeming simplicity but unable to analyze complex systems. All these methods can actually lead to a false sense of security. This chapter provides only a brief overview and the reader is advised to read the manuals provided free of charge on the MIT Partnership for System Safety and Security site.

As Leveson says, "the solution to both system safety and security lies in a comprehensive approach. Today most of the current attempts to solve these problems look like hundreds of fingers stuck in dikes on the verge of collapse. That is why we continue to have so many unpredictable accidents and other safety critical industries. STAMP provides a solution to solve the most complex problems we are facing today."

Dr. Leveson's ground-breaking work can be found through her lectures, textbooks, journal articles and the annual STAMP conference (Systems-Theoretic Accident Model and Processes) at MIT.

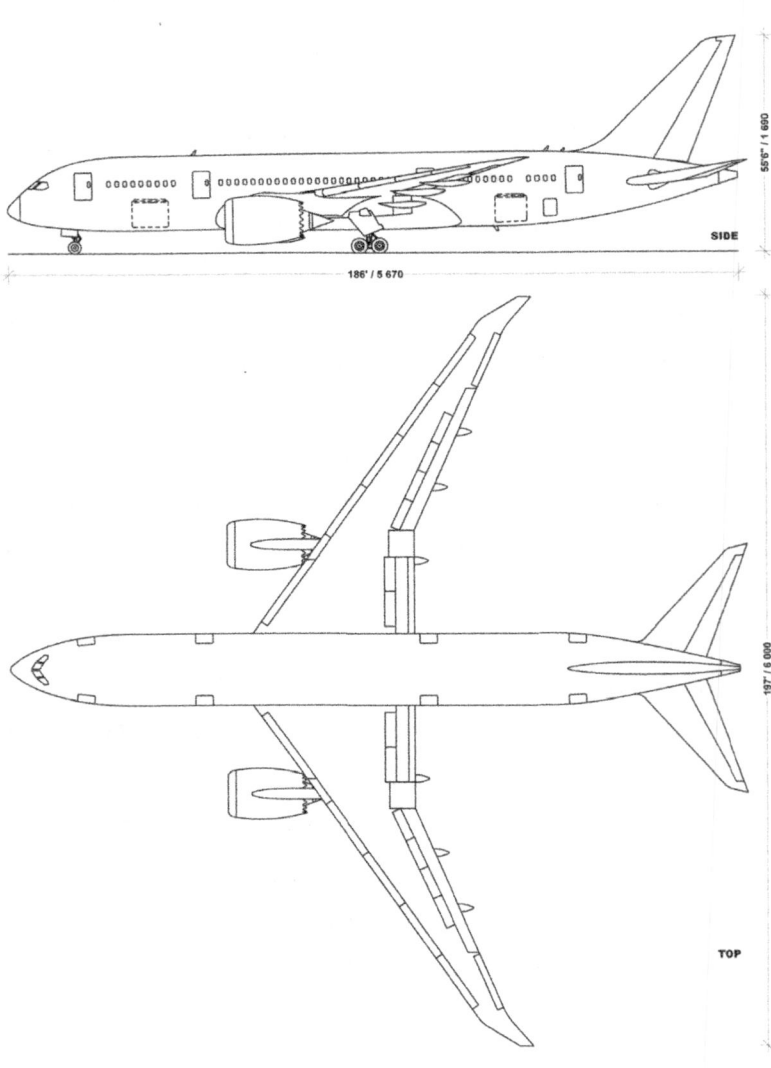

CHAPTER 20
Deus Ex Machina

Is the Gentleman who is the (head of the) FAA right now not a pilot? I don't know if he is a pilot or not. I'd like to find out. I think it would maybe be good to have a pilot, a really good pilot. My pilot, he's a smart guy and he knows what is going on...

President Donald Trump
meeting with airline executives February 6, 2017

Finally America had a President who got aviation. Although he had been burned on the Trump Shuttle and brushed aside by the banks on his takeover bid for American Airlines, Donald Trump believed that the nation's airlines and Boeing were destined to become cornerstones of his bold new economic strategy.

For Nick Calio, the President of Airlines of America, Washington's newest aviation enthusiast was a delight:

"We were encouraged by his in-depth understanding of our industry," said Calio after his first meeting with the President. "We share his administration's goals of growing jobs, reducing taxes and regulation and expanding our economy."

Although he had been in office for a mere 17 days, the commander in chief and his new Secretary of Transportation, Elaine Chao, were already thinking about privatizing the air traffic control system to save money and end those maddening tarmac delays that had threatened his on time performance at campaign rallies. Change began by replacing FAA Administrator Michael Huerta with a real pilot.

The new leader of the world's most leading aviation agency would be deus ex machina, a god flying in from on high, to unite Democrats and Republicans, labor and industry, consumer advocates and corporate bean counters. With any luck even the "fake" news media would recognize his genius. There was just too much at stake to leave the Federal Aviation Agency in the hands of a leader who didn't know the difference between an angle of attack indicator and a pitot tube. The United States of America needed a real pilot at the helm of the FAA.

In Florida, historic preservationist and environmentalist Trump had gone a few rounds with the FAA and Palm Beach County over the local airport. A 1995 lawsuit aimed at ending jet traffic above his Mar-a-Lago resort was dropped after the county agreed to lease Trump 280 acres for a new golf course.

In July 2010 he sued the airport and its director, Bruce Pelly, to block a new runway that would bring in more flights over his Mediterranean style mansion where guests like Jennifer Lopez and Sean "Diddy" Combs had been spotted making love on his beach. This case was filed a few months after Gregory Gish, an FAA air traffic employee, renamed navigation waypoints on the Palm Beach and departure route for singer/pilot Jimmy Buffet, Trump and his family.

Gish chose DONLD (Donald), TRMMP, IVANK ONE (Ivanka),

UFIRD (You're Fired) and BRTHR, apparently a reference to Trump's false "birther" claim that President Barack Obama was actually born in Kenya.

Trump, thrilled that his empire now included what the Palm Beach *Post* called "a piece of the heavens above South Florida," had kind words for his FAA flight controllers fans:

"They are very talented people."

Not everyone in the resort community was thrilled by this move. Airline pilot Paul Egan, head of the airport's noise advisory committee said:

"We've actually had reports of people refusing to fly these departures because they are so offended by the fact that Trump has been memorialized."

In 2011, after the FAA decided a new runway wasn't justified, Trump settled his suit with Palm Beach County. Four years later he was back in court demanding $100 million in compensation for "irreparable damage" to his historic mansion resort purchased for $7 million.

The complaint alleged that airport director Pelly had personally using his clout with the FAA to persuade controllers to route traffic over Trump's personal Xanadu.

"Pelly is seeking revenge by attacking Mar-a-Lago from the air," argued the plaintiff's attorney.

"I want to make sure it's protected and not destroyed by the noise, the pollution and the soot," added Trump.

In the summer of 2015, newly minted Presidential candidate Trump made headlines claiming that Mexican immigrants were "rapists" and "drug dealers." NBC canceled 'The Celebrity Apprentice', many businesses severed their ties with his companies and some pilots asked controllers not to fly routes using the Trump connected Palm Beach waypoints.

In early July 2015 the FAA, out of an abundance of caution decided to eliminate all the Trump related codes in the Palm Breach area.

"The FAA is taking steps to rename three 'fixes' near PBI," explained the agency. "In general, the FAA chooses names that are non-controversial and relate to the area in which the fixes are located." Fortunately for Jimmy Buffet fans, the musician linked flight code was left in place.

By the time of his 2016 meeting with Airlines for America, Trump had a sense that the fix was in at the FAA. It was time to replace Michael Heurta with an aviator he could trust, someone who understood the family business, the real estate empire, the golf courses, the hotels, his kids and their spouses now sharing helpful insights with the new West Wing team. The President had the perfect candidate in mind, someone who could get along with everyone and make American aviation great again in the face of stiff competition from Airbus.

The catch was that the pilot he was leaning toward, a dear friend, would be a very tough sell in Congress. It would take a little time to make it work but Trump was confident he could eventually persuade the Republican Congressional leadership to trust him on this one.

In the meantime he and Transportation Secretary Elaine Chao began grooming an adequate interim FAA administrator to replace Huerta. Like many of Trump's picks, he was a veteran industry lobbyist who also had impressive government experience, a former American Airlines pilot named Daniel Elwell.

From 2006 to 2008 he worked at the FAA as assistant administrator for policy, planning and the environment. Elwell went on to serve as vice-president of both the Aerospace Industries Association and Airlines For America where he remained close to Calio and his colleagues.

He also ran his own consulting business before rejoining the FAA in early 2017 as a "special government employee." While not Trump's dream choice for the top job, Elwell was a perfect fit for the "deregulation team" quickly hired by Transportation Secretary Chao to trim fat from the FAA. He was joined by a United Airlines attorney specializing in regulatory issues, as well as an auto executive working for green car companies overseen by the DOT.

A *Pro Publica/New York Times* investigation discovered that Trump's "deregulation teams" were "stacked with political appointees, some of whom may be reviewing rules their former employees sought to weaken or kill... Elwell's designation as a special-government employee also allowed him to continue his private consulting business even as he worked for his government."

On February 3, just three days before Trump's flashy summit with airline and airport executives, Elwell received an email inquiry the top lobbyist residing at his old employer, Airlines for America. She wanted to know if there was an update on the FAA's plan to roll back Obama administration rules on mishandled baggage and other fees. It didn't take long for her to get an answer. All these regulations were dropped within weeks.

In March, Elwell worked with Jet Blue, its lobbyist, the FAA and the media to push privatization of St. Louis Lambert International Airport management. In April, after United was forced to make a fast settlement with a ticket holding pulmonologist dragged off an overbooked flight in Chicago, Elwell quickly fired off a lighthearted note to Sasha Johnson, the FAA's former chief of staff.

"Looks like you guys have really taken leadership on this. Crossing my fingers for a denied boarding flight," he wrote Johnson , then serving as United's director of international regulatory and policy.

In June 2017, DOT Secretary Chao, proud of Elwell's quick work on the deregulation task force, welcomed him back on board as deputy FAA administrator:

He moved up to acting administrator after Michael Huerta left the FAA in January 2018. As Trump tried to build support for his dream FAA administrator candidate, Elwell and Chao successfully pushed a five year FAA Reauthorization Act through Congress. Although private pilots had killed Trump's attempt to privatize air traffic control, new regulations expanding air space for recreational drones, banning pet storage in overhead bins, barring the eviction of passengers from over-sold planes, and mandating a review of shrinking seat sizes all passed. The bill also gave Boeing a critical sales tool for the world marketplace.

At hearings a year earlier the company's vice-president of engineering, John Hamilton, sought a new type certificate meeting the standards of foreign regulatory authorities. Delivering thousands of new MAX planes to 83 airline customers in 43 countries required the FAA and Boeing to win advance approval from each foreign government. Only an act of Congress could solve this problem that was delaying foreign aviation authority validation for up to 14 months.

Elwell and his staff applauded this important regulatory reform, noting that the bill directed "the FAA to promote U.S. aerospace-related standards globally... (while it) allows the Agency to work with foreign partners to streamline certification processes for U.S. aircraft. The legislation also...ensures that U.S. aviation manufacturers can compete globally and get their products to market on time..."

Airlines for America's Calio proudly noted that the $90 billion reauthorization bill, which passed the House 398-23 and the Senate 93-6, "provides stability for the FAA to uphold the highest levels of safety... while providing certainty for... millions of passengers and countless businesses... every day."

The October 5, 2018 White House FAA bill signing ceremony was a bipartisan victory lap for Trump and Chao. House Transportation and Infrastructure Subcommittee ranking minority member, Oregon's Peter DeFazio (D-OR) was over the moon. The new bill, he proclaimed, "guarantees that the United States will continue to lead the world in all things aviation... improve aviation safety and the air travel experience for more than 900 million passengers who fly in the United States each year."

"Because of this bill," added Senate Commerce, Science and Transportation chairman John Thune (R-SD), "our economy and passengers will benefit as... aviation manufacturing gets a boost."

Just 24 days after Trump signed the FAA reauthorization bill, Lion Air lost a MAX in Indonesia. The parallel Ethiopian Airlines crash March 10 , 2019, quickly led to worldwide grounding of the MAX fleet.

Following these back to back disasters Boeing CEO Dennis Muilenberg conceded, in a series of statements and interviews, that flight automation on the MAX failed to meet his the high standards that made his company synonymous with air safety.

"The implementation of that software, we did not do it correctly.... We are fixing it now, and our communication on that was not what it should have been....We know ... that the public's confidence has been hurt by these accidents and that we have work to do to earn and re-earn the trust of the flying public, and we will do that. We are taking all actions necessary to make sure that accidents like those two ... never happen again."

At a March 27, 2019, Senate Science and Transportation Sub-committee hearing the FAA's Elwell insisted that his agency had correctly licensed the MAX. Neither the Lion Air nor Ethiopian Airlines crashes diminished his agency's success.

"Since 1997," he told the Senators, "the risk of a fatal commercial aviation accident in the United States has been cut by 95 percent. And in the past ten years, there has only been one commercial airline passenger fatality in the United States in over 90 million flights. Aviation remains the safest mode of transportation globally, and we promote this level of safety by sharing issues, trends, and lessons learned throughout the world.... Despite what you might read in the press, I believe the FAA still is the gold standard.... We fight for it all the time. Our goal is to raise the safety bar everywhere."

Senator Ted Cruz (R-TX), chair of the Commerce Committee's aviation subcommittee was worried about a pilot complaint alleging that the MAX flight manual was "almost criminally insufficient."

"As a passenger," said Cruz, "I would certainly find it troubling ... if the captain is describing the training manual as 'inadequate and almost criminally insufficient.' That is a pretty serious charge."

Senator Maria Cantwell (D-WA) asked Elwell about a Seattle Times report suggesting that FAA managers had pushed their engineers to delegate wide responsibility for assessing MAX safety to Boeing.

"We do not allow self-certification of any kind," replied the acting administrator.

On May 15, Rep, DeFazio led another hearing before the House Transportation and Infrastructure Subcommittee.

"How was this certified?" he asked the acting administrator. "We shouldn't have to be here today."

"Mr. Elwell, the FAA has a credibility problem," added Rep. Rick Larsen (D-WA). "The FAA needs to fix its credibility problem....if (people) don't fly, airlines don't need to buy airplanes (and) then there will be no jobs" in aircraft manufacturing.

Congresswoman Dina Titus, (D-NV). wanted to know why the aircraft's home country was the last one in the world to ground the plane:

"You were in bed with those you were supposed to be regulating, and that's why it took so long" to ground the planes.

Elwell, citing 10,000 FAA man and woman hours to the MAX licensing process, replied that it was wrong to blame 346 passengers fatalities on his agency.

"We are absolutely confident in the safety of this aircraft."

From his long experience as a pilot, industry lobbyist and FAA leader there was no question that the agency's licensing system is "part of the fabric of what we've used to become as safe as we are today."

"I'm proud of my team," added Earl Lawrence, the agency's director of aircraft certification, who, like Elwell, defended the work of 1,200 Boeing paid Designated Aviation Representatives representing the agency on this plane.

Committee members noted that the FAA's traditional system of delegating review work to manufacturers failed to prevent the MAX crashes. They voiced concern that the 45 FAA employees reviewing Boeing's data did not fully understand the need for pilot simulator training opposed by carriers like Southwest.

Elwell countered that ending the decades old DAR program at 79 aircraft manufacturing facilities would require hiring 10,000 new employees at a punishing cost of $1.8 billion annually.

Under tough questioning Elwell conceded that he was "not happy with the 13-month gap between finding that (MCAS software) anomaly and us finding out about it.... We are looking into that, and we will make sure software anomalies are reported more quickly."

As a former airline pilot himself, Elwell added: "When I first heard about this, I thought that there should have been more text in the manual about the MCAS."

At another Senate Transportation Subcommittee hearing in late July 2019 Ali Bahrami, the FAA's top safety official, made a strong case for treating industry fairly in the regulatory process.

Seven years earlier, while heading the FAA's Transport Airplane Directorate he was the sole government representative serving on a federal airplane certification process review committee.

"The eight other members," reported the Seattle Times, "were from industry including a co-chair from Boeing. It's recommendation, delegate more certification work to plane manufacturers....

"In 2013, Bahrami made a move reflecting the tightly inter-twined relationship between regulator and industry. Just months after overheated batteries in flight caused the worldwide grounding of Boeing's recently introduced 787 Dreamliner—a jet that Bahrami had shepherded through certification—he left the FAA for a lucrative lobbying job."

In his new position as vice president of Aerospace Industries Association, he represented many of the same aerospace companies on the 2012 committee reviewing the certification process.

"We urge the FAA to allow maximum use of delegation," lobbyist Bahrami told the House Subcommittee on Aviation shortly after changing jobs in 2013. "It would be detrimental to our competitiveness if foreign manufacturers are able to move improved products into the marketplace more quickly."

Back before the same committee in July 2019, the FAA's Bahrami insisted that the agency's delegation program had "a proven, quantifiable safety record. I was a designee of a company. I know what it is to be a designee. It's a badge of honor that once the greatest safety organization in the world tells you that you're trusted to do work on my behalf... that is probably the highlight of an individual's career. When we talk about delegation, delegation is sound."

When Senator Jack Reed, (D-RI) asked why the FAA hadn't provided pilots with important details on the MCAS system software following the October 2018 Lion Air MAX crash, Bahrami cited a confidentiality agreement.

"We do not disclose information or any indication of what may have gone wrong in that particular case, and that is a very delicate balance for us to play. So, we wanted to basically resolve the issue without having to disclose information that investigators did not want us to disclose. And from the safety perspective, we felt strongly that what we did was adequate."

Reed was not persuaded: "The implication was that this pilot change would be sufficient to provide airworthiness. There was no real mention of improvements and necessary changes to the MCAS system, leading.... most people to conclude that there was no long-term issue with the MCAS. That lack of transparency I think is not appropriate."

Bahrami disagreed: "We knew the eventual solution would have modifications. Based on the risk, we felt we had sufficient time to do modification and get the final fix."

Nadia Milleron, plaintiff in a lawsuit filed against Boeing and the FAA following the Ethiopian Airlines crash, did not buy Bahrami's live testimony. Grieving over the loss of her daughter, Ralph Nader's grand-niece Samya Stumo, she jumped in her car and drove overnight from her home in Sheffield, Massachusetts, to the FAA office in Washington. In a scene echoing Arthur Miller's *All My Sons* she and her son, with-out taking time to change clothes, began picketing the agency's head-quarters. Bahrami agreed to a meeting where Milleron demanded his resignation. After their talk the FAA issued a statement standing by its actions on the MAX crashes.

That same week the Senate Commerce, Science and Transportation Committee was interviewing Trump's pick for FAA Administrator, Delta Airlines Senior Vice-President of Flight Operations Steve Dickson. Playing the aviation version of musical chairs, nominee Dickson's prior job performance had been overseen by Delta's Directors including former FAA administrator Michael Huerta.

While not quite the God that Trump had in mind for the job,

Dickson, was, in the President's eyes, a potential angel. For more than a year Trump had tried to persuade key Republican senators to confirm his personal pilot, a man he trusted with his life, John Dunkin, for the top FAA post. Working for Trump off and on for two decades, he often flew the President's pride and joy, a $100 million Boeing 757.

"John Dunkin isn't just a pilot," an administration official told Axios. "He's managed airline and corporate flight departments, certified airlines from start-up under FAA regulations, and oversaw the Trump presidential campaign's air fleet, which included managing all aviation transportation for travel to 203 cities in 43 states over the course of 21 months."

There was just one catch. Although Trump had successfully hired his children, named his bankruptcy attorney Israeli ambassador and appointed his son's wedding planner to leadership of the Department of Housing and Urban Development's New York/New Jersey office, Dunkin was not a shoo-in.

This candidate's record of managerial oversight of the 2016 Trump campaign flight crews had been called in to question by *The Guardian*. The problem focused on Trump campaign charter pilot Vincent Caldara who flew vice-president Pence, his family, the press and the secret service to political rallies. This retired policeman, who chaired a group of conservative law enforcement Trump supporters in swing states, had not been thoroughly vetted by the campaign.

In July 2015 Caldara was indicted in Broward County, Florida, for alleged battery. According to a police report, Caldara repeatedly drove his dark blue Ford Victoria into business associate Jeff Shaley. *The Guardian* reported that the victim "underwent two surgeries, received a spinal stimulator and a fusion of his right hand." Caldara, was also a defendant in a case filed by a woman who claimed that she had been hit by his recklessly driven Harley-Davidson.

These disclosures, which led to Caldara's firing by Eastern Airlines, would have come into question during a potential John Dunkin confirmation hearing. Compromise FAA Administrator candidate, pilot Steve Dickson, appeared to be a much safer bet. Another plus was the fact that he would not be in a conflict of interest situation on the MAX, a plane Delta never bought.

At the time of his Senate confirmation hearing, Delta was benefiting directly from the fact that Southwest, American and United had canceled thousands of peak summer season flights due to the loss of their MAX fleets. The longer the MAX was grounded the better for Delta.

Dickson's confirmation looked like a shoo-in. Unfortunately for the White House, their vetting process had failed to catch a potential spoiler out in Seattle. Her name was Captain Karlene Petitt and she flew for Delta.

CHAPTER 21

Delta's "Bipolar" Pilot Who Nursed Too Much: Karlene Petitt's Whistleblower Case Against FAA Administrator Steve Dickson

"I will be working to "lock in" the Majority Leader's support tonight over dinner."

Elaine Chao
Senate Transportation Confirmation Hearing
January 11, 2016

For Donald Trump and Secretary Chao the spring of 2019 promised to be a rare kumbaya moment up on Capitol Hill. Airbus/Boeing/F-15 pilot Steve Dickson was clearly a hole-in-one for the top job at the world's leading aviation regulatory agency. Democrats, Republicans, trade associations, unions, even lobbyists that never stopped slugging it out on the Capitol steps, were preparing to expedite delivery of this FAA administrator nominee to the Senate where he would receive Mitch McConnell's blessing.

Endorsements poured in for the retired Delta Senior Vice-President of global flight operations. As the head of pilot training, crew resources, scheduling and compliance work with FAA regulators, Dickson appeared to be the right man to pull the agency out of PTMSD, post-traumatic MAX stress disorder. Paul Rinaldi, president of the National Air Traffic Controllers Association applauded the "well-deserved appointment for Steve who has been a staunch advocate for aviation safety."

National Business Aviation Association CEO Ed Bolen, who fought Trump on privatizing air traffic control, applauded Dickson's "comprehensive understanding of our national air transportation system."

Over at Airlines for America, the trade association that included Delta, CEO Nick Calio was thrilled that The Donald had picked this "uniquely qualified nominee."

The Airline Pilots Association congratulated the recently retired Delta vice-president on "his nomination to lead the safest and most complex aviation system in the world."

At the Helicopter Association International, CEO Matt Zuccaro was looking "forward to working with him on issues important to the helicopter community."

With a Republican majority in the Senate, Dickson appeared to be a much easier sell than other Trump picks like Supreme Court Justice Brett Kavanaugh. While his resume looked good, some Delta

218

pilots under his leadership worried about Dickson's commitment to open reporting of safety issues. They were concerned that his industry ties might undermine pilots who challenged the agency on key safety issues. This was a particularly sensitive issue in view of the fact that many MAX pilots had raised questions about their lack of training following the Lion Air crash in 2018.

Unlike other countries, such as France and Italy, American pilots do not face the possibility of reprisal, arrest or jail time for identifying safety problems at their airline, even after an accident. They can't be taken to court for pinpointing deficiencies in their carrier's safety management system. Comprehensive flight crew reporting of safety issues, often the first line of defense for the industry, is fully protected under the nation's AIR 21 Whistleblower Protection Program. Across the aviation industry experts who have studied this law, passed with strong bipartisan support in 2000, believe it is one of the reasons why the United States has been spared airline crashes in recent year.

One person who takes this law seriously is Senate Commerce Science and Transportation Committee ranking member Maria Cantwell (D-WA), who represents the state that leads the world in aircraft production. Reviewing the Trump/Chao nominee she discovered a key conflict of interest missed in the vetting process at the White House and the Department of Transportation. Failure to do their due diligence opened up a serious challenge to the nominee.

During the previous three years Delta Senior Vice President Dickson had been at the center of an ongoing whistleblower case filed by a veteran Delta pilot. One of her documented allegations had already prompted the FAA to revise a key safety requirement for the entire industry. Others were in the midst of a review by the Occupational Safety and Health Administration (OSHA).

"Stephen Dickson has had a long career in both the Air Force and at Delta Air Lines," said Cantwell. "I have no doubt he has the basic knowledge and technical qualifications to serve as FAA Administrator. Indeed, I was inclined to support his nomination based on this experience and expertise.

"But at this time of unprecedented challenges involving aviation safety, we also need to be absolutely certain that the person chosen to lead the FAA has a clean record on safety, and the ability to help restore the public's trust in the FAA. Unfortunately, information brought to our committee in recent weeks calls into question the safety culture that existed under Mr. Dickson that allowed a safety whistleblower to be retaliated against. The nominee's lack of candor about the issue was also troubling.

"I recently met with a Delta Air Lines pilot, First Officer Karlene Petitt, who has been flying for 40 years. Petitt told me she had repeatedly raised concerns about the safety culture at Delta to a number of executives, including Mr. Dickson. Instead of being celebrated for her potentially life-saving diligence, First Officer Petitt was sent for a compulsory mental health examination with a company-approved psychiatrist who incorrectly diagnosed her with bipolar disorder. This... cost her 18 months of flying. The doctor Delta chose for this compulsory exam has a record that includes serious red flags, which deepens my concern about this case.

"Mr. Dickson described the decision to refer First Officer Petitt for a compulsory mental health examination as 'sound.' In the course of following up on First Officer Petitt's allegations, Mr. Dickson has...

repeatedly sought to minimize his role in this extremely troubling episode. However, the written record... contradicts the picture Mr. Dickson has sought to paint of minimal involvement.

"Given the urgent need for stronger safety culture and transparency throughout the FAA, these incidents do not paint the picture of the type of leadership that we need. Mr. Dickson's oversight of these matters raises serious questions about his leadership, and therefore I will not support his nomination."

Petitt's concerns about "inadequate pilot training and not enough pilot rest were things that you thought would have maybe gotten her recognized," said Cantwell. "Instead she came under scrutiny and faced inappropriate questions from the psychiatrist brought in by Delta. "For example, the doctor cited that just because Officer Petitt had three kids, a job, and helped her husband with his career, she must be manic. The psychiatrist even had the nerve... to ask when the first officer was breast-pumping milk for her children," she said.

"According to a hearing transcript, the psychiatrist said: 'I asked her—and she was very upset about this—I asked: 'Did you express the milk,' because that's going to take more time. So, basically, she's doing all of this—I think that's well beyond what any woman I've ever met could do.' "

Cantwell rejected Dickson's claim that he was not a party to Petitt's review by Delta hired Skokie, Illinois psychiatrist Dr. David Altman: "It's very clear that Mr. Dickson did know, was involved with this pilot, did know what was happening and failed to disclose it to this committee. We certainly can't have organizations threaten pilots with this kind of retaliation."

After reviewing Petitt's case another medical expert at the Mayo Clinic, concluded:

"This has been a puzzle for our group—the evidence does not support presence of a psychiatric diagnosis but does support an organizational/corporate effort to remove this pilot from the rolls."

In a similar case, pilot Michael Protack also sued the airline claiming wrongful termination and retaliation after reporting safety deficiencies at the carrier. He too was deemed medically unfit to fly by Dr. Altman. Another whistleblower, Kurt Seuring, who also flew under Dickson's leadership, claimed he was fired for raising safety concerns about his company's maintenance work on a Chilean military plane.

Dickson defended his former employer's decision to pay $74,000 to Dr. David Altman, the Illinois psychiatrist who concluded Petitt was "bipolar" and unfit to fly for Delta. The same doctor allegedly threatened to use any complaint filed by Protack against him as the basis for a diagnosis that would bar him from flying for life.

Petitt, type rated to fly nine Boeing and Airbus aircraft including the B777, A350, A330, B747-400, B747-200, B767, B757, B737 and B727, has flown for Delta and Northwest for over 20 years. During that time she has also worked extensively as a training pilot. She wrote her 45-page safety report on Delta while studying for a PhD at the nation's premiere aviation school, Embry-Riddle Aeronautical University. In a meeting with Dickson and Vice-President of Flying Operations Jim Graham, she focused on numerous FAA compliance areas including:

(1) the falsification of pilot training records, (2) failure to conduct the required oral portion of an LOE (Line Oriented Evaluation), (3) the

practice of using line checks (flight exams) as a form of retaliation for reporting non-compliance with federal aviation standards, (4) forcing her to fly while fatigued, (5) a management pilot's unlawful use of a personal computer on an aircraft's flight deck, (6) withholding supplemental training after Petitt advised that she had received "inadequate training."

Other issues reported to Dickson and Graham included:

→ The airline's failure to notify federal officials that more than a dozen Delta Airbus 330 pilots reporting unreliable airspeed events prior to a similar automation failure that took down Air France 447 in June 2009. This information would have been useful to Air France and other A330 operators.

→ A need for pilots to do more training at high altitude.

→ Major errors in training manuals.

→ Check pilots' texting during pilot simulator exams.

→ Improper stall recovery procedures

→ Pilots receiving type ratings after studying at home on a computer flash drive and then being given all the exam questions by an instructor in advance to make sure they passed.

→ An instructor falsifying training records for an event he did not conduct. In a subsequent meeting with the airline's manager of equal opportunity, a non-pilot, Petitt complained of being forced to fly long transoceanic flights after inadequate rest. She alleged that at one intimidating session overworked pilots asking to be relieved from flight duty were warned they might be jeopardizing their careers. Her Delta instructor cautioned that fatigue was considered the "other F-word."

Petitt added that her airline failed to comply with federal aviation standards and mentioned potentially catastrophic events involving Delta flight operations. Following this meeting the Equal Opportunity manager told colleagues, including Delta attorney Meg Taylor, that Petitt would be a candidate for removal from duty pending the results of a psychiatric exam. One cited example of the whistle-blowing pilot's deteriorating mental health and bad judgment was her determination to give a copy of this safety report to someone outside the family of America's most admired airline, Petitt's mother.

Attorney Taylor, an important figure in Petitt's case traveled to Washington supporting Dickson's nomination in meetings with Senate Commerce Committee members. Refuting Senator Cantwell, spokeswoman Lisa Hanna assured the media that Delta and its managers never retaliated against Petitt:

"Her referral into a medical review process was out of concern for her well-being and consistent with our absolute commitment to safety. She was not retaliated against by anyone in any way."

"The very core of our safety program is employee reporting," added *Delta's Catherine Simmons. "Every single Delta employee is encouraged and empowered to report potential concerns and we do not tolerate retaliation against employees who raise concerns."*

Republican Commerce Committee Senators who had collectively received millions in campaign support from Airlines For America, as well as individuals and PACS connected with the nation's airlines, spoke passionately in defense of Dickson.

"We've never had a partisan vote on an FAA nominee in the past, and I believe that we should have found consensus on a nominee for the FAA, given all of the concerns the public has about flying safety," responded Senator Cantwell. *Voting against Dickson, she added, "will help us create an environment where whistleblowers will be listened to."*

Her view was seconded by "Miracle on The Hudson" Captain Chesley Sullenberger:

"This nominee while a senior executive at Delta Air Lines either caused or allowed a whistleblower with validated safety concerns to be retaliated against. Especially now with the safety of the 737 MAX under review, it is critically important that we have an FAA Administrator who will act with integrity and independence to protect everyone who flies. I strongly oppose his nomination."

The Republican dominated committee advanced Dickson's nomination to the Senate July 10, 2019, on a straight 14-12 party line vote. He was spared a contentious floor debate later that month thanks to cloture invoked by longtime Delta Political Action Committee sweetheart, Majority Leader Mitch McConnell. The former manager of Delta's regulatory compliance work at the FAA was confirmed by a party line full Senate vote of 52-40. Seven Democrats campaigning for the Presidency were absent from the roll call.

"Captain Dickson is highly qualified to lead the FAA," said McConnell's favorite dinner partner, Elaine Chao. "Safety is the Department's No. 1 priority, and he is committed to ensuring that the

FAA's safety culture, and safety record, continue to lead the world."

Petitt's lawyer Lee Seham disagreed and argued that the airline's assault on his client's fitness to fly had a chilling effect on the industry's safety culture as well as federally mandated open reporting: "What's the impact of safety in terms of the message to 12,000 pilots that after you submit a safety report you're off to a psychiatrist? Captain Dickson did nothing in terms of stopping what happened."

One of the key questions raised by this landmark case was Dickson's lack of transparency. The FAA substantiated Petitt's OSHA whistleblower complaint on the fatigue issue, agreeing that "dead-heading" to another location to pick up a flight counts toward the pilot's daily and weekly flight limit. The airlines subsequently modified scheduling to meet FAA regulations created to make sure pilots don't fly when overly fatigued. A victory for pilots and their passengers, this kind of prompt action also reduced the industry's potential exposure to accidents, fines or lawsuits.

The FAA rejected Petitt's broader OSHA whistleblower claim that the key aspects of the airline's "safety culture were not in compliance with the agency's 2013 outline requirements and core values." In his deposition for this case Dickson denied retaliation but acknowledged that many of Petitt's complaints would be a concern to any airline executive.

The company's failure to settle and his attempt to make it through confirmation without disclosing his role in this litigation opened an important discussion about the nation's aviation regulatory system. Should airlines do a better job of encouraging pilots to quickly say something when they see a potential safety violation? Does this form of retaliation discourage pilots from speaking out about the kinds of problems that led to the two MAX crashes and Air France 447?

Petitt's reports of incidents reflecting a lack of operational control, helplessness, and improper flight operations instructions make a strong case for refresher training. Unfortunately, said Petitt's attorney Seham, "None of these incidents were ever investigated by the responsible Delta management representative, Captain Graham, or by any other employee."

One the key elements of the airline case against her was the 366 page report submitted to Delta by their Skokie, Illinois psychiatric consultant Dr. David Altman. His research and interviews, which included one six-hour session with no breaks, convinced him that Petitt was bipolar and should be grounded by Delta after 36 years of flying. He said Petitt's introduction of her credentials as a pilot type rated to fly eight aircraft and her long training documented "her... grandiosity." Notwithstanding Delta's open door policy, he added that her decision to reach out directly to airline CEO Ed Bastian documented an "expansive mood" that further confirmed his bipolar diagnosis.

Here is how he explained his conclusion during a deposition taken by the pilot's attorney in her OSHA whistleblower case alleging harassment by Delta and FAA Administrator Dickson. At issue was Petitt's conduct thirty years earlier in the mid 1980s, when she was a young mother raising three children.

ALTMAN: ... to have mania you have to have elevated energy. You have to be able to do -- you have the energy to stay up, you have the energy to engage in activities which are well beyond normal. And the question is what's normal? So, during the interview she talked about that she and her husband decided to have three children under three. Okay. And she also, simultaneously, went to night school and got a 3.7. And she also worked at her husband's business. And I asked her: "Did you get any help?" "No, not really." I don't know any woman who could do that. I don't know any woman with three under three that isn't exhausted, let alone going to school. So, this, to me, was— oh, I asked her—and she was nursing—I asked her—and she was very upset about this—I asked: "Did you express the milk," because that's going to take more time. So, basically, she's doing all of this—I think that's well beyond what any woman I've ever met could do. And she acknowledged that in the transcript. She acknowledges: "I don't recommend that, I don't really know how I did it." It was sort of a puzzle. But she doesn't close the loop and say, there's something unusual about this.

So, there are these four elements, back then three under three, going to night school, getting a 3.7, working at her husband's business, some, and no help. I don't think that that's within the normal range of a person's energy.

JUDGE SCOTT MORRIS: Could it equally be just a determination that she's gifted? Do you know her IQ, for example?

ALTMAN: Wait. I don't know if IQ matters with three under three. Three under three is exhausting. Nursing means you're up every four hours. No help means no help. In other words, this is a clinical judgment. If you can show me a large cohort of women -- or ever talk to a woman who was able to do that and not be wiped out -- then we have different cultural experiences. That's -- so you base it on because -- what was talked about in the book is exactly the theme -- the pilots are defensive. So, if you're going to make the diagnosis and you just ask them -- you want to just ask them the symptoms, it's easy -- it's 'No, no, I don't have it.'

'Did you — your speech?'

'No.'

'Okay.'

"So, you have to look in the history to see are the symptoms there, manifest, in a way other than the direct examination. And that's what I believe I did. Now, others can have another opinion, that's perfectly legitimate. The data is there, I tried to give all the data based on every-thing, so that it could be determined. And others found it not convinc-ing. Well, I can accept that, because others have opinions that are not the same as mine."

After returning to duty as a Delta pilot, Petitt continued work-ing on the appeal of her OSHA whistleblower case, writing about flying and encouraging other pilots to aggressively report safety issues. Petitt filed a complaint with the Illinois State Medical Disciplinary Board against Dr. Altman who labeled her bipolar. It was merged with a second case filed by former Delta pilot Michael Protack after Altman wrote a report saying he was unfit to fly. A confidential consent decree with Dr. Altman was approved by the Disciplinary Board in response to these complaints on August 5, 2020. According to the department's Medical Prosecution Unit the result was a "permanent inactive license" for Dr. Altman. This "formal punitive public action" meant that he was no longer licensed to practice medicine in the state. Delta would have to look elsewhere for pilot psychiatric evaluations.

CHAPTER 22

Book With Confidence— Never a Better Time to Fly

From our experience of past outbreaks, airlines have well-developed standards and best practices to keep travel safe. Airlines are assisting the World Health Organization (WHO) and public health authorities in efforts to contain the outbreak in line with the International Health Regulations. There currently is no advice from WHO to restrict travel or trade.

International Air Transport Association,
February 6, 2020

"Though the headlines may be worrisome, experts continue to say the overall coronavirus risk in the U.S. remains low. "The latest expert guidance indicates that for the overwhelming majority, it's OK to live, work, play and travel in the U.S.

National Air Association
With a coalition of 150 travel-related organizations,
March 10, 2020

"We are not a public health agency."
FAA Administrator Steve Dickson
April 14, 2020

231

In October 2019 the International Air Transportation Association released an optimistic report in Rome predicting competition could generate an additional 200,000 Italian aviation jobs by 2037. At the end of the year carriers worldwide reported an impressive 4.2 percent jump in passenger traffic. With an 83.7 load factor, air carriers were packing in passengers by the billions. Worldwide airline profits for 2019 were a remarkable $28 billion. A reassuring FAA administrator Steve Dickson guaranteed that he would personally pilot a Boeing 737 MAX before allowing Southwest, American, United or any other carrier to take it back up into the friendly skies.

No wonder that the world's booming airlines had become a darling of securities analysts around the world. There was no arguing with a record $220 billion in net profits between 2010-2019. Undoubtedly 2020 was on its way to becoming another banner year, especially in the United States. America's airlines continued spending nearly all of their billions in free cash on stock buybacks. Building a rainy day fund was less important than boosting their key performance benchmark, earnings per share.

In Washington, Transportation Secretary Elaine Chao proudly confirmed that the New Year was proving, once again, that deregulation worked. January's on-time arrival rate was 84.6 percent, up 8 percent from the same period a year earlier. Flight cancellations for the month declined to just 1.3 percent and tarmac delays exceeding three hours fell from 24 to a mere four. The mishandled baggage rate had also gone down to just 5.48 per thousand. The only disappointment came in the companion animals category. That month carriers "reported three incidents involving the death, injury or loss of an animal while traveling by air."

On February 20, a buoyant Secretary Chao headlined the International Air Transport Association Legal Symposium at the New York Marriott, overlooking the Brooklyn Bridge. After quickly thanking the airlines for "helping government authorities address this (Covid-19) public health emergency" and promising that the FAA would lift its 737 MAX grounding order "when it was safe to do so," she launched into the heart of her speech:

At the top of her list was "proposed rule making... to ensure the safety of everyone who travels by air," as it related to "bringing service animals on board aircraft." Under her leadership a big shake up was in progress on the DOT's "definition of a service animal for purposes of air transportation.... The only service animals airlines would be required to accommodate would be dogs... individually trained to assist the passenger with a physical or mental disability."

By the time the comment period for this proposed FAA service animal policy revision closed on April 6, some members of Secretary Chao's February IATA audience were focused on a higher priority, their own jobs. That day a mere 108,310 passengers boarded flights at America's 440 airports, a 95 percent drop from the same day a year earlier.

Except for the fact that Secretary Chao's diligent TSA agents continued arresting passengers at checkpoints for carrying loaded guns at a fast clip—23 at Orlando International alone during the first four months of the year—America's airports were almost unrecognizable. Empty terminals looked like they were all prepping for the arrival of

Hollywood disaster movie location scouts.

Captain Shem Malmquist, flying medical supplies, hospital equipment, and other personal protection equipment to first responders around the world, found the airways surreal. On many flights his Boeing 777 was the only aircraft on the air traffic control frequency. Walking through dark airport terminals tripping light sensors felt like touring a haunted house on Halloween.

With service animal rule making off the front burner, Secretary Chao refocused on rebuilding the decimated American transportation industry. At dinner she had a chance to talk this over with her husband, Senate Majority Leader Mitch McConnell. Thanks in part to his leadership, the United States Congress had rushed through a $54 billion airline bailout and loan package like a guided missile. While taxpayers checked their bank accounts daily for their $1,200 stimulus checks, American Airlines, which had spent $45 billion on stock buybacks and dividends since 2015, didn't need to worry about the lack of a rainy day fund. Despite a catastrophic drop in business they were they were able to keep flying and pay their employees until September 2020.

Around the world airlines postponed or cancelled tens of billions in Boeing and Airbus order. In France the Airbus CEO warned employees that the future of their company was in danger. Boeing temporarily suspended Puget Sound area production after an employee died of complications related to Covid-19. Critical to national security Boeing was being considered for a $17 billion federal loan from Congress. The good news was that not one cent of this money would go to Boeing management including, Dennis Muilenberg. He was fired two days before Christmas, 2019.

This CEO, who had apologized to families of 346 people lost in the two MAX crashes, left the company with a decent consolation prize, $62 million in pension and stock benefits. Succeeding Muilenberg, an engineer was Boeing Board Chairman David Calhoun, an accountant. For the past decade he had run the private equity firm Blackstone Group.

Muilenberg's platinum parachute did not sit well with angry critics like Zipporah Kuria, still grieving over the death of her father, a passenger on ill-fated Ethiopian Airlines flight 302:

"Boeing executives should be walking away in handcuffs, not with millions of dollars."

On op-ed pages, in magazines and business publications across the land, critics blasted the bailout and loan packages for America's airlines. Particularly galling was the $157 million handout to 70 private jet companies. Among them were two firms owned by substantial donors to the Trump campaign. The founder of California based Clay Lacy Aviation, recipient of $27 million under the CARES Act, donated almost $50,000 to the Republican National Committee and the President. In Omaha Jet Linx Management owner John Denny Carreker received $20 million from the taxpayers. He and his wife donated $68,100 to the Trump Victory Committee.

Pro Publica, which broke this story, noted that these major donors fared far better than the other 68 jet charter operators receiving grants from the CARES Act: "The average grant amount for the 70 private jet companies to receive aid was $2.2 million, about a tenth of what Jet Linx and Clay Lacy each received.

This controversial handout to companies that charge as much as $4,500 an hour for plane rentals, was similar to the $15 billion airline bailout that followed a three-day grounding post 9/11

Critics echoed the skepticism of Senator Peter Fitzgerald (R-IL) after the earlier bill was hustled through in 2001.

"Congress just got out the ladle and shoveled it all over the place."

That $15 billion bailout 19 years earlier included $20 million for bankrupt airlines Midway, Vanguard and Reliant. Nearly $165 million was handed out to freight carriers like Fed Ex and UPS. There were also generous payments to companies running Grand Canyon helicopter flyovers as well as millions for tour operators operating trips to destinations like Cuba.

Some of the big recipients like American, Northwest and United went on to file for bankruptcy years later. In a worst case scenario, United pilots, who had paid big money for partial airline ownership, ended up being crushed in bankruptcy and lost much of their pension benefits.

Consumer advocacy groups were angry that the new $54 billion bailout and loan package did not come with any concessions from airlines that were continuing to raise bag fees. While companies flying nearly empty planes temporarily waived cancellation policies, some made it difficult to get refunds. When business picked back up the airlines still had the freedom to pack customers more tightly in cramped seats that could contribute to blood clots on long flights. Passengers could still be overcharged for seat reservations necessary to sit next to their own kids in "basic economy" and be stuck with steep fares for short flights on government subsidized "essential air services routes".

While the Center For Disease Control had issued an emergency "Do Not Sail" order for cruise ships, carriers like Spirit and Frontier were actively promoting bargain flights starting as low as $11.

"Never A Better Time To Fly," claimed a Spirit promotion.

"Book with confidence," announced Frontier as it launched a 2 million-seat sale with a 90 percent discount.

This double standard made it clear that the FAA took a much different approach to public health than the CDC. Why was the Trump administration making the case that flying for hours next to an asymptomatic Covid-19 passenger was less risky than dining with one on the high seas?

This question underscores what passengers realize every time they board: the airline industry is, in many ways, a monopoly exempt from any serious antitrust action. Everything about the flying experience shows precisely what happens when political leaders give an influential industry the ability to make and live by many of their own rules. As Bloomberg *Business Week*'s Joseph Nocera put it, "The FAA is a classic case of 'regulatory capture.'"

For example, only after carriers around the world agreed to ground the Boeing 737 MAX in March 2019, did the Federal Aviation Agency, Secretary Chao and President Trump finally heed the complaints of Southwest and American pilots worried about the absence of simulator training for the new aircraft.

Denying persuasive testimony in Congress, FAA officials, including acting administrator Daniel Elwell (who would become the agency's representative on the White House coronavirus task force before resigning in November 2020) and safety chief Ali Bahrami insisted they had not made a single mistake in the aircraft's licensing process. Unlike Boeing, which conceded that the MCAS software system was not up to its high standards, the FAA continued to insist that it had licensed the plane to the letter of the law. Accepting this view further confirmed that the FAA's requirements were not meeting the expectations of the traveling public.

Exactly how did the regulatory process fail? Why couldn't it keep up with advancing technology? It's easy to find fault with Boeing and the FAA. But simply blaming these companies is a dangerous trap. We believe that blame is always the enemy of safety. Historically the problem goes all the way back to the dawn of aviation when Samuel Langley, the third Secretary of the Smithsonian made repeated attempts to launch the first human-piloted aircraft. His work on an aerodrome caught the attention of President William McKinley. With a $50,000 grant ($1.5 million today) from the War Department, Langley built a machine designed to launch his plane into the air from a houseboat. Repeated tries, including two failed attempts in late 1903, ended his dream. After Langley's dazed pilot was fished out the freezing Potomac in early December, the assembled crowd wanted to find out what caused the crash. The inventor was quick to blame failure on "the launch mechanism."

Was he right?

Without an accident investigation we'll never know what went wrong. In the absence of a regulatory system, there were no effective safety controls in place on Langley's Aerodrome. As the industry flourished events such as the 1956 United/TWA collision over the Grand Canyon, Air France 447 and the MAX crashes raised the same question. In every case someone somewhere found a way to shift responsibility to a bad actor, a bad mechanic, bad equipment, bad weather, or a second hand aviation parts shop in Florida selling a defective angle of attack indicator to an Indonesia MAX operator... the list never ends.

The common denominator in all these events was missing or poorly designed control systems. From the folly of the California Naval war team that couldn't get their torpedoes to work to the MCAS tragedy, responsibility ultimately lies with the people who control the regulatory system, our own elected officials.

Today government agencies, such as the FAA license aircraft and the people who fly them. They and all the other actors in the aviation industry do this to the best of their ability. Business leaders are expected to make money for their shareholders. Designers and pilots follow the rules. Government officials work under Congressional authority. The vast sums spent on campaigns by corporations and their lobbyists are subject to federal oversight. Even lobbyists chosen to lead government agencies are subject to full disclosure. Whistleblowers, inspector generals, Congressional investigators and the media can expose people who break the rules.

In the end, the "blame" traces back to failed government policies. Obsolete or ineffective regulations are at the heart of our present crisis in aviation. In almost every case failure in aviation can be traced back to industry rule making that didn't work, or as we've seen in Samuel Langley's case, rules that didn't exist.

This is where a heavily lobbied Congress comes in. For far too long too many of these officials have genuflected to industry, trade associations, airlines, manufacturers and other companies. Permits, licenses, regulations, enforcement actions and waivers, are all created under the authority of officials who fly on government-sanctioned aircraft. Boeing, the company that serves customers in 150 countries was allowed by the FAA to delete information about the MCAS software system in the MAX manual. The same manufacturer took a much different approach to the pair of converted 747s serving President Trump as Air Force One. In that case the Defense Department tightly controlled the $82 million flight manual used for these planes that Boeing built for $4 billion.

Those of us who are fortunate to live in democracies believe we are far safer than people who fly in third world countries or autocracies like Russia. We assume that freely elected leaders are less vulnerable to corruption than despots who can be bribed by airline owners. We are told that the free enterprise system creates prosperous industries flourishing thanks to the diligent oversight of government agencies such as the Food and Drug Administration or the Center for Disease Control.

When capitalism fails, as it does from time to time, socialist ideology in the form of bailouts and subsidies for the airlines and Boeing, quickly wins the support of Congressional conservatives, libertarians and liberals alike. From the Senate and House Majority Leaders on down Republicans and Democrats are eager to resuscitate this protected industry, to show the world what we do for them when it's time to travel by air. They fight hard for corporate interests that donate generously to their campaigns. They are eager to resuscitate this challenged industry, to show the world what we can do for them when it's time to travel by air.

There is just one catch. When it comes to science, new technology is always a wild card. Indeed, the very success of Airbus fly-by-wire design and the Boeing 737 led to the kind of overconfidence that can backfire in a safety critical industry. Anyone who argues that flying is risk free has not studied the case of Air France 447, the MAX or the Covid-19 crisis.

No one wants to be infected by an asymptomatic passenger. The impossibility of social distancing on a full aircraft makes some passengers reluctant to fly. Flight attendants, pilots, baggage handlers, gate agents, TSA agents, air traffic controllers and other employees also face challenges trying to stay safe during a pandemic.

When air travel spreads a virus around the world, flight safety is no longer just the responsibility of the airline or the FAA. Every passenger has a personal obligation to board healthy. As the Covid-19 pandemic spread around the world during the first part of 2020, customers in countries like the United States needed to show symptoms to qualify for screening. Asymptomatic passengers were assumed to be healthy, even though some were not. This problem created special risks, especially since one infected passenger with no apparent symptoms could, through multiple contacts infect as many as 40 people.

Senior pilots and flight attendants losing colleagues to Covid-19 had good reason to be worried. Then why, in the face of shelter in place orders, were so many passengers free to board planes without effective Covid-19 screening. The answer, clearly, is lack of planning. For example in January 2020 the Chinese government banned domestic flights from the pandemic's epicenter, Wuhan but allowed foreign flights to transport infected passengers around the world. Some of the hardest hit cities such as Detroit, which connects closely with the Chinese auto industry, were accessed by direct flights from Wuhan. Iran and Italy were also hit hard by outbreaks connected to travel from the same region. Despite a late January 2020 ban on Chinese air passenger travel to the United States, over 300,000 people flew from China to America in the early part of 2020.

One of the unanswered questions is how many people caught Covid-19 from asymptomatic airline passengers. Unlike Taiwan, Japan, Singapore and Germany there was no effective contact tracing in the United States as the pandemic began to take a hold. Thanks to years of remarkably effective airline lobbying at the FAA, numerous attempts to initiate contact tracing at the carriers were systematically defeated.

Even after the number of Americans lost to Covid-19 quickly exceeded combat deaths during the Vietnam War, the industry and the federal government refused to initiate aviation contact tracing. Could there be a better example of what can go wrong when effective controls are not in place?

It's likely that quickly limiting the airlines to essential workers, repatriation and freight could have slowed community spread to island nations. Even in places where arriving passengers were required to self-quarantine for two weeks, this system was difficult to regulate.

This public health crisis combined with economic decline decimated commercial aviation. Why, when major carriers around the world were shutting down and some countries were halting virtually all air traffic out of an abundance of caution, did a bipartisan Congress force airlines to keep flying at a huge loss? Why didn't airlines curb non-essential travel and immediately initiate contract tracing for potentially infected passengers?

The answer is they had no choice. As a condition of the March 2020 bailout Congress required airlines to maintain existing routes at a time when there simply weren't enough Covid-19 test kits to meet huge demand. While countries like Greece were testing arriving passengers for Covid-19 before admitting them to the country, American airports were handicapped by the lack of clear federal guidelines on screening for the pandemic. Only in September 2020 did major airports like Tampa begin offering comprehensive screening for all passengers. The considerable danger of flying non-essential passengers carrying Covid-19 asymptomatically was never discussed on the floor of Mitch McConnell's Senate or Nancy Pelosi's House of Representatives. In the midst of stay at home orders across the country airlines were ordered, as a condition of their bailout, to keep flying domestic routes.

After hundreds of reports of pilots testing positive for Covid-19 the Airline Pilots Association demanded that FAA Administrator Steve Dickson step up protections for flight crews. Hundreds of employees at his former employer, Delta, were in self-quarantine with the virus. In a single April week, 15 employees at American airlines perished. Pilots at companies like Fed Ex, Turkish Airlines, and Kenya Airways also died. Among them was Captain Daudi Kimuyu Kibati, who flew the latter carrier's last repatriation flight from New York to Nairobi.

With many air traffic control centers across the country shut down from time to time due to the pandemic and hundreds of TSA employees infected, contact tracing became critical. America's airlines and the government completely failed to do the kind of tracing working well in countries like Taiwan. One lame excuse frequently cited by the carriers was their inability to get this information from third party websites booking tickets.

Here is one example of how the system should work. A New York Department of Public Health contact tracer focused on sexually transmitted disease told us that part of her job required reaching out to people who had engaged in extra-marital affairs. This meant notifying spouses that they could become infected. Stopping community spread, was, in some cases, totally dependent on the worker's ability to reach every single contact.

In one case, a young man connecting with as many as five potential partners per day had created a spread sheet adding up to more than 150 names. When asked by the state STD specialist why he had gone to so much trouble, he had a good answer:

"I knew I was eventually going to be infected."

One of the reasons airline lobbyists helped kill long overdue attempts to put in place a contact tracing system was cost. This is a frightening example of the federal government putting the financial interests of airline stockholders and management ahead of public and employee safety. People who may have been unknowingly infected by asymptomatic passengers on flights were simply not warned to self-quarantine, putting family, friends and colleagues at risk.

It gets worse. Passengers repatriating in March 2020 to a handful of designated American airports such as Chicago's O'Hare were forced to break social distancing rules for hours as they queued up at customs.

The complete lack of planning for these surges exposed many people lacking PPE to potential infections.

Members of Congress have the authority to compel contact tracing that would help contain an outbreak and save lives in their own district. Failure to limit travel to emergency responders, government officials and people repatriating contributed to the terrifying community spread of Covid-19. This is one reason so many passengers discovered alternatives to air travel, including simply staying home.

At the FAA, an agency created in 1958 to protect the traveling public and promote commercial aviation, an inherent conflict of interest mirrors exactly what happened to the Smithsonian's Samuel Langley. One agency like the DOT cannot simultaneously govern and regulate air safety while promoting commercial aviation. These roles need to be separate.

All the reassurances and discount, videos promoting the efficiency of HEPA air filtration systems, abandoning inflight magazines, handing out free face masks and hand sanitizer, wiping down touch screens, ending duty free sales, food and drink service isn't terribly reassuring. Even if the airlines started passing out free Hazmat suits there is still that tricky little problem of sharing that tiny little lavatory with strangers who forgot to wash their hands.

Because the Department of Transportation and the FAA are in air safety leadership positions worldwide, it's critical for them to regain public trust. Generous bailouts are no substitute for bipartisan reform. Monopoly and deregulation have given the American airlines and Boeing too much latitude. Regulation has not kept up with new challenges created by automation. Failure to sensibly prepare for pandemics has exposed all air travelers to needless risk.

Far from saving the industry from itself, the Congressional bail-out forced flight crews to risk their health and safety. Pilot and flight attendants continued to criticize FAA Administrator Steve Dickson over multiple issues, including failure to immediately mandate Covid-19 testing, PPE and other workplace protections. As flight attendants warned the media that leisure travel passengers should stay home, and more pilots died from the virus, the industry suffered. On some days passenger cancellations exceeded bookings. The International Air Transportation Association forecast 4.5 million flight cancellations and a $314 billion industry loss for 2020. Prospects for the return of the MAX were undercut by a survey showing that more than half of the potential market preferred to wait six months before flying the plane.

The underlying structural problems in aviation began long before the MAX was on the drawing board and Covid-19 Patient Zero showed up in America. For many years air safety advocates at the National Transportation Safety Board, universities, pilot organizations and consumer advocacy groups have warned about the hidden dangers of automation. Presidents George W. Bush and Barack Obama, Microsoft co-founder Bill Gates, the World Health Organization and many other international agencies all called for a robust worldwide pandemic response plan. Numerous documentaries and feature films like *Contagion* also sketched out the many ways a pandemic could devastate communities worldwide.

No one at Elaine Chao's Department of Transportation or the White House was prepared to prevent the nation's air transportation system from becoming a primary source of Covid-19 community spread. The FAA could no longer fulfill its congressionally mandated obligation to promote commercial aviation while also overseeing safety. Due to the pandemic even preflight safety demonstrations were eliminated to protect flight attendants.

Prior to the advent of automated systems like fly-by-wire, Congress had many effective tools available to assess the performance of the DOT. Analog systems were vetted in a dependable way that proved their reliability. This proved far more difficult with state of the art avionics that became the victim of unexpected and uncontained failures. Pilots did not always have the experience or the training necessary to save the day.

In an age where automation dominates air travel, an agency like the FAA can no longer succeed as cheerleader and beat cop. Regulations watered down by brilliant lobbyists, including some who have migrated from industry and the FAA, don't work As we've seen with Air France 447, the Boeing Max and the Covid-19 virus, officials at the FAA and the Department of Transportation cannot afford to be distracted by the bottom line.

For over 60 years Congress and the electorate have been seduced by the false notion that the best way to make air traffic safe is to progressively give the aviation industry more control over its own destiny. This useful experiment has failed in a way that even pioneering Boeing test pilot Tex Johnson wouldn't have expected. He understood that the best way to reassure the traveling public following the British Comet disasters was to tell the truth.

When pilots distribute press releases saying they need more simulator training to confidently fly the MAX, they are sending an irrefutable message to passengers. The same thing happens when the head of the National Institute of Health's allergy and infectious disease division tells the public to avoid flying during a pandemic.

Public trust in air safety has broken in a way even 707 acrobatic pilots like Tex Johnson could never have imagined. Luring people back on board will take more than a couple of MAX barrel rolls over Lake Washington, even if they are performed by the FAA Administrator.

CONCLUSION
Aviation's Future

Nervous about flying?

Don't be. As long as the two million parts of the plane, all supplied by the lowest bidder, work perfectly for the 100,000 hours of their design life, and the multi-tonne, gravity-defying, cylindrical building travels at close to the speed of sound through thin, minus 50°C air, propelled by jet gas turbine engines managing a continuous fossil fuel explosion, suspended by four bolts on a pylon under the wing, two meters below hundreds of thousands of liters of highly flammable volatile fuel contained in the wings (the entire wing is a flying fuel tank).

In the jet engine, razor sharp metal compressor blades rotate at 13,000rpm in temperatures exceeding 500°C within the continuous fuel explosion, spinning the compressors and fan blades...the exiting exhaust speed exceeds 603km/h immediately aft of the engine exhaust nozzle.

The engines drive the air-conditioning and heating systems, keeping the air breathable and temperatures livable ... just. The time of useful consciousness at 40,000ft and

-50°C is counted in seconds.

All while you sit in a seat, sipping beer, somewhere over the vast ocean, traveling 12km above the Earth's surface at the pressure altitude of the peak of a mountain with only 5mm of aluminum and a thin glass window between you and the -50°C, 1000kph, cold and unforgiving air outside.

Beneath your feet is the cargo hold, which contains multiple flammable cargos and a fire suppression system which can certainly put some types of cargo out.

If the cabin is ruptured and decompressed, you have 15 minutes of chemical oxygen generated to breathe

If everything works, you'll be absolutely fine.

Darren Straker
Former Chief Accident and Safety Investigator
Hong Kong Air Accident Investigation Authority

hen we finished our previous book, *Angle of Attack*, the Boeing 737 MAX had already become the fastest selling new commercial aircraft in history. Neither of us imagined that *Grounded* would be published at a time when more than half the world's aircraft were parked, some major airlines around the world were in bankruptcy or close to it and no one would be able to predict when commercial air traffic would rebound.

We have amplified the idea that blame is the enemy of safety and that chain of events analysis misrepresents the cause of aviation accidents. What has brought the airlines to this turning point was both predictable and, sadly, preventable. From the very dawn of commercial jet aviation the industry has done everything in its power to convince both the regulators and the traveling public that flying is safe. This is a complex argument, undercut to some extent by the fact that thousands of aviation accidents have taken the lives of tens of thousands of people on good airlines and bad ones.

Yes, we agree that flying is a safer way to travel long distances than competing forms of transit. Nonetheless the industry's commercial success has been built on the fact that virtually every accident is explained as a one off, something that will never be repeated thanks to lessons learned.

While the two MAX crashes dealt an economic blow, the industry's tepid and underwhelming initial response to the risks posed by Covid-19 demonstrate its inability to respond effectively to a challenge in the moment. After many years of successfully lobbying against contact tracing, the airlines have discovered that this shortsighted decision undermined one of the most effective tools for protecting the health and well being of its passengers.

More to the point, the complexity of dealing with the economic and public health fallout of Covid-19 has undermined public confidence in the safety of flying. People would rather stay home than run the risk of catching a dangerous virus. The fact that air travel of asymptomatic passengers made it possible to quickly spread Covid-19 around the world is a cruel irony. Clearly international air travel was curtailed far too late to prevent the pandemic from spreading across the globe.

Countries such as the United States tried to limit domestic air travel on the honor system. With the exception of states like Hawaii, which imposed a mandatory 14-day quarantine on all arrivals, this approach failed miserably. Instead of limiting traffic to essential workers and repatriation travel, the industry, was required, as part of a $54 billion bailout, to keep flying. This kind of government hand-holding compounded the industry's marketing problem. Although hundreds of airline employees contracted Covid-19 and some died from it, carriers were unable to screen out asymptomatic passengers as traffic began to rebound. Even carriers like Delta, which wisely blocked middle seats as competitors such as United and American filled their planes, reported 500 employee Covid infections and ten deaths during the first months of the pandemic.

The fact that more customers were returning to the air did not miti-gate the fact that the airlines were still losing money. In effect they were subsidizing the spread of the virus with taxpayer bailouts, doing the very best they could to enforce safety protocols. The problem was that forces mostly beyond airline control such as public transit to the airport, check in lines, security lines, waiting lounges, public restrooms, boarding lines and other points of exposure increased the risk of transmission.

Collectively all of these factors contributed to the spread of Covid-19 while shaking public confidence in the airlines. Some passengers diverted to driving while others simply stayed home. With respected epidemiologists and other scientific experts declining to fly themselves, the industry was clearly on the defensive. For the first time it was forced to defend the safety of air travel in terms of social distancing, something that is impossible on a crowded airplane.

To the best of their ability some airlines and even some countries such as New Zealand and Greece limited exposure by simply turning away international air travelers or forcing arriving passengers to submit to an instant Covid-19 test before they could leave a containment area.

Although the airlines took admirable steps to reduce risk there was no way to eliminate it. The lessons learned from events such as Air France 447, the Boeing 737 MAX and the Covid-19 pandemic transcend traditional probability studies and risk management theories. Neither capitalist nor socialist governments have short or long term answers to the current aviation crisis. What worked in the past is not necessarily going to rebuild public trust in flying. Add in numerous flight safety challenges and the fact that the industry depends on serving the two percent of the world's population that flies frequently (including us), you have an unprecedented situation.

Further complicating the situation is that some European nations, as a condition of their multi billion-dollar airline bailouts have taken partial ownership of big airlines. That means that environmentalists working to stop climate change are pushing the airlines to reduce shorter trips as part of an effort to move passenger traffic to rail. This approach would reduce carbon emissions and also push the airlines toward aircraft powered by hydrogen and other cleaner fuels.

In fall 2020 ZeroAvia proudly flew the world's maiden hydrogen powered flight on a six seater Piper plane in Cranfield, England. A few weeks later Airbus announced plans to create three hydrogen fueled zero-emission planes by 2035. These short and long range aircraft were touted as a turning point in aviation history. CEO Guillaume Faury said the jet and turboprop hydrogen powered aircraft would become a "historic moment" marking "the most important transition this industry has ever seen." A key part of this plan was government backing to pay for early retirement of fossil fuel powered aircraft.

All of these challenges create an opportunity to rebuild the aviation industry on a more sustainable model. Here are some of the areas where we see room for improvement in an industry victimized by an obsolete approach to escalating problems.

Flight safety

While flying has become safer new problems introduced by automation challenges require better training. Fixing the automation to prevent such problems is not likely to happen any time soon. Paying for that training in the midst of a sharp economic downtown is problematic.

Regulation

Flight safety expert Elaine Parker who consults with governments and airlines worldwide for her company Beyond Risk Management, makes it clear that the exponential pace of automation innovation has created a difficult problem: "In the two years it takes to teach someone how to be a good regulator, that person starts falling farther and farther behind. Once you move into regulation you are not longer the top guy in your field. With complex systems it's difficult for a regulator to stay ahead. It's very difficult to keep up with complex avionics. It's hard to think like a regulator when your knowledge of technology is out of date."

Government oversight

Airline contributions to the reelection campaign of the former Trump Shuttle President turned out to be a great return on investment. According to Salon "American, which is getting $5.8 billion, contributed $264,366 to Trump's re-election effort. Delta, which is getting $5.4 billion, donated $201,098. Southwest, which is in line for a

$3.2 billion bailout, donated $125,655. JetBlue, which is expected to receive just under $1 billion, contributed more than $42,000." In addition these equal opportunity carriers also donated heavily to Democratic members of the Congressional Transportation committees. This kind of money makes it harder to protect the public interest. Positioning lobbyists, industry executives and leaders of trade associations in leadership positions makes conflicts of interests inevitable. To make matters worse federal inspector generals hired to protect the public interest are being sacked and replaced by loyal agency employees.

Private contractors have also gone to the top to hold on to lucrative contracts and win new ones. Facing the possible loss of a $10 billion State Department aviation service contract, AAR Corp. executive David Storch took to the Mar-a-Lago links with newly elected President Donald Trump during the 2016 Thanksgiving holiday. The Illinois businessmen sharply boosted his lobbying with a pair of Trump connected firms after the Republican leader was sworn in. AAR booked a six figure corporate retreat at the Trump National Doral golf course and an event at Trump's Chicago hotel. According to the *New York Times* both events "were intended to encourage the president to view the company favorably."

This strategy worked perfectly. Not only did AAR retain its lucrative State Department contract, it picked up $1.35 billion worth of new federal contracts under the Trump administration. Storch insisted there was absolutely no conflict of interest here. He made it clear that his time on the links with the commander-in-chief had nothing to do with his expanded government business. "I was not aware that President-elect would be at the club" on that 2016 holiday weekend, "nor was I expecting the president-elect to join our group on the course."

Loss of public confidence in current industry and regulatory leadership is one of the reasons the aviation industry is in financial trouble. The best way to end this charade is to completely eliminate all political donations from any source to lawmakers regulating government transportation agencies. Protecting public safety means putting an end to contributions from big money interests focused on the bottom line. This subverts critically necessary oversight, especially when elected officials should be investigating transportation agency leaders who appear to be in a potential conflict of interest with elected officials.

Restoring public trust

If the industry has the tools to make flying safer and screen out passengers who may be transmitting a deadly virus, why doesn't it implement new safeguards immediately? More training is certainly part of the answer. Following the example of other airlines that have successfully screened out passengers with Covid-19 is certainly easier with a diminished passenger load. Failure to take these critical steps implies that the industry suffers from a lack of imagination.

By contributing vast sums to elected officials on both sides of the aisle the industry has, until recently, been able to dominate the political process. Instant success in rushing a $54 billion bailout/loan package through congress simply pushed back a day of reckoning. Far from solving the problem, it has given corporate boards the wherewithal to perpetuate their magical thinking. Flying millions of nonessential passengers to destinations like Mardi Gras or Disney World in the midst of a pandemic is counterproductive and potentially dangerous.

Rebuilding public trust begins with recognizing the consequences of disastrous board policies. Investing nearly all of its tens of billions in free cash into stock buybacks during the past decade contributed directly to their current financial crisis. During the same period Boeing invested 74 percent of its free cash, 43.4 percent of its free cash in stock buybacks. To make matters worse deregulated airlines essentially gave nothing of value back to the traveling public in exchange for the unprecedented bailout. In fact, flying has become a much worse experience as airlines have eliminated virtually all inflight service.

Bailing out airlines won't persuade passengers to return to the air if they don't feel safe. Subsidies can backfire because they reinforce the industry's irresponsible response to the need for better training, new technology oversight and public health challenges. Because no one has all the answers and time is short, it's important for safety experts to work independently of corporate managers and boards of directors. That means politicians need to listen carefully to people who are not under the thumb of corporate marketing departments or advocating for self-serving trade organizations.

The best solution would be collaboration between all stakeholders including the government, the airlines, the manufacturers, and unions representing all members of the work force, consumers and the insurance industry. Independent experts from agencies such as the National Transportation Safety Board, epidemiologists from universities like Johns Hopkins, technical experts like MIT's Nancy Leveson and leaders from the National Institutes of Health and the Center for Disease Control are central to this process. A comprehensive national health policy governing air travel during a pandemic should be mandatory.

STAMP

As Nancy Leveson outlines, the safety success of the airline industry is only party due to the design of the airplanes. Critically important (and as highlighted in the Max debacle), the role of government and industry associations are as much, or perhaps, more important. Absent government oversight and industry guidelines (the latter generally very closely aligned with regulation serve as methods to comply with regulations), there would be far more accidents. Factors such as fatigue, which is a constant tradeoff between safety and efficiency, were addressed in a haphazard way prior to the introduction of regulations. The framework of government and industry is designed to control everything from aircraft design and how pilots are trained to their key roles in airline management. This framework has had a profound effect on safety.

As previously outlined, Leveson's System Theoretic Accident Models and Processes, STAMP, can be utilized to greatly increase our chances of identifying a hazard before an accident. The methods based on STAMP capture both the technical and socio-technical system, including the roles of government and industry organizations. We may still miss some, but that number will be far fewer than current methods, which is why we endorse it so strongly. Even absent this, engineers, through their scientific approach, have been a large part of making air travel remarkably safe through the management of hazards.

The engineers do know their limitations. Engineers, as we've shown, do expect pilots to manage those hazards they either cannot engineer out, or have not anticipated. Engineers know that they have not captured everything. With or without STAMP, there may still be hidden hazards. STAMP can eliminate most of them, but nothing is 100%. That means humans are expected to fill those gaps, and in an airplane, the bulk of that work falls on the shoulders of pilots. How can we ensure pilots have the tools they need to accomplish this? The answer is through training.

Training

As outlined in the previous chapters, much can be done to improve the resilience of pilots—their ability to manage the unexpected. Today much time is spent training pilots to manage those hazards that we do expect, but that we cannot engineer out of the system. However, as aircraft systems and the airline system as a whole have become more reliable, those skills are much more rarely needed. In the future, the big problems will be ones we don't expect. Training a person to manage an unknown problem is much more of a challenge, but not impossible. Pilots need to integrate their knowledge of both systems and aerodynamics through the higher levels of what is known as Bloom's Taxonomy.

For those that are not familiar, Benjamin Bloom chaired a committee that devised a hierarchy of learning objectives. The original levels of Bloom's Taxonomy, as posted by Patricia Armstrong of Vanderbilt University's Center for Teaching, start with knowledge of specifics, facts, terms and basic concepts. Next is comprehension, which involves a demonstrated understanding of the facts and ideas—being able to state the main ideas. The third is the application of that knowledge. Solving problems in new situations using the prior knowledge.

Next comes analysis. This requires examining and breaking the information up into parts and understanding how those parts relate to one another, and then making inferences. Above that is synthesis, which allows for the person to derive abstract relations. The person is able to take the component parts and make them into a whole. Finally, there is the evaluation level. At this level the person can make informed judgments, understanding the "why" behind the concepts, and forming opinions on the validity of ideas.

These were revised, as Armstrong writes, in 2001, to be:

↷ Remember
  ↷ Recognizing
  ↷ Recalling
↷ Understand
  ↷ Interpreting
  ↷ Exemplifying
  ↷ Classifying
  ↷ Summarizing
  ↷ Inferring
  ↷ Comparing
  ↷ Explaining
↷ Apply
  ↷ Executing
  ↷ Implementing
↷ Analyze
  ↷ Differentiating
  ↷ Organizing
  ↷ Attributing
↷ Evaluate
  ↷ Checking
  ↷ Critiquing
↷ Create
  ↷ Generating

→ Planning

→ Producing

Clearly we want pilots at the highest level here. How can we best achieve this?

Accelerated expertise

One of the best methods we have seen are those advocated by Dr. Robert Hoffman in his books and articles on Accelerated Expertise. Through extensive research, Dr. Hoffman has identified methods that show incredible promise in creating training methods that can bring people up to very high levels of expertise in very short periods of time. These methods will not only improve safety and human performance, but also save training costs due to their efficiency.

Pandemic

It is hard to imagine that putting a human in a container, and hurling them at nearly the speed of sound through an environment where just outside their thin capsule is air colder than a winder in Antarctica, and so thin they would lose consciousness in mere seconds, could be made surprisingly safe. Yet humans have done a remarkable job of it. The same approach can be applied to a virus.

Flying a human in a container at high speeds in freezing conditions is dangerous. Fortunately we've been able to successfully reduce risk to a level the public accepts. Can the same thing be done with a pandemic? What if we were to treat the society at large as a system and then take a look at how an engineer might reduce the hazard of an infectious disease to the flying public? How might the hazards be reduced? What can we control and what aspects can we not? What controls might there be? If you were an engineer, what might you do?

The first aspect is to understand the hazard. In the case of COVID-19, as of this writing, the indications are that the most prominent vector path is via airborne water droplets from breathing. In addition, it appears that a person can be infectious several days before they have symptoms (pre-symptomatic). It is less clear if someone who is entirely asymptomatic can spread the virus, although why not design controls that can prevent the spread regardless?

Although an airplane is an enclosed environment, the air is changed quite rapidly. The air in the cabin is dumped overboard and replaced with fresh outside air about every two to three minutes. In addition, the recirculated air is passed through hospital intensive care unit (ICU) quality air filters, the combination making the overall air quality cleaner than most hospital ICUs. In addition, the air moves through the cabin from the top to the bottom, so any exhalations are drawn towards the floor. These design features already give us a tremendous advantage for an airborne virus.

The factors that can offset this are anything that might create more turbulence in the air inside the cabin. A person talking loudly enough might do it, but a cough or a sneeze is much more likely. A person walking by in the aisle will also have some effect. How might we mitigate these risks? Two obvious factors would be to reduce, to the extent possible, people walking in the aisles, and requiring people to wear masks. The masks prevent the airflow from going horizontal when a person talks, sneezes or coughs. Regulators should mandate mask use for all passengers and limit the movement of passengers and flight attendants, moving up and down the aisles.

To prevent the possible spread through surface contract, hand-sanitizing liquid should be made easily available, and passengers instructed to wash their hands carefully for at least 20 seconds when they use a lavatory. In addition, closing the lid when flushing can greatly reduce the amount of virus that is released (as an aside, the toilet lid can also reduce bacteria from spreading onto surfaces through the area). Vacuum toilets clearly help, and passengers can use tissue to line the toilet bowl to reduce anything from adhering to the sides and not going down during the flush.

This leaves the boarding areas. The two factors that work here, in addition to the hand cleaning, are masks and social distancing. This works. In one case in the spring of 2020, two hairstylists in a Missouri establishment both had active COVID-19 and served 140 customers. Due to strict distancing requirements between customers, coupled with facemasks being required for both the stylists and the customers, not one person was infected. This is remarkable, and demonstrates that this can work.

On board, enforcing separation of passengers, enforcing the use of masks and eventually improving the design (a current topic of research) to limit the spread of disease are all ways to move forward while reducing the risk to a more acceptable level.

Like any risk in flying, the best way to avoid it would be to not fly. However, it is entirely possible to mitigate the risk to an extent we can work with. Some airlines are doing so, requiring all employees to wear masks, enforcing social distancing (even by going so far as blocking restroom stalls and sinks on company facilities to enforce it), temperature screening,

COVID-19 testing of employees, providing sanitizers for crew members to ensure that their hotel rooms are clean, sanitizing the aircraft and all facilities. This can be done. The airline industry is a master as managing hazards, and if infection risk is treated as another hazard it can be mitigated.

At the individual level, as pilots are admonished, we must not become complacent. Pilots understand risk and tradeoffs. The first task is to understand the risk, where the risk factors are large and where they are not. Do not ignore the risk, but do not succumb to hype either. Everything we do entails some risk. Leaving the house, taking a bath, even eating, adds risk. Is the added risk to us and the community justified?

Humans need companionship as social creatures. Total isolation can be hazardous, even for an extreme introvert. We must develop habit patterns to keep us safe such as learning new ways to properly wash hands, wearing masks, keeping a distance and not touching our faces. These are all new habits, but once ingrained, like seatbelts, we don't even think about them in the future. We must balance the risk with all of these factors. Approached from a system safety perspective flying can reduce risk to an acceptable level. This partnership begins with public acceptance of the idea that science gives us the tools to deal with seemingly hidden dangers. The industry has a very deep bench capable of all the risks highlighted in these pages.

Attempts by business people and politicians to "protect" the industry make it difficult for scientists and pilots to do their jobs to the best of their ability. We look forward to the day when the problems discussed in these pages become history. In the long run aviation can become a role model for other industries driven by high technology.

Epilogue

Testing 1-2-3

When you have a group of engineers, a group of pilots, in my book the last thing you want is groupthink. We want to challenge each other. We want to challenge assumptions and ultimately we have to make a decision about how we are going to move forward together. Consensus is actually pretty rare in these processes... I think it's a healthy debate to have. We will continue to have it and foster an environment of transparency and openness so that we can make the best possible safety decisions in these situations.

Steve Dickson,
FAA Administrator

Like 707 test pilot Tex Johnson 65 years earlier, FAA Administrator Steve Dickson rolled down a Seattle runway on September 30, 2020, confident in his Boeing 737 MAX aircraft. This time the whole world was watching his flawless takeoff. After his second landing Captain Dixon told the assembled press corps he "liked what he saw" and was impressed by Boeing's the preflight simulator training that was not available to the flight crews on the lost Lion Air and Ethiopian Airlines MAX planes.

A big vote of confidence for the Trump administration's handling of the MAX relaunch in the midst of a presidential election campaign, Dickson assessment was viewed worldwide by potential passengers on an FAA streaming link. The FAA boss made it clear that his agency was dedicated to restoring its image as the "gold standard" in air safety.

Dickson was determined to make sure passengers could board the MAX with confidence anywhere in the world.

"Shortly after I took the helm at the FAA, I made a promise that I would fly the 737 MAX and that I wouldn't sign off on its return to service until I was comfortable putting my family on it.... The FAA — I — will not approve the plane for return to passenger service until I'm satisfied that we've adequately addressed all of the known safety issues....This is not a publicity stunt."

Dickson's flight and press conference was a sharp rebuttal to the House Committee on Transportation and Infrastructure's review of the MAX crashes in a report issued several weeks earlier. Begging to differ with the administrator's endorsement of the FAA as the "gold standard" in aviation safety, the committee was particularly tough on the agency's Ali Bahrami.

"In December 2019, in a transcribed interview with Committee staff, Bahrami, the FAA's Associate Administrator for Aviation Safety, seemed unaware of key issues related to the 737 MAX accidents.

For instance, he said he had not seen Boeing's November 6, 2018 Flight Crew Operations Manual Bulletin that Boeing had provided as an update to flight crews following the Lion Air crash.

"He said he was not familiar with the details of FAA's post Lion Air TARAM analysis that predicted 15 more fatal accidents without a fix to MCAS over the lifetime of the MAX fleet. He was also unaware of the fact that Boeing had conducted its own tests that showed it took a Boeing test pilot 10 seconds to respond to uncommanded MCAS activation in a flight simulator, which the pilot described as 'catastrophic,' despite the fact that this information had been made public at a high profile Committee hearing on the 737 MAX on October 30, 2019, and widely covered by the media.

"Separately, Mr. Bahrami claimed he could not recall a single conversation with Boeing officials about the MAX in between the Lion Air and Ethiopian Airlines crashes. The FAA's head of aviation safety said, 'I don't recall a conversation about that between the two accidents.'

"Despite that, documents Boeing provided to the Committee show that recollection was not accurate..."

The contrast between Administrator Dickson's effort to rebrand the FAA's image and the house report was illuminating. Watching his MAX flight on the agency's website and reading the *House* analysis of what went wrong underscores the central question being asked by the flying (and non-flying) public. The *House* document, summarized in the appendix to our book suggests that the agency ignored, again and again, significant warnings about hidden dangers in the MAX's MCAS system. Even after the 2018 Lion Air MAX crash in Indonesia, the agency failed to assert its regulatory prerogatives in a disciplined way.

The FAA's helter-skelter approach to the MAX challenge documented by the *House* committee analysis suggests that Dickson's commitment to healthy debate between scientific experts, pilots and engineers always makes good sense. We agree and would love to see the day when Captain Dickson and Delta Captain Karlene Petitt make a joint Congressional appearance on Capitol Hill to discuss these important issues.

Appendix

Final House Committee Report
The Design, Development & Certification Of The Boeing 737 MAX

Executive Summary

Technical design flaws, faulty assumptions about pilot responses, and management failures by both The Boeing Company (Boeing) and the Federal Aviation Administration (FAA) played instrumental and causative roles in the chain of errors that led to the crashes of Lion Air flight 610 in October 2018, and Ethiopian Airlines flight 302 in March 2019, that resulted in the tragic and preventable deaths of 346 people. Both crashes involved Boeing 737 MAX airplanes.

On March 8, 2017, the FAA granted an amended type certificate to Boeing for the 737-8 aircraft, the first of the 737 MAX family. The MAX is the 4th generation 737 model airplane and is the successor to the company's 737 Next Generation (NG) family of aircraft. The 737 MAX was the 12th derivative model of the 737 aircraft, which was first certified half a century earlier in 1967. In May 2017, the 737 MAX first entered revenue passenger service with Malindo Air, a Malaysian air carrier, two months after its FAA certification. Seventeen months later the 737 MAX suffered its first fatal crash.

On October 29, 2018, Lion Air flight 610 flying from Soekarno–Hatta International Airport in Jakarta, Indonesia, to Depati Amir Airport in Pangkal Pinang, Indonesia, crashed into the Java Sea 13 minutes after takeoff, killing all 189 passengers and crew. One Indonesian rescue diver also died during recovery efforts. Less than five months later, on March 10, 2019, in strikingly similar circumstances, Ethiopian Airlines flight 302 crashed six minutes after takeoff on a flight from Addis Ababa, Ethiopia, to Nairobi, Kenya, killing all 157 passengers and crew, including eight U.S. citizens.

In March 2019, within days of the crash of Ethiopian Airlines flight 302, the House Committee on Transportation and Infrastructure (Committee), under the leadership of Chair Peter

A. DeFazio and Subcommittee on Aviation Chair Rick Larsen, launched an investigation into the design, development, and certification of the 737 MAX aircraft and related matters that led to these crashes. Since then, the Committee has held five hearings on issues related to the 737 MAX program; written 23 oversight letters, including 12 records request letters; received an estimated 600,000 pages of records from Boeing, the FAA, airlines, and others; and conducted two dozen official interviews with current Boeing and FAA employees and others. This included transcribed interviews with Michael Teal, former vice president, chief project engineer and deputy program manager of the 737 MAX program; Keith Leverkuhn, former vice president and former general manager of Boeing's 737 MAX program;16 and Ali Bahrami, the FAA's current Associate Administrator for Aviation Safety. Committee staff have also spoken with a wide range of aviation experts, engineers, software developers, and former FAA and Boeing employees. In addition, the Committee's investigation has been informed by records and information provided by numerous whistleblowers who have contacted the Committee directly with their concerns.

This report was produced by Democratic staff of the Committee and is the culmination of the Committee's investigative efforts assessing the costs, consequences, and lessons from the design, development, and certification of Boeing's 737 MAX aircraft. The report reveals several unmistakable facts. The MAX crashes were not the result of a singular failure, technical mistake, or mismanaged event. They were the horrific culmination of a series of faulty technical assumptions by Boeing's engineers, a lack of transparency on the part of Boeing's management, and grossly insufficient oversight by the FAA—the pernicious result of regulatory capture on the part of the FAA with respect to its responsibilities to perform robust oversight of Boeing and to ensure the safety of the flying public. The facts laid out in this report document a disturbing pattern of technical miscalculations and troubling management misjudgments made by Boeing. It also illuminates numerous oversight lapses and accountability gaps by the FAA that played a significant role in the 737 MAX crashes.

The MAX Crashes

Ethiopian Airlines, which is wholly owned by the government of Ethiopia, has flourished over the last two decades as it has capitalized on a strategy to connect primary and secondary markets across the African continent with North American, European, and Asian destinations via its hub in Addis Ababa. The carrier's pilot training programs and facilities have garnered praise from seasoned American pilots. Before the crash of flight 302, Ethiopian Airlines' last major accident occurred in January 2010 and involved a Boeing 737-800 departing Beirut at night bound for Addis Ababa; it was determined that the flight crew likely experienced spatial disorientation during climb out over the Mediterranean Sea in the darkness, and that the crew failed to manage the flight path of the airplane and lost control, leading to an impact with the sea. All 90 passengers and crew died.

Lion Air is an Indonesian airline which provides fast, inexpensive travel across the massive Indonesian archipelago. Unfortunately, Lion Air has a checkered safety record and has earned a reputation among some observers of hiring inexperienced pilots and working them hard. For example, before the crash of flight 610, Lion Air airplanes had been involved in 10 accidents that led to the death of 25 people since the company's founding in 1999.23 Moreover, between 2007 and 2016, the European Union (EU) blacklisted the carrier, prohibiting it from operating into EU member states.

In November 2011, Lion Air signed a $22 billion order with Boeing for 230 units of the 737—including 201 737 MAX aircraft—the largest single order in Boeing's history.25 However, while Lion Air's business model was built around the use of the Boeing 737 and its pilots were used to flying the airplane, the 737 MAX contained a new feature in its flight control computer—the Maneuvering Characteristics Augmentation System (MCAS)—that has become the center of scrutiny for both MAX crashes. The new system had the ability to trigger non-pilot-commanded flight control movements that could place the airplane into a dangerous nose-down attitude that challenged the pilots' ability to control the aircraft. In addition, the MCAS software operated on input from one of the two angle-of-attack (AOA) sensors externally mounted on the fuselage on either side of the airplane.

The day before the crash of Lion Air flight 610, a mechanic in Denpasar, Indonesia, replaced the AOA sensor on the left side of the accident airplane, prior to its 90-minute flight from Denpasar to Jakarta. The mechanic used a refurbished AOA sensor that had previously been used on a Boeing 737-900ER (NG) aircraft operated by Lion Air's Malaysian sister company, Malindo Air, and rebuilt in late 2017 by Xtra Aerospace in Miramar, Florida.

On the flight to Jakarta, MCAS activated based on an erroneous reading from the newly installed AOA sensor and commanded the airplane's horizontal stabilizer to push the nose down while the pilots struggled against it to stabilize the airplane. In this case, a third "deadheading" pilot who occupied the jump seat inside the flight deck recognized what was occurring and provided instructions to the two active pilots that enabled them to regain control of the airplane and fly it safely to Jakarta by depressing two "stabilizer trim cutout" switches, thereby removing electrical power from the flight control that MCAS was erroneously activating.

Upon landing in Jakarta, the captain made entries in the airplane's maintenance log about cautions and warnings that appeared during the flight. However, he did not report the flight crew's use of the stabilizer trim cutout switches to address the unexpected horizontal stabilizer movement.

On the following day, October 29, 2018, Lion Air flight 610 departed Jakarta. Again, the AOA sensor provided inaccurate information to the flight control computer which triggered MCAS to move the horizontal stabilizer which pushed the airplane's nose down. This occurred more than 20 times as the pilots fought MCAS while struggling to maintain control of the aircraft. Unfortunately, because the previous flight crew did not document its use of the stabilizer trim cutout switches to address the same condition, the new flight crew did not have an important piece of information that could have helped them to identify and respond to the problem. Amid a cacophony of confusing warnings and alerts on the flight deck, the horizontal stabilizer ultimately forced the airplane into a nose-down attitude from which the pilots were unable to recover.

Nearly five months later, on March 10, 2019, once again a faulty AOA sensor and subsequent triggering of MCAS led to the downing of Ethiopian Airlines flight 302. As opposed to the Lion Air accident airplane on which cautions and warnings on its earlier flights had given some indication of a problem, the 737 MAX operated by Ethiopian Airlines had no known technical troubles. However, after a normal takeoff, the left AOA sensor began producing erroneous readings. Over the approximately six minutes that Ethiopian Airlines flight 302 was airborne following its departure from Addis Ababa, Ethiopia, MCAS triggered four times as a result of the false AOA readings and caused the airplane's horizontal stabilizer to force the airplane into a nose-down attitude from which the pilots were unable to recover. Faulty AOA data that erroneously triggered MCAS to repeatedly activate played critical roles in both MAX crashes.

There have been some allegations made against both Lion Air and Ethiopian Airlines regarding poor maintenance and even cover-ups. For example, investigators determined that photos provided by the Lion Air mechanic that purported to document the AOA sensor repair on the accident airplane depicted a different airplane and dismissed the photos as invalid evidence. In addition, a whistleblower with knowledge of Ethiopian Airlines' actions in the aftermath of the March 2019 crash alleged that staff of the carrier accessed the airplane's maintenance records the day after the accident. Such action is contrary to protocols that call for records to be immediately sealed following a crash. However, while it is not known how, if at all, the records were altered, the whistleblower contends that this action was part of a pattern of faulty repairs and erroneous records that call into question the reliability of Ethiopian Airlines' maintenance practices.

In addition to maintenance concerns, some negative aspersions have arisen about the abilities of the pilots who commanded the ill-fated Lion Air and Ethiopian Airlines flights. While Lion Air has a reputation for hiring inexperienced pilots and quickly promoting them, the 31-year-old captain of Lion Air flight 610 had accumulated over 5,100 hours of flight time on Boeing 737 airplanes, and the 41-year-old first officer had more than 4,200 hours on Boeing 737 models, indicating that they were seasoned pilots.49 Further, while the 29-year-old captain of Ethiopian Airlines flight 302 had reportedly not received training on the airline's 737 MAX simulator—even though Ethiopian Airlines was one of the first airlines worldwide to purchase a 737 MAX specific simulator—the young pilot had amassed over 5,500 flying hours on Boeing 737 airplanes, including 103 hours on the 737 MAX. Even the 25-year-old first officer of flight 302—who was the least experienced of the pilots—had accumulated 207 hours flying Boeing 737 airplanes since obtaining his commercial pilot's license in December 2018, just three months before the fatal crash.

Addressing the qualifications of these pilots at a June 2019 Subcommittee on Aviation hearing, Captain Dan Carey, a 35-year career pilot and then president of the Allied Pilots Association, which represents 15,000 American Airlines pilots, said in his written statement:

> To make the claim that these accidents would not happen to U.S.-trained pilots is presumptuous and not supported by fact. Vilifying non-U.S. pilots is disrespectful and not solution-based, nor is it in line with a sorely needed global safety culture that delivers one standard of safety and training. Simply put, Boeing does not produce aircraft for U.S. pilots vs. pilots from the rest of the world.

Retired airline captain Chesley B. "Sully" Sullenberger III, who landed U.S. Airways flight 1549 on the Hudson River in 2009 saving all 155 people on board in what came to be known as the "Miracle on the Hudson," also testified at that hearing. He offered similar sentiments about the qualifications of these pilots as part of his remarks about the two crashes. In his prepared testimony Captain Sullenberger wrote:

> These crashes are demonstrable evidence that our current system of aircraft design and certification has failed us... It is obvious that grave errors were made that have had grave consequences, claiming 346 lives... Accidents are the end result of a causal chain of events, and in the case of the Boeing 737 MAX, the chain began with decisions that had been made years before, to update a half-century-old design... We owe it to everyone who flies, passengers and crews alike, to do much better than to design aircraft with inherent flaws that we intend pilots will have to compensate for and overcome. Pilots must be able to handle an unexpected emergency and still keep their passengers and crew safe, but we should first design aircraft for them to fly that do not have inadvertent traps set for them.

For two brand-new airplanes, of a brand-new derivative model, to crash within five months of each other was extraordinary given significant advances in aviation safety over the last two decades. While certain facts and circumstances surrounding the accidents differed, a common component in both of the accident airplanes was the new flight control feature: MCAS. Boeing developed MCAS to address stability issues in certain flight conditions induced by the plane's new, larger engines, and their relative placement on the 737 MAX aircraft compared to the engines' placement on the 737 NG. On March 13, 2019, the FAA grounded the 737 MAX three days after the Ethiopian Airlines crash, following similar actions taken by China, the EU, and Canada, among others. Despite optimistic predictions at the time—that a simple software fix for MCAS would allow the 737 MAX to return quickly to service—the aircraft has been grounded for 18 months, with even more, newly discovered safety issues emerging since. (See "New Issues Emerge" below).

This report identifies the key technical flaws and management failures the Committee has discovered at both Boeing and the FAA during its investigation of the design, development, and certification of the 737 MAX, and related issues. We anticipate that the factual evidence our investigation has uncovered and the findings we present in this report will help the Members of the Committee as they consider legislative actions to (1) rectify the problems our investigation has revealed, (2) create a more robust FAA oversight structure and improved certification process, and (3) enhance the safety of the flying public.

Investigative Themes

The Committee's investigative findings identify five central themes that affected the design, development, and certification of the 737 MAX and FAA's oversight of Boeing. Acts, omissions, and errors occurred across multiple stages and areas of the development and certification process of the 737 MAX. These themes are present throughout this report. They include:

1   **Production Pressures.** There was tremendous financial pressure on Boeing and the 737 MAX program to compete with Airbus' new A320neo aircraft. Among other things, this pressure resulted in extensive efforts to cut costs, maintain the 737 MAX program schedule, and avoid slowing the 737 MAX production line. The Committee's investigation has identified several instances where the desire to meet these goals and expectations jeopardized the safety of the flying public.

2   **Faulty Design and Performance Assumptions.** Boeing made fundamentally faulty assumptions about critical technologies on the 737 MAX, most notably with MCAS. Based on these faulty assumptions, Boeing permitted MCAS— software designed to automatically push the airplane's nose down in certain conditions—to activate on input from a single angle of attack (AOA) sensor. It also expected that pilots, who were largely unaware that the system existed, would be able to mitigate any potential malfunction. Boeing also failed to classify MCAS as a safety-critical system, which would have attracted greater FAA scrutiny during the certification process. The operation of MCAS also violated Boeing's own internal design guidelines related to the 737 MAX's development which stated that the system should "not have any objectionable interaction with the piloting of the airplane" and "not interfere with dive recovery."

3   **Culture of Concealment.** In several critical instances, Boeing withheld crucial information from the FAA, its customers, and 737 MAX pilots. This included concealing the very existence of MCAS from 737 MAX pilots and failing to disclose that the AOA Disagree alert was inoperable on the vast majority of the 737 MAX fleet, despite having been certified as a standard aircraft feature. The AOA Disagree alert is intended to notify the crew if the aircraft's two AOA sensor readings disagree, an event that can occur if one sensor is malfunctioning or providing faulty AOA data. Boeing not only

concealed this information from both the FAA and pilots, but also continued to deliver MAX aircraft to its customers knowing that the AOA Disagree alert was inoperable on most of these aircraft. Further, Boeing concealed internal test data it had that revealed it took a Boeing test pilot more than 10 seconds to diagnose and respond to uncommanded MCAS activation in a flight simulator, a condition the pilot found to be "catastrophic[.]" While it was not required to share this information with the FAA or Boeing customers, it is inconceivable and inexcusable that Boeing withheld this information from them. It also argues strongly for a disclosure requirement. Federal guidelines assume pilots will respond to this condition within four seconds.

4   Conflicted Representation. The Committee found that the FAA's current oversight structure with respect to Boeing creates inherent conflicts of interest that have jeopardized the safety of the flying public. The Committee's investigation documented several instances where Boeing Authorized Representatives (ARs)—Boeing employees who are granted special permission to represent the interests of the FAA and to act on the agency's behalf in validating aircraft systems and designs' compliance with FAA requirements—failed to disclose important information to the FAA that could have enhanced the safety of the 737 MAX aircraft. In some instances, a Boeing AR raised concerns internally in 2016 but did not relay these issues to the FAA, and the concerns failed to result in adequate design changes. Some of the issues that were raised by the AR and not thoroughly investigated or dismissed by his Boeing employees, such as concerns about repetitive MCAS activation and the impact of faulty AOA data on MCAS, were the core contributing factors that led to the Lion Air and Ethiopian Airlines crashes more than two years later.

5   Boeing's Influence Over the FAA's Oversight Structure. Multiple career FAA officials have documented examples where FAA management overruled a determination of the FAA's own technical experts at the behest of Boeing. In these cases, FAA technical and safety experts determined that certain Boeing design approaches on its transport category aircraft were potentially unsafe and failed to comply with FAA regulations, only to have FAA management overrule them and side with Boeing instead. These incidents have had a detrimental impact on the morale of FAA's technical and subject matter experts that compromises the integrity and independence of the FAA's oversight abilities and the safety of airline passengers. A recent draft internal FAA "safety culture survey" of employees in the agency's Aviation Safety Organization (AVS) drew similar conclusions. "Many believe that AVS senior leaders are overly concerned with achieving the business-oriented outcomes of industry stakeholders and are not held accountable for safety-related decisions," the survey observed.

These five recurring themes point to a troubling pattern of problems that affected

Boeing's development and production of the 737 MAX and the FAA's ability to provide appropriate oversight of Boeing and the agency's certification process. These issues must be addressed by both Boeing and the FAA in order to correct poor certification practices that have emerged, reassess key assumptions that affect safety, and enhance transparency to enable more effective oversight.

Investigative Findings

Listed below are the Committee's investigative findings grouped into six distinct categories:

1   FAA oversight
2   Boeing production pressures,
3   Maneuvering Characteristics Augmentation System (MCAS),
4   AOA Disagree alert,
5   737 MAX pilot training, and
6   Post-accident responses by Boeing and the FAA.

FAA Oversight
The FAA failed to ensure the safety of the traveling public

+   The FAA's recent draft "safety culture survey" has made it clear that the agency is struggling to effectively fulfill its core regulatory and oversight mission to enhance aviation safety. According to the survey results, 49 percent of the FAA employees responding said they believe "safety concerns/incidents" will not be addressed, 43 percent believe the FAA delegates too many certification activities to industry and 34 percent said "fear of retribution" is one reason employees don't report safety issues. These results correspond with many of the Committee's own investigative findings.

+   Excessive FAA delegation to Boeing has eroded FAA's oversight capabilities.

+   Boeing's Authorized Representatives (ARs) may be impaired from acting independently.

+   A 2016 Boeing internal survey of its ARs, who are supposed to represent the interests of the FAA, conducted at the height of the 737 MAX's certification activities, and provided to the Committee from a whistleblower, found that 39 percent of Boeing ARs that responded perceived "undue pressure" and 29 percent were concerned about consequences if they reported potential "undue pressure."

+   The Committee has documented four instances in Boeing's 737 MAX program where Boeing ARs failed to represent the interests of the FAA in carrying out their FAA-delegated functions. In one instance, in 2013, an AR concurred on a decision not to emphasize MCAS as a "new function" because of Boeing's fears that doing so would increase "costs" and lead to "a greater certification and training impact" on the 737 MAX program. The Committee has no evidence that the AR shared this information with the FAA. In addition, the Committee found no evidence that any of the four Boeing ARs who knew that Boeing had evidence demonstrating that in 2012 it took a Boeing test pilot more than 10 seconds to respond to uncommanded MCAS activation in a flight simulator, a condition the pilot found to be "catastrophic[,]" informed the FAA of this critical information. In 2016, a Boeing AR also raised concerns regarding the ability of MAX pilots to respond to repetitive MCAS activation and the impact of faulty AOA data on MCAS. Those concerns were not properly addressed, and the AR did not inform the FAA of the concerns. The Committee also discovered that one AR who was aware that Boeing knowingly delivered aircraft with inoperable AOA Disagree alerts to its customers in 2017 and 2018 took no action to inform the FAA.

✈ Not all of these instances violated FAA regulations or guidance. However, every one of them indicates that Boeing ARs are not communicating fundamentally important information about safety, certification or conformity-related issues to the FAA that could drastically enhance the agency's oversight functions and greatly improve its understanding of potential safety issues on aircraft it is obligated to certify as safe.

✈ FAA management has undercut the authority and judgment of its own technical experts and sided with Boeing on design issues that failed to adequately address safety issues and appear to have violated FAA regulations or guidance, in some instances. These issues go beyond the 737 MAX program. The Committee is aware of at least one example where FAA technical experts were overruled by FAA management regarding a lightning protection safety feature on another Boeing aircraft, the 787 Dreamliner.

✈ The FAA's oversight was hampered by poor, disjointed FAA communication among the agency's own internal offices responsible for certifying new critical 737 MAX systems, such as MCAS. This lack of information impeded the ability of FAA employees to make fully informed decisions about the MAX. From FAA leadership down, ineffective communication and lack of coordination on key certification and safety issues jeopardized the safety of the flying public.

✈ The FAA failed to fully exercise its oversight authority and this failure adversely affected safety. The agency did not ask enough questions or sufficiently scrutinize Boeing responses regarding critical certification-related issues involving pilot training and technical design. The FAA has, for instance, as of the publishing of this report, failed in its duty to hold Boeing accountable for delivering airplanes with non-functioning AOA Disagree alerts that Boeing knew were inoperable. According to then-Acting FAA Administrator Dan Elwell, Boeing was required to deliver airplanes with functioning AOA Disagree alerts because they were part of the 737 MAX's approved type design.

→ Boeing received an FAA exception to allow the company to not install on the 737 MAX an Engine Indicating and Crew Alerting System (EICAS)—a system common in newly type certificated aircraft since 1982 that displays for pilots aircraft system faults and failures and helps pilots prioritize their response to multiple or simultaneous indications, warnings, and alerts. The FAA accepted Boeing's argument about the impracticality and the economic expense of installing EICAS on the 737 MAX. The 737 family, including the 737 MAX, is the only Boeing commercial aircraft line that does not have an EICAS installed, which may have helped to alleviate pilot confusion in both the Lion Air and Ethiopian Airlines accidents.

Boeing Production Pressure
Costs, schedule, and production pressures at Boeing undermined safety of the 737 MAX.

→ Schedule pressure was visible to all Boeing employees working on the 737 MAX program.

→ To emphasize the significance of the 737 MAX program's schedule to Boeing employees, the Committee learned that senior program officials kept a "countdown clock" in their conference room. Keith Leverkuhn, the former Vice President and General Manager of the MAX program, described the clock as an "excitement generator" for Boeing's staff. But he also acknowledged it was to remind staff about the MAX's schedule. "One of the mantras that we had was the value of a day," he said, "and making sure that we were being prudent with our time, that we were being thorough, but yet, that there was a schedule that needed to be met...." He said the countdown clock was used to mark two major milestones: power on, when the MAX was powered up for the first time in the factory, and first flight.

→ In 2012, in order to lower costs of the 737 MAX program, Boeing reduced the work hours involved in avionics regression testing on the 737 MAX by 2,000 hours. It also examined other reductions to save costs, including a reduction to flight test support by 3,000 hours and a reduction to the engineering flight deck simulator (E-CAB) by 8,000 hours.

→ In 2013, a Boeing engineer raised the issue of installing on the 737 MAX a synthetic airspeed indicator—a computer-based indicator of speed that can be compared to actual airspeed measures—as had been done on the 787 Dreamliner. However, this request was rejected by Boeing management due to cost concerns and because adding synthetic airspeed could have jeopardized the 737 MAX program's directive to avoid pilot simulator training requirements.

→ The Committee has learned that to thank him for keeping to the MAX's production schedule, Boeing gave Michael Teal, the former Chief Project Engineer on the 737 MAX program, restricted stock options after the airplane's first flight in 2016 to show its appreciation for his work.

✦ In June 2018, Ed Pierson, a senior Boeing plant supervisor at the company's Renton, Washington 737 MAX production factory, emailed Scott Campbell, the 737 General Manager, requesting a meeting about "safety concerns." Mr. Pierson described multiple concerns about production and schedule pressures that were impacting quality control and safety issues. "As a retired Naval Officer and former Squadron Commanding Officer," wrote Pierson, "I know how dangerous even the smallest of defects can be to the safety of an airplane. Frankly right now all my internal warning bells are going off. And for the first time in my life, I'm sorry to say that I'm hesitant about putting my family on a Boeing airplane."

✦ In July 2018, five weeks after Mr. Pierson's email, he finally met with Mr. Campbell in Mr. Campbell's office. According to Mr. Pierson's testimony to the Committee, he told Mr. Campbell that in the military they would temporarily halt production if they had the kinds of safety problems that Mr. Pierson was seeing on the MAX factory floor. Mr. Campbell allegedly responded: "The military is not a profit-making organization." Rather than heeding Mr. Pierson's dire warnings and thoroughly evaluating his safety concerns, Boeing continued to ramp up production on the 737 MAX and rehired retired Boeing employees to keep the production lines moving at the Renton plant. Lion Air flight 610 crashed three months later in October 2018.

Maneuvering Characteristics Augmentation System (MCAS)
Boeing failed to appropriately classify MCAS as a safety-critical system, concealed critical information about MCAS from pilots, and sought to diminish focus on MCAS as a "new function" in order to avoid increased costs, and "greater certification and training impact."

✦ Both Boeing and the FAA failed to appropriately designate MCAS a safety-critical system. In May 2019, then-Acting FAA Administrator Dan Elwell acknowledged this point at a hearing before the Committee.

✦ In 2012, Boeing developed initial concepts for an MCAS annunciator to inform pilots when MCAS failed to activate, but never implemented it. Instead, Boeing designed the "speed trim fail" alert to incorporate the MCAS failure functionality. Human factors experts have argued that an MCAS-specific display that went beyond just indicating MCAS's "failure" could have helped to negate pilot confusion in the MAX accidents.

✦ In June 2013, Boeing employees formulated a plan to help avoid increased "cost," and "greater certification and training impact" for the 737 MAX by describing MCAS as "an addition to [the existing] Speed Trim [system]." The Boeing meeting minutes warned: "If we emphasize MCAS is a new function there may be a greater certification and training impact." According to the email that summarized the meeting minutes, a Boeing AR concurred with this plan.

✈ In 2015, a Boeing AR raised the question of whether MCAS was "vulnerable to single AOA sensor failures...." Despite this, the aircraft was delivered with MCAS dependent on a single AOA sensor. Boeing's decision to allow MCAS to operate off of a single AOA sensor has been roundly criticized by a wide range of aviation safety experts.

✈ In March 2016, the General Manager of Boeing's 737 MAX program, Keith Leverkuhn, and Michael Teal, the former Chief Project Engineer on the 737 MAX program, both approved a redesign of MCAS to increase its authority to move the aircraft's stabilizer at low speed, in order to address "stall characteristics" requirements necessary for FAA certification.

✈ Just hours after the approval for MCAS's redesign was granted, Boeing sought, and the FAA approved, the removal of references to MCAS from Boeing's Flight Crew Operations Manual (FCOM)—a document that provides procedures, performance, and systems information to flight crews to enable their safe and efficient operation of the airplane. As a result, 737 MAX pilots were precluded from knowing of the existence of MCAS and its potential effect on aircraft handling without pilot command. Meanwhile, the FAA officials who authorized this request remained unaware of the redesign of MCAS until after the crash of the Lion Air flight. Although Boeing's approval of the redesign of MCAS and its efforts to remove references to MCAS from pilot training material occurred nearly simultaneously it is unclear if these actions were coordinated.

✈ After Boeing redesigned MCAS in 2016 to increase its authority to move the aircraft's stabilizer at lower speeds, Boeing failed to reevaluate the system or perform single- or multiple-failure analyses of MCAS.

✈ In June 2016, a Boeing AR raised concerns following a test flight of the 737 MAX during which MCAS countered the pilot's attempts to trim the airplane, including concerns related to the vulnerability caused by faulty AOA readings. These concerns were discounted by the AR's Boeing colleagues, particularly Boeing's test pilots. However, faulty AOA data that resulted in uncommanded MCAS activation was a significant contributing factor in the crashes of both the Lion Air and Ethiopian Airlines flights.

✈ Following the same test flight, another Boeing engineer asked if repetitive MCAS activation was a safety issue. A colleague responded: "I don't think this is safety, other then (sic) the pilot could fight the MCAS input and over time find themselves in a large mistrim." In both the Lion Air and Ethiopian Airlines flights, the pilots struggled to overcome MCAS, partly because of MCAS's repetitive activations that forced the airplanes into a nose-down configuration from which the pilots were unable to recover.

✈ In a transcribed interview with Committee staff, Michael Teal, the former Chief Project Engineer on the 737 MAX program, acknowledged that when he approved the MCAS redesign in March 2016 he was unaware:

1) that MCAS operated from a single AOA sensor, 2) that MCAS could activate repeatedly, or 3) that Boeing had internal test data showing that one of its own test pilots took more than 10 seconds to react to uncommanded MCAS activation in a flight simulator, and described the results as "catastrophic."

✦ Mr. Teal defended his lack of awareness of these key attributes on a system he approved saying he relied on the advice of the engineers on the MAX program. Although Mr. Teal was the program's Chief Project Engineer responsible for signing off and approving of key design decisions on the MAX, he did not actually supervise any engineers. "[Y]ou could say that none of them worked for me but all of them worked for me," he said.112 This reporting structure contributed to an overall lack of accountability on the MAX program.

✦ The operating parameters of the MCAS system eventually placed on the 737 MAX aircraft violated Boeing's own internal design requirements which demanded that MCAS "not have any objectionable interaction with the piloting of the airplane" and "not interfere with dive recovery," which occurred in both 737 MAX crashes.

AOA Disagree Alert

Boeing concealed information from the FAA, its customers, and pilots that the AOA Disagree alerts were inoperable on most of the 737 MAX fleet, despite their operation being "mandatory" on all 737 MAX aircraft. To date, FAA has failed to hold Boeing accountable for these actions.

✦ Boeing has publicly blamed its software supplier for an issue that tied the AOA Disagree alert, which was supposed to be standard on all 737 MAX aircraft, to an optional AOA Indicator display, the result of which was to render the AOA Disagree alert inoperable on more than 80 percent of the MAX aircraft. However, the Committee has learned that in July 2015, Boeing tested this software and failed to detect the problem.

✦ In August 2017, five months after the 737 MAX was certified by the FAA and three months after it entered revenue service, Boeing issued a problem report to its supplier complaining that the 737 MAX's AOA Disagree alert was tied to the optional AOA Indicator and therefore was not functioning on the vast majority of the 737 MAX fleet worldwide. Yet Boeing had previously approved of the version of the software that tied the AOA Disagree alert to the optional AOA Indicator display in July 2015.

✦ Rather than immediately informing the FAA and Boeing customers about this issue when it was discovered in August 2017, and advising Boeing to fix the problem via a software update as soon as possible, a Boeing AR consented to Boeing's plan to postpone the software update until 2020, three years later, so it could be done in conjunction with the rollout of Boeing's planned 737 MAX-10 aircraft.

✈ Although Boeing prepared a "Fleet Team Digest" to inform its customers about the inoperable AOA Disagree alert, Boeing never sent it, keeping Boeing's customers in the dark about the inoperable alert until after the Lion Air crash.

✈ Boeing's software supplier, Collins Aerospace, also falsely believed that Boeing had communicated the AOA Disagree alert issue to its 737 MAX customers.

✈ Boeing provided Lion Air with a Flight Crew Operations Manual (FCOM) for its 737-8 MAX aircraft dated August 16, 2018, one year after learning that the AOA Disagree alert was not functioning on most 737 MAX aircraft, including those operated by Lion Air. The FCOM explained how the AOA Disagree alert was intended to work and provided absolutely no indication that Boeing was fully aware that the AOA Disagree alert on the Lion Air 737 MAX aircraft was not operational. As a result, Lion Air pilots who referenced Boeing's FCOM would have falsely believed that the AOA Disagree alert was functioning properly and would reliably warn them of a malfunctioning AOA sensor. Boeing knowingly deceived these pilots and its customer airlines.

✈ Boeing did not acknowledge that the AOA Disagree alerts on more than 80 percent of the 737 MAX fleet were inoperative until after the Lion Air crash in October 2018.

✈ By the time of the Lion Air crash, Boeing had knowingly delivered approximately 200 MAX aircraft to customers around the world with non-functioning AOA Disagree alerts.

✈ In July 2019, then-Acting FAA Administrator Dan Elwell informed the Committee that "[a]lthough an AOA Disagree message was not necessary to meet FAA safety regulations, once it was made part of the approved type design, it was required to be installed and functional on all 737 MAX airplanes Boeing produced."

✈ Although the AOA Disagree alert was not considered a safety critical component, Boeing knowingly delivered 737 MAX aircraft to its customers with inoperable AOA Disagree alerts that did not conform to the airplane's amended type certificate. As far as the Committee understands, the FAA has failed to take any measures whatsoever to hold Boeing accountable for knowingly delivering aircraft with non-functioning AOA Disagree alerts to their customer airlines and failing to inform MAX pilots or the FAA that an item that was supposed to be a standard feature in the cockpit was inoperable.

737 MAX Pilot Training

Boeing's economic incentives led the company to a significant lack of transparency with the FAA, its customers, and 737 MAX pilots regarding pilot training requirements and negatively compromised safety.

✈ Boeing had tremendous financial incentive to ensure that no regulatory determination requiring pilot simulator training for the 737 MAX was made. Under a contract signed in December 2011 with Southwest Airlines, the U.S. launch customer for the 737 MAX, Boeing was financially obligated to have discounted the price of each MAX airplane it delivered to Southwest by at least $1 million if the FAA had required simulator training for pilots transitioning from the 737 NG to the 737 MAX.

✈ Southwest had 200 firm orders for the MAX with the option to purchase an additional 191 MAX aircraft. Thus, if Boeing failed to obtain Level B (non-simulator) training requirements or less from the FAA it would have owed Southwest between $200 to nearly $400 million. This helped incentivize Boeing and its leadership to forestall any simulator training for 737 MAX pilots. This had the impact of evading and averting the inclusion of at least one technology that could have affected Boeing's directive to avoid simulator training.

✈ In November 2012, for instance, it took a Boeing test pilot more than 10 seconds to respond to uncommanded MCAS activation during a flight simulator test, a condition the pilot found to be "catastrophic[.]" The FAA has provided guidance that pilots should be able to respond to this condition within four seconds. This event should have focused Boeing's attention on the need for enhanced pilot training for MAX pilots. It didn't.

✈ From 2015 to 2018, the information regarding the fact that Boeing's own test pilot took more than 10 seconds to respond to uncommanded MCAS activation in a flight simulator leading to potentially "catastrophic" consequences was included in at least six separate internal Boeing Coordination Sheets on MCAS's requirements. This indicates Boeing's keen awareness of the importance of this information.

✈ The Committee has found no evidence that Boeing shared this information with the FAA, its customers, or 737 MAX pilots and Boeing has confirmed to the Committee that it found no record showing it shared any of these MCAS Coordination Sheets with the FAA because they were not required to do so.

✈ At least four Boeing ARs were aware of these findings and never reported them to the FAA.

✈ One of Boeing's key goals for the 737 MAX program was that simulator-based training would not be required for pilots transitioning to the 737 MAX from the 737 NG. That goal undermined appropriate pilot training requirements, hampered the development of safety features that conflicted with that goal and created management incentives to downplay the risks of technologies that jeopardized that goal.

→ Early in the 737 MAX program, for instance, Boeing recognized that the addition of MCAS to the pilot's flight controls system posed a risk to qualifying for Level B (non-simulator) training.

→ However, the chief project engineer on the MAX program told Committee staff that obtaining Level B (non-simulator) pilot training requirements from the FAA was a "design objective" of the MAX program. That directive demanded that differences training for pilots transitioning from the 737 NG to the 737 MAX would be limited to 16 hours—or less—of computer based training requirements.

→ In July 2014, two years before the FAA made a determination regarding pilot training requirements for the 737 MAX, and at a time when the FAA was actively questioning Boeing on its presumption that no simulator training would be required, Boeing issued a press release asserting: "Pilots already certified on the Next-Generation 737 will not require a simulator course to transition to the 737 MAX." Boeing made similar claims in marketing materials it provided to potential customers.

→ In February 2015, Boeing's 737 Chief Technical Pilot wrote that MAX simulator training would be "unrecoverable" for some Boeing customers due to the lack of simulators.

→ In August 2016, the FAA granted provisional approval for Level B (non-simulator) differences training requirements for pilots transitioning between the 737 NG and the 737 MAX. The FAA estimated that its approved computer-based training for the MAX could be completed in approximately two hours, a drastic reduction from the 16 hours Boeing was anticipating.

→ The following month, in September 2016, Boeing granted its team of technical pilots the company's Commercial Aviation Services (CAS) Service Excellence Award for their role in "developing the MAX Level B [non-simulator] differences training..."

→ In March 2017, the month the 737 MAX was certified by the FAA, Boeing's 737 Chief Technical Pilot responded to colleagues about the prospects of 737 MAX simulator training, writing: "Boeing will not allow that to happen. We'll go face to face with any regulator who tries to make that a requirement."

→ In May and June 2017, as some foreign carriers asked Boeing about providing simulator training for their pilots transitioning to the 737 MAX from the 737 NG, emails show Boeing's 737 Chief Technical Pilot strongly opposed such training, and in one case even successfully talked a carrier out of using such training for its pilots on the 737 MAX.

→ In December 2017, the Chief Technical Pilot referring to his efforts to talk airlines out of the need for simulator training wrote to a Boeing colleague: "I save this company a sick amount of $$$$."

→ Even after the fatal Lion Air crash, Boeing maintained that its "rationale" for removing references to MCAS from the 737 MAX training manual was still "valid," and Boeing asserted that the addition of MCAS on the 737 MAX did "not affect pilot knowledge, skills, abilities, or flight safety."

✈ After the Lion Air crash, Boeing also recommended that FAA only require Level A training on MCAS. This is the training level with the fewest obligations, and would only require pilots to review printed materials that described MCAS as part of their transition from the 737 NG to the 737 MAX.

✈ On March 1, 2019, the FAA reminded Boeing that the original level of differences training proposed in 2016 by Boeing—before the Lion Air crash—was Level B. The FAA informed Boeing that the software changes to MCAS "may not meet the definition of Level A differences" training and advised Boeing that the company's "evaluation is proceeding at risk." Nine days later, Ethiopian Airlines flight 302 crashed.

Post-Accident Response
Both Boeing and the FAA gambled with the public's safety in the aftermath of the Lion Air crash, resulting in the death of 157 more individuals on Ethiopian Airlines flight 302, less than five months later.

✈ After the Lion Air crash, Boeing and the FAA failed to take the actions needed to avert a second crash. In November 2018, days after the Lion Air crash, both Boeing and the FAA issued advisories for 737 MAX pilots that failed to even mention the existence of MCAS by name. Only after receiving inquiries about MCAS from airlines did Boeing describe MCAS in a Multi Operator Message (MOM), on November 10, 2018, that went to Boeing's MAX customers but was not otherwise made public.

✈ The FAA acknowledged to the Committee that it had drafted—and then deleted—reference to MCAS that had originally appeared in a draft of its Emergency Airworthiness Directive (AD).

✈ There were multiple red flags and clear data points that should have informed the FAA's decision-making after the Lion Air crash. The FAA learned, for instance, that not only had Boeing failed to fix an inoperable AOA Disagree alert on more than 80 percent of the 737 MAX fleet, but that it had also decided not to inform the FAA or its customers about the non-functioning alert for more than 14 months—until after the Lion Air crash.

✈ Moreover, in December 2018, the FAA received a briefing from Boeing in which the company acknowledged that prior to certification, Boeing had not evaluated the effects of a combination of failures leading to unintended MCAS activation in simulator tests nor their combined flight deck effects on pilots. Boeing also acknowledged that it did not reevaluate its single- and multiple-failure assessments of MCAS after its engineers made design changes to the MCAS software in 2016. Further, because Boeing determined that the loss of one AOA sensor followed by erroneous readings from the other AOA sensor to be extremely improbable, it did not analyze this failure scenario even though it had determined that delayed pilot reaction in this situation was "potentially catastrophic."

✈ These issues should have raised warning signs for the FAA, but none of these issues were deemed noncompliant with FAA regulations by the FAA.

✈ In December 2018, the FAA conducted a risk assessment based on its Transport Aircraft Risk Assessment Methodology (TARAM) and estimated that without a fix to MCAS, during the lifetime of the 737 MAX fleet, there could potentially be 15 additional fatal crashes resulting in over 2,900 deaths.

✈ Despite that assessment, the FAA permitted the 737 MAX to continue flying while Boeing and the FAA worked on designing and validating, respectively, a fix to the MCAS software. During the period between the crashes, the FAA repeatedly justified its decision not to ground the 737 MAX saying that it did not have appropriate data to make that determination. That judgment proved tragically wrong.

✈ In December 2019, in a transcribed interview with Committee staff, Ali Bahrami, the FAA's Associate Administrator for Aviation Safety, seemed unaware of key issues related to the 737 MAX accidents. For instance, he said he had not seen Boeing's November 6, 2018 Flight Crew Operations Manual Bulletin that Boeing had provided as an update to flight crews following the Lion Air crash. He said he was not familiar with the details of FAA's post Lion Air TARAM analysis that predicted 15 more fatal accidents without a fix to MCAS over the lifetime of the MAX fleet. He was also unaware of the fact that Boeing had conducted its own tests that showed it took a Boeing test pilot 10 seconds to respond to uncommanded MCAS activation in a flight simulator, which the pilot described as "catastrophic," despite the fact that this information had been made public at a high profile Committee hearing on the 737 MAX on October 30, 2019, and widely covered by the media.

✈ Separately, Mr. Bahrami claimed he could not recall a single conversation with Boeing officials about the MAX in between the Lion Air and Ethiopian Airlines crashes. The FAA's head of aviation safety said, "I don't recall a conversation about that between the two accidents."

✈ Despite that, documents Boeing provided to the Committee show that recollection was not accurate. On January 24, 2019, Elizabeth ("Beth") Pasztor, Boeing's ODA Lead Administrator, and one of Boeing's most senior officials regarding FAA regulatory compliance, emailed Mr. Bahrami about setting up a phone call. "I would appreciate a few minutes of your time, the topic is Lion Air," wrote Pasztor. According to Mr. Bahrami's response, the two planned to speak the following day. It is unclear if the call ultimately took place and if it did, what was discussed, and who else, if anyone from FAA or Boeing was on the call. However, one week after that email requesting the call with Mr. Bahrami, Ms. Pasztor's deputy wrote to the FAA's Aircraft Evaluation Group (AEG) on Ms. Pasztor's Boeing letterhead arguing that the FAA should grant Boeing Level A training for MCAS in its post Lion Air evaluation.

✈ The Department of Transportation (DOT) has provided the Committee with substantial FAA records in response to Chair DeFazio and Subcommittee Chair Larsen's original April 2019 records request. However, this process has been inexplicably slow, seemingly incomplete and it is still unclear to the Committee—17 months later—where the agency is in its response since it has repeatedly and consistently refused to provide the Committee with clear updates on the status of these requests. The Senate Committee on Commerce, Science, and Transportation has experienced remarkably similar problems according to public statements from that Committee's Chairman, Senator Wicker.

✈ After the Lion Air crash, the FAA's Boeing Aviation Safety Oversight Office (BASOO) started an internal review of its MCAS certification process on the 737 MAX. The review was the first time FAA performed its own detailed analysis of MCAS and the first time FAA received a complete picture of how MCAS operated, according to the Department of Transportation Office of Inspector General (DOT OIG).

✈ The draft report, titled, "737-8 MAX Maneuvering Characteristics Augmentation System Oversight Report," concluded that Boeing was compliant with FAA regulations in the certification of the 737 MAX aircraft. "The oversight activity did not reveal any noncompliances," the report said, "but did observe some assumptions used by the Applicant and accepted by the FAA." The report implied that these "assumptions" by both Boeing and the FAA regarding pilot reaction time, for instance, were faulty. The FAA review also found that there was nothing discovered that required "corrective action," although they cited some areas for potential "improvement." The draft report's analysis showed that the MAX was compliant with FAA regulations, raising serious questions about the FAA certification process and its oversight of Boeing.

✈ This internal FAA review of MCAS began on January 9, 2019, and the last version of the draft report was dated February 8, 2019. The FAA never finalized this report. The FAA told the DOT OIG that the report was going through management review at the time of the Ethiopian Airlines accident and that it was simply overtaken by events.

✈ The metadata of this report showed that the report was accessed and printed by an FAA employee on March 11, 2019, the day after Ethiopian Airlines flight 302 crashed.

✈ Because this report was a "draft" and a final copy was never produced the DOT refused to provide a copy to the Committee. However, Committee staff were given the opportunity to review the document.

Investigative Findings Conclusion

Boeing's design and development of the 737 MAX was marred by technical design failures, lack of transparency with both regulators and customers, and efforts to downplay or disregard concerns about the operation of the aircraft. During development of the 737 MAX, a Boeing engineer raised safety concerns about MCAS being tied to a single AOA sensor.177 Another Boeing engineer raised concerns about not having a synthetic airspeed system on the 737 MAX. Concerns were also raised about the impact of faulty AOA data on MCAS and repetitive MCAS activations on the ability of 737 MAX pilots to maintain control of the aircraft. Ultimately, all of those safety concerns were either inadequately addressed or simply dismissed by Boeing.

In the wake of the Lion Air and Ethiopian Airlines tragedies, Boeing has now acknowledged some of these issues through its actions. For instance, Boeing now plans to have two AOA sensors feed into MCAS. Boeing has also said that MCAS will no longer activate repeatedly. In January 2020, Boeing dramatically reversed course yet again, by recommending that pilots undergo simulator training on the 737 MAX once the airplane returns to service. That decision violated one of the premier principles of the MAX program, to avoid pilot simulator training. Unfortunately, Boeing's responses to safety issues raised in the 737 MAX program have consistently been too late.

The Committee's investigation has also found that the FAA's certification review of Boeing's 737 MAX was grossly insufficient and that the FAA failed in its duty to identify key safety problems and to ensure that they were adequately addressed during the certification process. The combination of these problems doomed the Lion Air and Ethiopian Airlines flights.

The following pages detail the factual evidence gathered by the Committee during its investigation that highlight the actions and events that undermined the design, development, and certification of the 737 MAX aircraft and led to the tragic death of 346 people.

The complete report is available to read in full at https://transportation.house.gov/committee-activity/boeing-737-max-investigation

Bibliography

Books

Dekker, Sidney: (2014) *The Field Guide to Understanding Human Error*, Boca Raton: CRC Press

Kahneman, D. (2011). *Thinking Fast and Slow*. New York: Ferrar, Strauss and Giroux.

Leveson, Nancy: (2012) *Engineering a Safer World*, Cambridge: MIT Press

Rapoport, Roger; Malmquist, Shem (2017) *Angle of Attack*, Chicago: Lexographic Press

Sparaco, Pierre (2006) *Airbus The True Story, Toulouse*, France: Editions Privat.

Sullenberger, Chesley (2009) *Highest Duty*, New York, USA: William Morrow

Tobin, James (2003) *To Conquer The Air*, New York, USA: Free Press.

Documentaries

Darlow Smithson Productions (2010) 'Lost: The Mystery of Flight 447'. London: BBC.

PBS (2011) 'Crash of Air France 447'. Arlington, Virginia.
www.pbs.org/wgbh/nova/space/crash-flight-447.html

GOVERNMENT HEARINGS AND REPORTS

www.commerce.senate.gov/2019/5/nomination-hearing-for-administrator-of-federal-aviation-administration

www.commerce.senate.gov/services/files/52b13b14-29ec-436b-89ab-9de0efd29ea5

transportation.house.gov/committee-activity/hearings/
the-boeing-737-max-examining-the-federal-aviation-administrations-oversight-of-the-aircrafts-certification

appropriations.house.gov/events/hearings/oversight-hearing-faa-aviation-certification

Bureau d'Enquêtes et d'Analyses pour la Sécurité de l'Aviation Civile:

Air France 447 Interim Report July 2, 2009 www.bea.aero/docspa/2009/f-cp090601e1.en/pdf/f-cp090601e1.en.pdf Air France 447 Second Interim Report December 17, 2009

www.bea.aero/docspa/2009/f-cp090601e2.en/pdf/f-cp090601e2.en.pdf Air France 447, Third Interim Report #3 July 29, 2011

www.bea.aero/docspa/2009/f-cp090601e3.en/pdf/f-cp090601e3.en.pdf Sea Search Operation Phase One: June 10- July 10, 2009

www.bea.aero/en/enquetes/flight.af.447/sea.search.ops.phase.1.php Sea Search Operation Phase

Two: July 17-August 17, 2009

www.bea.aero/en/enquetes/flight.af.447/sea.search.ops.phase.2.php Sea Search Operation Phase 3: April 2-May 24, 2010

www.bea.aero/en/enquetes/flight.af.447/sea.search.ops.phase.3.php Sea Search Operation Phase 4: March 2011 to summer 2011

www.bea.aero/en/enquetes/flight.af.447/sea.search.ops.phase.4.php

www.bea.aero/docspa/2008/d-la081127.en/pdf/d-la081127.en.pdf Metron Search Analysis January 20, 2011

www.bea.aero/fr/enquetes/vol.af.447/metron.search.analysis.pdf

Ministry of Planning, Housing, Transport and Maritime Affairs, Investigation Commission concerning the accident which occurred on 26 June 1988 at Mulhouse-Habsheim to the Airbus A320, registered F-GFKC. Final Report, November 29, 1989. Air France Pitot Probe Chronology corporate.airfrance.com/en/press/af447/pitot-probes/#c1983

WEBSITES

Captain Malmquist's many articles on aviation safety can be found at airlinesafety.blog/ www.airdisaster.com/reports/ntsb/AAR86-05.pdf

SCIENTIFIC PAPERS & REPORTS

Arkes, H. R., & Blumer, C. (1985). The psychology of sunk cost. Organizational behavior and human decision processes, 35(1), 124-140.

Baron, J., & Frisch, D. (1994). Ambiguous probabilities and the paradoxes of expected utility. Subjective probability, 273-294

Bureau d'Enquêtes et d'Analyses. (2012). Final Report on AF 447. Le Bourget, FR.: BEA.

Chandler, C. C., Greening, L., Robison, L. J., & Stoppelbein, L. (1999). It can't happen to me ... or can it? conditional base rates affect subjective probability judgments. Journal of Experimental Psychology: Applied, 5(4), 361-378. doi: http://dx.doi.org/10.1037/1076-898X.5.4.361

Carroll, J. S. (1978). The effect of imagining an event on expectations for the event: An interpretation in terms of the availability heuristic. Journal of experimental social psychology, 14(1), 88-96

Commercial Aviation Safety Team (2003). Cast Plan and Metrics 09-29-03. Retrieved from www.google.com/url?sa=t&rct=j&q=&esrc=s&source=web&cd=1&cad=rja&ved=0CD-MQFjAA&url=http%3A%2F%2Fwww.icao.int%2Ffsix%2Fcast%2FCAST%2520Plan%2520and%2520Met-rics%25209-29-03.ppt&ei=DG5oUbm5CJCC9QTS2IAg&usg=AFQjCNE33DVJr9hOL6w8A4sVYgm9zVooy-Q&sig2=5N43hFFDr2vqX7QYXvrEdg&bvm=bv.45175338,d.eWU

DeJoy, D. M. (1989). The optimism bias and traffic accident risk perception. Accident Analysis & Prevention, 21(4), 333-340.

Cooper, G. E., White, M. D., & Lauber, J. K. (Eds). (1980). Resource management on the flightdeck: Proceedings of a NASA/industry workshop (NASA CP-2120). Moffett Field, CA: NASA-Ames Research Center.

Dismukes, R.K., Berman, B., and Loukopoulos, L. (2007). The Limits of Expertise. Burlington, VT: Ashgate.

Dodhia, R.M. and Dismukes, R.K. (2008). Interruptions Create Prospective Memory Tasks. Applied Cognitive Psychology. 23: 73-89 (2009).

Dunning, D., & Story, A. L. (1991). Depression, realism, and the overconfidence effect: Are the sadder wiser when predicting future actions and events? Journal of Personality and Social Psychology, 61(4), 521-532. doi: http://dx.doi.org/10.1037/0022-3514.61.4.521

Goldstein, E.B. (2010). Sensation and Perception, Eighth Edition. Belmont, CA: Wadsworth

Hoffrage, U., Hertwig, R., & Gigerenzer, G. (2000). Hindsight bias. Journal of Experimental Psychology: Learning, Memory and Cognition [PsycARTICLES], 26(3), 566-566. doi: http://dx.doi.org/10.1037/0278-7393.26.3.566

Jeng, M. (2006). A selected history of expectation bias in physics. American journal of physics, 74, 578.

Kahneman, D., and Klein, G. (2009). Conditions for Intuitive Expertise: A Failure to Disagree. American Psychologist. 64(6), 515-526.

Kuran, T., & Sunstein, C. R. (1999). Availability cascades and risk regulation. Stanford Law Review, 683-768.

MacLeod, C., Mathews, A., & Tata, P. (1986). Attentional bias in emotional disorders. Journal of abnormal psychology, 95(1), 15-20

Mahajan, J. (1992). The overconfidence effect in marketing management predictions. JMR, Journal of Marketing Research, 29(3), 329-329. Retrieved from search.proquest.com/docview/235228569?accountid=27313

Massad, C. M., Hubbard, M., & Newtson, D. (1979). Selective perception of events. Journal of Experimental Social Psychology, 15(6), 513-532.

McCoy, C. E., & Mickunas, A. (2000, July). The role of context and progressive commitment in plan continuation error. In Proceedings of the Human Factors and Ergonomics Society Annual Meeting (Vol. 44, No. 1, pp. 26-29). SAGE Publications.

Moore, D. A., & Small, D. A. (2007). Error and bias in comparative judgment: On being both better and worse than we think we are. Journal of Personality and Social Psychology, 92(6), 972-989. doi: http://dx.doi.org/10.1037/0022-3514.92.6.972

National Transportation Safety Board. (1972). Aircraft Accident Report, AAR-73-14. Washington, D.C.: NTSB

National Transportation Safety Board. (1985). Brief of Accident, DCA97MA049. Washington, D.C.: NTSB

National Transportation Safety Board. (1997). Aircraft Accident Report. AAR-86/05. Washington, D.C.: NTSB

Nickerson, R. S. (1998). Confirmation bias: A ubiquitous phenomenon in many guises. Review of General Psychology, 2(2), 175

Pascual, R., Mills, M., & Henderson, S. (2001). Training and technology for teams. IEE CONTROL ENGINEERING SERIES, 133-149.

Schwarz, N., Bless, H., Strack, F., Klumpp, G., Rittenauer-Schatka, H., & Simons, A. (1991). Ease of retrieval as information: Another look at the availability heuristic. Journal of Personality and Social psychology, 61(2), 195-202.

Thomas P. Harding, Psychiatric disability and clinical decision making: The impact of judgment error and bias, Clinical Psychology Review, Volume 24, Issue 6, October 2004, Pages 707-729, ISSN 0272-7358, 10.1016/j.cpr.2004.06.003. (www.sciencedirect. com/science/article/pii/S0272735804000807)

West, R., Krompinger, J., & Bowry, R. (2005). Disruptions of preparatory attention contribute to failures of prospective memory. Psychonomic Bulletin & Review (Pre-2011), 12(3), 502-7. Retrieved from http://search.proquest.com/ docview/204940379?accountid=27313

USAF. (ND). C-5 Stall Incident—Diego Garcia, F3214-VTC-98-0017 PIN# 613554 http://www.youtube.com/watch?v=Tqo8Fq6zz3M

Wickens, C. D., & Alexander, A. L. (2009). Attentional Tunneling and Task Management in Synthetic Vision Displays. International Journal Of Aviation Psychology, 19(2), 182-199. doi: 10.1080/10508410902766549

ARTICLES

New Republic: https://bit.ly/3dpZK8Vn

archive.aviationweek.com/issue/19950130

slate.com/business/2020/03/airlines-bailout-coronavirus.html

www.nytimes.com/2020/01/10/business/boeing-dennis-muilenburg-severance.html

www.bloomberg.com/news/articles/2020-03-16/u-s-airlines-spent-96-of-free-cash-flow-on-buybacks-chart

Forbes: https://bit.ly/3iWIrNF

airlines.iata.org/news/coronavirus-outbreak-set-to-cost-airlines-30bn-in-revenue

www.bloomberg.com/news/articles/2020-03-16/u-s-airlines-spent-96-of-free-cash-flow-on-buybacks-chart

Forbes: https://bit.ly/3iKdka2

Business Insider: https://bit.ly/2GSemCe#

www.latimes.com/business/la-fi-airline-profits-20180507-story.html

Endnotes

xi   I don't think: Dallas News https://bit.ly/3OJfFtF

1   After netting a record $37.6 billion: www.statista.com/statistics/232513/
     net-profit-of-commercial-airlines-worldwide/

2   Not a bad return www.forbes.com/sites/greatspeculations/2019/01/28/
     what-headwinds-airlines-to-book-their-10th-straight-year-of-profitability/#34fc77372965

2   The same was true: www.transtats.bts.gov/Data_Elements_Financial.aspx?Data=6

4   One of the ways: Block, Fred L (2018): *Capitalism: The Future of An Illusion*
     (Berkeley: University of California Press)

10   Now it is true: http://www.baaa-acro.com/crash-archives

10   Making it clear: Final House Transportation Committee Report 'The Design,
     Development & Certification of The Boeing 737 MAX'

11   One of them was: www.seattletimes.com/
     seattle-news/60-years-ago-the-famous-boeing-707-barrel-roll-over-lake-washington/

12   In 1965: www.transportation.gov/50/halaby-letter-proposing-creation-department-transportation

12   Johnson's pick www.enotrans.org/article/conversation-alan-boyd-first-secretary-transportation/

15   'The Challenge: Rapoport' interview with Dr. Gary Helmer.

16   As society progressed: Rapoport interview with senior Boeing designated aviation
     representative.

16   Eager to build: www.newsweek.com/guru-and-faa-180712
     www.washingtonpost.com/business/2020/05/07/real-reason-boeing-didnt-take-coronavirus-bailout/

31   The June 1 2009 loss: Rapoport, Malmquist (2017): *Angle of Attack: Air France 447
     and the Future of Aviation Safety* (Chicago: Lexographic Press)

47   In his April 2018 letter: Factbox: In Boeing internal messages, employees distrust
     the 737 MAX and mock regulators | Reuters FAA https://bit.ly/34wtFYU

47   With more than: aviation-safety.net/database/

48   The President's empathy: www.thedailybeast.com/the-crash-of-trump-air

51   In return: ITEP https://bit.ly/3dFEO8U

51   Southwest were sitting: www.ibtimes.com/southwest-airlines-cash-burn-improves-again-3049191

64   Eager to push up: www.washingtonpost.com/business/2020/05/07/
     real-reason-boeing-didnt-take-coronavirus-bailout/

64   In 2012 Boeing: Final House Transportation Committee Report 'The Design,
     Development & Certification of The Boeing 737 MAX'.

65   Certain this would never happen: www.reuters.com/article/us-boeing-airplane-south-
     west-idUSKBN1X92D4 and *The New Republic* https://bit.ly/2SArGND

66 We'll go face to face: www.reuters.com/article/us-boeing-737max-factbox-idUSKBN1Z90NP
    Roger Rapoport interview with Boeing Designated Aviation Representative,
    Forbes: https://bit.ly/33Pak6g

67 "I don't know how": Forbes: https://bit.ly/33Pak6g

67 "Now friggin": *Ibid.*

68 "I just Jedi mind tricked." USA Today https://bit.ly/30FDhzC

68 Captain Pedro Herrera: Aviation Pros https://bit.ly/2SxQO7R

68 Brazil went even further: USA Today https://bit.ly/34AorLS
    Also ANAC https://bit.ly/34yBHAr and https://bit.ly/33PsmFf

69 "Honesty is the only way": *LA Times* https://lat.ms/30XL0cp

69 "As designed": Roger Rapoport interview.

71 "Herb was much more": nader.org/2019/01/09/southwest-airlines-herb-kelleher-one-of-a-kind/

74 "In the beginning": www.reuters.com/article/us-boeing-737max-training-idUSKBN1ZL0EH

80 Fred George explains: George, F. (April 2019) *Aviation Week* https://bit.ly/3dEjFRu

86 As MIT'S: Leveson, N. G. (2016). *Engineering a Safer World: Systems thinking
    applied to safety* (p 560). Cambridge, The MIT Press

94 As pointed out: Leveson, *ibid.,* Woods, D.D. (2018) The theory of graceful exten-
    sibility: basic rules that govern adaptive systems. Environ Syst Decis 38, 433–457
    https://doi.org/10.1007/s10669-018-9708-3

113 Fortunately for us: Leveson, *ibid*

117 Graceful extensibility: Woods, *ibid*

145 Accelerated expertise: Robert Hoffman, Hoffman, R. R., Ward, P., Feltovich, P. J.,
    DiBello, L., Fiore, S. M., & Andrews, D. H. (2013). *Accelerated expertise: Training for
    high proficiency in a complex world.* UK: Oxford, Psychology Press

158 Lincoln Lab: Wolfson, M. M., Delanoy, R. L., Forman, B. E., Hallowell, R. G.,
    Pawlak, M. L., & Smith, P. D. (1994). Automated microburst wind-shear predic-
    tion. *Lincoln Laboratory Journal,* 7(2).

203 Is the Gentleman: www.politico.com/story/2017/02/trump-criticize-faa-234849

204 A 1995 lawsuit: www.sun-sentinel.com/news/fl-xpm-1997-05-22-9705210833-story.html

204 Gish chose DONLD: AV Stop https://bit.ly/3iAyuW1

205 In 2011: www.palmbeachpost.com/news/20150109/trump-files-100-million-suit-claiming-jets-are-
    destroying-mar-a-lago and *Forbes* https://bit.ly/3nzSWub

207 *ProPublica*: www.propublica.org/article/secrecy-and-suspicion-surround-trumps-deregulation-teams

209 Following these back to back: UPI https://bit.ly/34xTLe5

212 In 2013: *Seattle Times* https://bit.ly/30XADFl

214 Nadia Milleron: NPR https://bit.ly/2SzPyRt and theberkshireedge.com/
    samya-stumo-who-grew-up-in-sheffield-dies-in-ethiopia-plane-crash/

215 John Dunkin isn't just a pilot: AXIOS https://bit.ly/30JHVfL

215 The problem focused on: *The Guardian* https://bit.ly/2Fd1XI8 & *Patch* https://bit.ly/2SA2zdV

219 Comprehensive flight crew reporting: www.faa.gov/about/initiatives/whistleblower/

220 "Stephen Dickson had a long career": https://bit.ly/33FoJSi

222 After Reviewing Petitt's Case: https://wapo.st/2GOLjiA **February 6 1995** | *Aviation Week,* https://cnn.it/30JCzRH and AP NEWS https://bit.ly/34yqHDh

222 In a similar case: www.ajc.com/business/former-delta-exec-for-faa-job-faces-scrutiny-over-pilot-osha-case/Tr2RDntjdIvIK2pABUe9CP/

222 Another Whistleblower: christinenegroni.com/second-delta-pilot-claims-retaliatory-action-by-faa-nominee/ and www.flyingmag.com/second-whistleblower-speaks-out-about-delta/

222 Dickson defended: dockets.justia.com/docket/michigan/miedce/2:2017cv13937/325571

222 The same doctor: www.ssmplaw.com/wp-content/uploads/2019/05/PETITT1.pdf, www.ssmplaw.com/wp-content/uploads/2019/05/PETITT2.pdf and www.ssmplaw.com/wp-content/uploads/2019/05/PETITT3.pdf

224 Refuting Cantwell: https://wapo.st/3nnLtOJl and https://wapo.st/30H3oWN

225 Her view was seconded: *Ibid.*

227 None of these incidents: Rapoport interview with Petitt attorney Lee Seham.

227 Here is how he explained: Petitt v. Delta 2018-AIR-00041 U.S. Department of Labor OSHA case October 31, 2018 www.ssmplaw.com/wp-content/uploads/2019/06/2957534-Dickson.Stephen-M.-103118.fullprint.pdf

229: A confidential consent order: www.idfpr.com/profs/Meetings/Minutes/8-5-2020%20MDB%20Minutes.pdf A freedom of information request has been filed to release this consent order.

229 Illinois Department of Financial and Professional Regulation Case # 2017-06378 www.idfpr.com/profs/Meetings/Minutes/8-5-2020%20MDB%20Minutes.pdf

229 Confidential Consent Decree: Illinois Department of Financial and Professional Regulation Case # 2017-06378 www.idfpr.com/profs/Meetings/Minutes/8-5-2020%20MDB%20Minutes.pdf

230 "Permanent Inactive License": Email October 7, 2020 from Medical Prosecution Unit, Illinois Dept. of Financial and Professional Regulation

232 There was no arguing: Statista https://bit.ly/3jaEOUL

235 This CEO: www.nytimes.com/2020/01/10/business/boeing-dennis-muilenburg-severance.html

235 Particularly galling: *ProPublica* https://bit.ly/3lyOA4v

236 The $15 billion bailout: edition.cnn.com/2001/US/09/21/rec.congress.airline.deal/

238 Historically the problem dates back: www.smithsonianmag.com/history/langleys-feat-and-folly-145999254/

253 In fall 2020: New Atlas https://bit.ly/31lPKiT

253 A few weeks later: *The Guardian* https://bit.ly/3kdP4N2

255 I was not aware: www.nytimes.com/interactive/2020/10/10/us/trump-properties-swamp.html

257 Boeing invested: https://on.mktw.net/3d7fw8s

Acknowledgments

Many people across the aviation industry helped us on this book reported around the world. Frank Browning, Dr. Nicklas Dahlstrom, Robert Goodrich, Dr. Gary Helmer, David Hughes, Peter Knudson, Jean Paries, Lee Seham, the late Pierre Sparaco, the late Art Torosian and David Woods all kindly contributed their expertise to this book. At Lexographic Press publisher James Sparling was a valued partner in the creation of this book. We also thank Mary Bisbee and Adam Lowenstein for helping us get the word out. My wife Marty Ferriby was an invaluable partner on this book bringing both her wisdom and wit to these pages. I also want to thank my children Jonathan, Elizabeth and Will for their support.

Working with Shem Malmquist, who I first met when he joined a screening of *Pilot Error* in Memphis, has been an honor. As he travels the world each month on 777s Shem has brought home valuable insights from the aviation community. His creativity and insights have benefited pilots everywhere. I'd fly with him anywhere. I would also like to put in a word for some of the great journalists covering these important stories including Dominic Gates at the Seattle Times and Bloomberg's Alan Levin. We also owe thanks to Curt Lewis at *Flight Safety Information*. It's been an honor to work with him on the important aviation stories of our time. Finally to you, the reader, thanks so much for joining us on this journey. As always we appreciate your insights, thoughts and ideas.

Roger Rapoport

About Curt Lewis Books

Over the past 25 years Curt Lewis's *Flight Safety Information*, has become an indispensable daily read across the aviation industry. CEOs at airlines and manufacturers, heads of regulatory agencies, university faculty, and their students, accident investigators, Air Force Generals, lawyers, engineers, and frequent flyers worldwide consider his daily journal a must read. Thanks to his passion for air safety, he has become one of the most trusted names in aviation writers. Curt Lewis Books, launched in association with Lexographic Press and General Editor Roger Rapoport, offers readers the same kind of up to the minute analysis and writing they have come to expect with *Flight Safety Information*. Available in print or via the web worldwide, Curt Lewis Books offer a balanced look at critical aviation safety issues. All of our authors work with a veteran team of aviation editors, training pilots and academic experts.